Zbigniew Drozdowicz

Rationality Standards of Social Life

Development in Humanities

edited by

Zbigniew Drozdowicz
(General Editor)

and Sławomir Sztajer

Volume 7

LIT

Zbigniew Drozdowicz

Rationality Standards of Social Life

Traditions and the Present

LIT

NARODOWY PROGRAM
ROZWOJU HUMANISTYKI

The present thesis has been financed as a part of a programme of the Ministry of Science and Higher Education, which is called: the National Programme for the Development of Humanities (NPRH)

Translated by Aleksandra Cichocka and Piotr Cichocki

Typeset by Michał Staniszewski

This book is printed on acid-free paper.

Bibliographic information published by the Deutsche Nationalbibliothek
The Deutsche Nationalbibliothek lists this publication in the Deutsche Nationalbibliografie; detailed bibliographic data are available in the Internet at http://dnb.d-nb.de.

ISBN 978-3-643-90376-1

Verlagskontakt:
Fresnostr. 2 D-48159 Münster
Tel. +49 (0) 2 51-62 03 20 Fax +49 (0) 2 51-23 19 72
E-Mail: lit@lit-verlag.de http://www.lit-verlag.de

Auslieferung:
Deutschland: LIT Verlag Fresnostr. 2, D-48159 Münster
Tel. +49 (0) 2 51-620 32 22, Fax +49 (0) 2 51-922 60 99, E-Mail: vertrieb@lit-verlag.de

Österreich: Medienlogistik Pichler-ÖBZ, E-Mail: mlo@medien-logistik.at
E-Books sind erhältlich unter www.litwebshop.de

Contents

Author's note

Various standards of rationality have typically played the role of regulating social life. If we were to imagine life as a great voyage on high seas and oceans, which are not always sympathetic towards humanity, then those standards could be seen as the rudders of the great vessels constituted by human communities.[1] It goes without saying that the better these instruments are crafted and operated, the lower will the risk be of a catastrophe, or navigational errors preventing the ships from finding the right harbours. It was an opinion already common among the ancients that the vital social task of crafting and operating such instruments should be performed by rational beings, i.e., such beings that, thanks to good fortune and great personal effort, possess the skills for reasoning. Moving beyond this conclusion would always entail controversy. There were those who maintained that such reason and ability can only be possessed by higher beings – identified with God or gods – and that humans should resign themselves to listening to them and following their orders. Yet, one could always find those who were certain that human reason and abilities should be sufficient for such tasks. Among the points of contention, one question typically concerned the problem that very few individuals or social groups seem to be endowed with the requisite reasoning ability and other qualifications. Another problem related to the issue of whether the roles of rudder constructors and helmsmen should be combined or separated, or – to drop the metaphoric expression – whether some are fit for designing the various rationality standards of social life, while others should implement them in practice, with perhaps yet others supervising this implementation. Of course, the list of controversies extends far beyond these two examples.

In my explorations I stick to a tradition that might be considered the secular way of thinking about the rationality of social life. I attribute a special

[1] This comparison was inspired by the polemics between the liberal J. Rawls, and the communitarian A. MacIntyre, which is explored in the final part of the book.

role in these considerations to philosophers, as they were among the most outspoken on the topic, but also because their ideas influenced modes of thinking and actions of non-philosophers. The latter might not even have had much respect for philosophy, and would become convinced of the validity of philosophical advice motivated by concrete needs rather than some overall esteem for philosophers and philosophy. This is not to say that this distancing from philosophy and philosophers was of no importance. Among its consequences one could for instance find significant differences between the rationality standards developed within idealised philosophical structures and their practical implementation in the course of social life. Some of these practical applications turned out to be so different from their philosophical sources that their authors were not willing to claim responsibility for them.

To analyse and describe everything in an unambiguous way when it comes to such a complex and socio-culturally entangled matter as standards of rationality is an utterly impossible task. Furthermore, some crucial elements can only be sketched in a delicate and vague manner, so as not to up the ante on points which have merely intuitive foundations, and for whose full understanding and appreciation one needs not only the intellectual efforts of successive generations of philosophers but also multigenerational testing by various practitioners. There is also the need to study the arguments of the other side and in case they are necessary and sufficient to correct pre-existing convictions, frameworks and postulated courses of action. At this point, we seem to be touching on the very core of rationalism and rationality: at least within the European intellectual culture it seems impossible to have a meaningful discussion on the topic without referring to the concept of reasons – not only in the sense of necessity and sufficiency, but also in determining, justifying, explaining, finalising and other aspects. This brings to mind G.W. Leibniz with his rule of philosophical rationality expressed in the formula: *nihil esse sine ratione* ("nothing is without a reason"), but also many other thinkers, who were looking for such a principle not in human thought but in practical action or attitudes of rational criticism and self-criticism (e.g. K.R. Popper). The problems mentioned at this point are meant to serve as an introduction and general justification for the historico-philosophical retrospective adopted in this book.

My exploration begins with the presentation of the rationality standards put forward by Plato. His idea of rationality and rationalisation of social life generally amounted to a conviction that the road towards these outcomes leads through the concentration of power in the hands of a select few, i.e., philosophers endowed with the task of designing the rudder of social life, and assuming the roles of both captain and helmsmen of this specific ship. As for others, he assigned them subservient yet important roles without which the ship would be unable to sail in the right direction. They could be compared to the crew members who take care of the sails or supervise this type of work. Plato was personally convinced that the more rigorously these roles were divided, the more accurately they would be executed, and the ship would thus move in the desired direction efficiently. His most prolific pupil, Aristotle, seemed to have some crucial doubts in this respect, and he was eager to grant more rights to those not on the bridge of a ship and, while not likely to be invited there in any foreseeable future, may or rather should assume greater responsibility than simply following orders from above.

The Renaissance was traditionally perceived as the period juxtaposed to the "Dark Middle Ages," and yet, nowadays it is seen as largely continuous with the culture of the Medieval Era under the spell of Christianity. It was at this time that a number of thinkers appeared whose ideas about the regulation of social life indicated that either the sailing requires corrections, or that changes ought to occur on the bridge of the ship. The former option was forwarded by L. B. Alberti, the latter is strongly associated with N. Machiavelli. Both presented justifications and explanations for the need to implement the changes they postulated. While these might be evaluated in various ways, it seems indisputable that all of these thinkers were right to recognise that the winds were starting to change. These new winds brought about a storm in the 16th century, in the form of the protestant revolution, as well as a progressive secularisation of social life in subsequent centuries.

The idea of secularisation obviously had many founding fathers. As early as the 17th century, there were philosophers whose ideas diminish the social order of either the aura of sanctity, or undermine its pillars of stability such as the Christian Church and Christian beliefs. The first of these applied to the legacy of T. Hobbes, the latter can be found in the writings of J. Locke. An even larger socially influential group of philosophers of this type appeared in the Enlightenment – the period known as the era of *reason* and *rationality*. This pushed leading thinkers to the conclusion that not only must the orientation of sailing be changed – from heavenly to earthly harbours – but also that the entire officer core must be replaced. This of course raises the question as to the grounds on which the enlightened philosophers demanded such radical changes. These doubts were addressed, for instance, by Ch. Montesquieu and C. Beccaria, whose ideas will be explored in this publication. Another question concerned the problem of which forces could and had the right to replace those who had hitherto been considered the representatives of complete or at least sufficient rationality, whose rationality was now being either denied altogether or judged incompatible with steering the ship in the right direction. These doubts were addressed by Enlightenment economists, including

F. Quesnay and A. Smith. Their answers did not, however, resonate with each other, as the former would typically look for the vital force in the agricultural economy, while the latter turned to the economy of large urban centres. And yet, both of them took it for granted that without the rationally organised economy and rational economic activity there cannot be any rational sailing within the other spheres of social life.

In the 19th and 20th centuries, this conclusion would not only be endorsed by liberals, one of the most important ideological and political formations in society, but also by the otherwise opposing communists and socialists. Especially among the socialists, there was no shortage of those looking towards heaven while thinking about earthly affairs and proposing solutions which in their view could make human life more bearable, and social relations more rational, and consequently more just. Still they were in the minority, as most socialists and communists were not only unconcerned with heaven, but even considered such concerns detrimental, and those who express them not fit to influence public life. Their demands were not only restricted to the elimination of religion and religiosity from social life: they went much further, postulating a general overhaul of social relations in their totality. In light of these demands, voice should be given to those who traditionally toiled on the deck performing the most physically demanding chores, i.e., to use the Marxist lingo, the "Workers of the world." Still, they needed to have someone on the bridge: the ideological, political and economic leaders – individuals who could show understanding for the needs of those who promoted them to such an exalted place (or who were brought there due to their resourcefulness or lucky coincidence). The question as to the proper way of achieving such deep social change would be answered by the socialists with reference to the force of arguments, whereas the communists would maintain that this is typically not sufficient and force would have to be resorted to – force that might often prove brutal and cause many deaths.

The above-mentioned ideas concerning rationalising social life and their practical implementations in various countries were criticised by liberals, who would point out that they do not constitute a step forward in social thought, but rather a regressive move, in many ways founded on the solutions of ancient philosophers such as Plato. K. R. Popper called them "utopian social engineers" engaged in great projects of social change, while F. A. von Hayek referred to them as "central planners" striving to run the economy from the top. The activity of such "engineers" and "planners" was not always seen by liberals to be socially detrimental, however it would be damaging if the collective reason and collective rationality is depreciated, supplanting it with the reason and rationality of the "engineers" and "planners." According to liberals, this is a sure road not only to social serfdom and totalitarianism, but also to social injustice and irrationality. Such at least seems to be the general message of the works of J. Rawls.

Chapter I

Rationality of social life according to the ancient philosophers

The list of philosophers in antiquity who were in search of social rationality is long and diverse in terms of worldview. Among the most eminent ones are Plato and Aristotle. They often differed in their essential assumptions and the solutions they suggested. They all agreed, however, that social life should be rational, or at least should aim at being rational. The possibility of attaining complete rationality of social life was presented and assessed in different ways.

1. Plato

Plato (427/8–347 BC) belonged to an aristocratic family from Athens. From a young age he was influenced by the philosophy of Socrates (which was supported by the relatives who were raising him, Critias and Charmides). He was considering a political career, but was discouraged by acts of political terror on the part of Athenian oligarchs. After the conviction of Socrates (399) he left Athens and took shelter in Megara – he became affiliated with the school of philosophy founded by Euclides. He subsequently went on a tour to other Greek cities as well as Italy and Egypt. While in Syracuse he won over Dion, the brother-in-law of Dionysus I the Elder, a tyrant who ruled over the city. However, the conflict with the ruler resulted in him leaving Sicily. He returned to Athens and around the year 387 he founded his own school of philosophy, called Plato's Academy, in the Grove of Academus. To the end of his life he remained its head (master) and a lecturer. In 367, at the invitation of his disciple, Dion, he set off on another journey to Sicily, where he tutored Dionysus II the Younger. He attempted to make him a philosopher who would be able to put into effect his concept of the rational state. The attempt ended in complete failure – Dionysus became disheartened with the concept, and it proved practically ineffective (it did not help the tyrant in his fight against the Carthaginians who threatened Sicily). This experiment also ended badly for his friend Dion (he was banished from Sicily, and his wealth was confiscated). The last years of Plato's life were devoted to lecturing and writing down his ideas. His literary output is particularly vast (it comprises thirty-six dissertations) and all of his works survived.[1] Three of them are crucial to the reconstruction of his concept of social life, i.e., *The Republic: Statesman* and *Laws.*

In the first of the above-mentioned works, Plato attempts to indicate that social life is rational only when, firstly, it occurs within the framework of a state, and, secondly, when it is orderly. It is orderly only when the respective social groups fulfil the duties they are allowed to, trained to and expected to fulfill. These potentials, skills and obligations were based on the tripartite theory of the human soul. Those who are motivated mainly by its rational aspect are wise men, and those who are dominated by the spiritual part are the warriors. In the case of farmers and craftsmen, it is the impulsive (appetitive) part that comes to the fore. The primacy of individual parts of the soul were treated by Plato not as inborn features, but rather as something developed in the course of a proper education conducted by the state.

It is possible to see Plato's rational society as a community of people educated and raised in such a way that each of its members knows his or her place and fulfills the duties arising from it, and is willing to and able to co-operate with other members of it. In one of the dialogues in *The Republic*, Socrates explains to Adeimantus: "a city, I believe, comes into being because each of us is not self-sufficient, but is in need of much. [...] So, then, when one man takes on another for one need and another for another need, and, since many things are needed, many men gather in one settlement as partners and helpers, to this common settlement we give the name city [...]." It is obviously a community of people who render services to each other – "one man [...] a farmer, another the housebuilder, and still another, a weaver [...] each one of them [should] put his work at the disposition of all in common – for example, [...] the farmer, one man, [should] provide food for four and spend four times as much time and labor in the provision of food and then give it in common to the others; or he must [...] produce a fourth part of the food in a fourth part of the time." A rational division of social roles among the professionals

[1] On the topic of the problems relating to the systematisation and interpretation of these works cf. G. Reale, *A History of Ancient Philosophy. II: Plato and Aristotle*, Albany 1990, p. 17 ff.

should mean that everything they produce is not only made faster, but is also finer ("the farmer, it seems, won't make his own plough himself, if it's going to be a fine one, or his hoe, or the rest of the tools for farming").[2]

Plato considered mental qualifications the most important, and intellectual ones in particular – such as those of both mathematics (which he sees as a propaedeutic discipline in educating the mind), and dialectics (which he considered to be directly dependent on reason and related to logic). These were to enable the possessor to reach the heart of the matter each time. The process of studying these methods is both time- and labour-consuming. In *The Republic*, Plato states that in mathematical science (arithmetic, geometry and astronomy), education should last ten years and in dialectics another five years. However, if one commits a lot of effort into overcoming these obstacles, one may eventually join the philosophers, who constitute a part of the ruling elite. In the above-cited work, Socrates tries to convince Glaucon that, as long as the elite does not take over the power, or at least does not have a fundamental influence on the ruling authorities, it will not be possible to prevent various social misfortunes. Thereby, Plato equated rationality with the happiness of citizens.

In *Statesman*, the topic of Plato's interest is the problem of rational conduct of those who rule and those who are ruled. The condition of this kind of rationality is that the former are properly educated and the latter skilfully disciplined. There is of course a need to address the meaning of proper education for those who rule. An attempt to answer this question was already made by Plato in *The Republic* and it was continued in *Statesman*. In the former work a properly educated statesman is a person who has the best interest of the subordinate at heart, and what follows is that "every kind of rule, insofar as it is rule, considers what is best for nothing other than for what is ruled and cared for."[3] On the other hand, in *Statesman*, the art of ruling does not consist in indulging the ruled but rather in enforcing the laws, and in managing social life in such a way that various human characters could be brought together to co-operate with each other wilfully and skilfully for the common good. It is obvious that the statesmen who act otherwise behave irrationally. Plato refers to them as Plato refers to them as "common statesmen" and criticises their conduct. He describes this type of a statesman as busy expanding the state, without seeing that this expansion is based on corruption and everything that statesmen in the past used to engage politics with (harbours, military arsenals, walls, levy, and other trivialities), forgetting about temperance and justice.[4]

[2] Cf. Plato, *The Republic*, New York 1991, pp. 45–47.

[3] Ibidem, p. 23.

[4] Cf. Plato, *Statesman*, New York 1901.

In the same work he explicated his views on the most rational social system, which turns out to be a specifically construed monarchy. Its specificity lies in, among others, concentrating all the power over a large number of subjects in the hands of a small number of philosophers. The most irrational system he considered to be democracy, in other words the rule of the common people – which was actually present in Athens of his time.

In *Laws* the main subject of the debate is the shape of the ideal or – which amounts to the same thing – completely rational state. Here social life is organised in such a way that nothing is left to chance and cannot exist outside the laws established by those who rule. The laws introduce, for instance, gender equality (including the imposition of obligatory military service), but at the same time a total ban on homosexual and polygamous relations, as well as the universal obligation to educate citizens, with the state taking responsibility for the upbringing of children. In this work, Plato may have departed from the idea, presented in *The Republic*, of temporary marriages within privileged social groups, but he was still of the opinion that all children were born for the sake of the state, and they all constituted the common good of all citizens.

A citizen who is responsible and behaves in a rational way ought to be cautious not to have more children than the state needs, and divide their social roles in such a way that every one of them does what they ought to do from the perspective of these needs. In order to explain the rules of this rational regulation, he wrote: if "a surplus of females or males occurs, or on the other hand a lack, there will be a designated magistracy – the greatest and most honoured, in fact – which should, after looking into all aspects, devise means of assisting those who have an excess or lack of offspring, so as to always, insofar as is possible, maintain the 5040 households intact. This is accomplished by means of various devices, including birth control for those who conceive too many children, or otherwise various ways of encouraging and stimulating a greater number of conceptions, for example the use of honors and dishonors, as well as the encouraging words of elders addressed to young people [...] Finally, if we're at a complete loss as to how to deal with the inequalities among the 5040 households, if we have an overflow of citizens because of the warmth of feeling among those who live together in households, and can't devise any other way out, there is the old device we've often spoken of: the dispatch of colonists from among those who seem suitable [...]."[5]

In Book V of *The Republic*, Plato enumerates a number of detailed recommendations related to rational procreation in a rationally organised state – such as a recommendation for "the best men to have intercourse as often as

[5] Cf. Plato, *The Laws of Plato*, Chicago and London 1988, pp. 127–128.

possible with the best women, and vice versa for the most ordinary men and the most ordinary women; and the offspring of the former must be reared but not that of the others, if the flock is going to be of the most eminent quality," or a recommendation that "they take the offspring of the good and bring them into the pen to certain nurses who live apart in certain sections of the city. And those of the worse, and any of the others born deformed, they will hide away in an unspeakable and unseen place, as is seemly." It should also be added that these suggestions concern people in their optimal reproductive period – which, according to Plato is 20 to 40 years old in the case of women and up to 50 in the case of men. "Now I suppose that when the men are beyond the age of procreation, we will, of course, leave them free to have intercourse with whomever they wish, except with a daughter, a mother, the children of their daughters and the ancestors of their mother, and as for the women, except with a son and a father and the descendants of the one and the ancestors of the other; and all this only after they have been told to be especially careful never to let even a single foetus see the light of day, if one should be conceived, to deal with it on the understanding that there's to be no rearing of such a child."[6] These are obviously only a part of the recommendations provided by Plato, which are to guarantee the rationality of social life. The list is so long and varied that only the greatest of minds are capable of comprehending its meaning. These are to be possessed only by philosophers of the Platonic type, i.e., those who are driven primarily by their intellect. Therefore, Plato placed them on the highest level of the social hierarchy.

Postscript

At present attempts to justify the assumptions and solutions proposed by Plato as well as critique are commonly found. The former appear for instance in the commentaries provided by Władysław Witwicki to the Polish edition of *The Republic*. Its author is not willing to accept all Plato's ideas, but presents justification for at least some of them. According to W. Witwicki "this major work of Plato raises various themes and does so in no specific order. [...] His point is, above all, what the a good man and a proper political system should be like." A proper system, according to Plato, is based on solid institutions, and these "do not serve the pleasure of all individuals. Individuals serve institutions [...] Hence, his ideal state resembles some great monastic order, a prison, a concentration camp or a totalitarian state, implying a project of harsh rigorous censorship, dishonesty in politics and absolute constraints even

[6] Cf. Plato, *The Republic*, op. cit., p. 138 ff.

in the most private spheres of life..." In his attempt to answer the question: where do these controversial beliefs come from?, Witwicki replies: they come from the fact that the citizens of Athens, driven by their sense of justice and the lawful rules of their state, sentenced Socrates to death. 'Hence the understandable protest in the soul of the young Plato and the necessity to rethink thoroughly the problems of justice and injustice. If the best individual in the state must die as a result of a verdict of the state, who is unjust? Socrates or the state? Obviously and undoubtedly the present state – democracy, which puts individuals and groups which are not well-born and not prepared for ruling first."[7] This "protest in the soul of the young Plato" is to constitute if not the most important then certainly one of the most important arguments justifying his standards for a rational state.

The next arguments appear in the shape of specific problems and ideas expounded by Plato. For example, in footnote 19 to the theses included in Book I of the work, Witwicki develops and brings up to date Plato's suggestion that "people who hold public office nowadays do so for the money, honours and dirty profits, they are evil people, ambitious, vain, thieves. Good people, who think, who are as they should be, would engage in ruling out of their sense of duty and out of fear that they could be ruled by lesser people. It ought to be so, but it is not." In footnote 9 to Plato's opinion on popular beliefs, which is added in Book II, the author explains that these beliefs "do not constitute a moral ground for a man who thinks. Honesty is quietly treated as an excess, something not actually indispensable, and something which costs more than it is worth." In footnote 23 to Book III, the author highlights the fact that Plato "does not demonstrate great trust in human nature and knows that people will not out of their own volition organise a state of which he would approve." In footnote 7 to the enfranchisement of women in military service proposed in Book V, Witwicki reminds us that "it was written by a homosexual who never loved a woman, nor had any children, though he appreciated the charm of a child and was skilful in describing it..." In the next footnote, he adds: "Plato is very far from deliberating on debauchery or liberty of sexual life. On the contrary, one must arrange these kind of relations strictly and keep register of it, according to numbers and dates. What is more, they must be sanctified, as it might *prove to be useful* [emphasis – W. W.], says Plato two lines above, before describing a system of mating hunting dogs, horses and noble birds which is to constitute an example for breeding people; hence, the sober naturalistic position." Even for such controversial solutions as Plato's proposal

[7] Cf. W. Witwicki, "Wstęp od tłumacza" [Translator's foreword], in *Państwo* [Republic], Kęty 2006, p. 5 ff.

of a "community of women and children" or "leaving in the pen or killing the less valued children," Witwicki provides, if not arguments justifying it, then at least such which indicate its origin. In his opinion they can be traced to the character features of this philosopher, such as "the aridity of a schizothymic, which inhibits him from exploring other people's feelings," or an inclination towards imposing on others what is close to him ("he patronises people's souls; he is eager to impose on them what he considers proper, and he does not take into account whether it is going to be painful or not").[8]

Obviously, the footnotes to this translation of the work contain many more such explanations of the solutions to immanent social problems which were adopted and proposed by Plato. They sometimes assume a form of explication of what the author of *The Republic* did not want to or was not able to state in certain terms. Some of the arguments, however, attempt to justify this concept of a state that is to be hierarchical, authoritarian and in some respects dictatorial. Although Witwicki claims that Plato's support for dictatorship in Book VIII of the work, and references to it as a form of government that is "so beautiful" are nothing more than a hoax which he is surprised was treated seriously by Cicero, it remains sure that this philosopher questioned such fundamental values as civil liberty, and the form of political system which Athenian democracy of the time was.

The latter Plato presented, among others, a form of state where "the teacher is afraid of his pupils and begins to flatter them, and the pupils do not respect their teacher, or the servants who take them to the school. In general young people begin to resemble the old and they begin to compete with them with regard to words and actions, and the old join the young, they display their wits and play tricks, imitating the youth, so as not to seem grim or excessively domineering."[9] Nowadays such behaviour does not only seem rational to us, but also normal and proper. Plato, however, viewed them as a threat to the social structures of a rationally organised state.

One might of course try to find the reasons why Witwicki devised this specific defence of Plato. On the basis of comments such as those included in footnote 15 to Book VIII (social groups are mentioned there whose "aversion to any kind of enforcement paves the way for dictatorship") as well as footnote 16 in the same Book (both the proletariat and its party leaders are mentioned, the latter becoming specific kinds of dictators by promising wonders to the former) one can conclude that the arguments are not only derived from the analysis of Plato's *Republic*, and not even only from the analysis of the

[8] Ibidem, p. 163 ff.

[9] Ibidem, p. 272 ff.

social circumstances in which it was written, but also from personal feelings and reflections of the author of the Polish translation of this work, including reflections on the so-called people's democracy of the countries which used to be part of the common political bloc of Central and Eastern Europe. Disentangling this complicated knot of interdependencies in the arguments that Witwicki provides to justify the Platonic standards for the rational state is possible. However, it requires a broader analysis.

Extensive commentaries on Plato's views also appear in various dissertations of K. R. Popper, in *The Open Society and its Enemies* in particular. This work constitutes a significant *votum separatum* with respect not only to the type of state which is mentioned in the works of this philosopher, but also to communist states which emerged as political units in the 20th century. Hence, it has at least two negative protagonists – Plato and Karl Marx. The latter is presented by Popper as a constructive continuator of the vision of a rational state which is presented in the works of the former – constructive in the sense that he formulated "an allegedly scientific prophecy: the era of socialism (or communism – subtleties in terminology are not important) will arrive in all certainty. One certain conclusion could be derived from this: the secure victory of the socialist revolution of the workers will mark the beginning of a social world with only one class. [...] The conviction was held that, if this line of reasoning is correct, then we have an unquestionable duty to do anything possible to accelerate the arrival of socialism so that its inevitable reign could come about as mildly and peacefully as possible."[10] According to Popper this line of reasoning is invalid and the "allegedly scientific prediction" constitutes one great historical lie. Not the first one, however, as one of the first to do this was Plato.

In order to unravel this mental shortcut one needs to refer, among others, to the Popperian concept of "historicism." He carried out a detailed analysis and critique of this term in the dissertation *The Poverty of Historicism*. In the *Introduction* to *Open Society*, Popper states that the first task of this book is "to contribute to a better understanding of totalitarianism and the meaning of the eternal fight against it. The other task of the book is to analyse the possibility of applying critical and rational scientific methods to the issues related to the open society. Therefore, by analysing the rules of a democratic reconstruction of society [...] I attempt to explain some of the obstacles that stand in the

[10] "By writing this book I wanted to accomplish two goals: firstly, I wanted to demonstrate that Marx's prophecy is incorrect, and secondly, I wanted to present a different and a more attractive alternative to the society of the future. I named it open society. I introduced the term as a synonym for a less fortunate term: 'democracy.'" Cf. K. R. Popper, "Przedmowa do czytelnika polskiego" [A foreword to the Polish reader], in *Społeczeństwo otwarte i jego wrogowie* [The Open Society and its Enemies], vol. 1, Warsaw 1993, p. 10 ff.

way of a rational approach towards the problems of social reconstruction, and I do this by criticising those social philosophies which are responsible for a widespread negative attitude towards the possibility of democratic reforms. The most powerful of these philosophies is the one called historicism."[11]

What seems to identify historicism best is a belief in "Inexorable Laws of Historical Destiny." Popper dedicates *The Poverty of Historicism* to all victims of this belief. And in this book he attempts to demonstrate that "historicism is a poor method – a method which does not bear any fruit." In the Foreword to this dissertation he provides an overview of his line of reasoning against historicism. Thus it may be noted that the Popperian critique of this method of thinking about social life is based on the following assumptions: "1. The course of human history is strongly influenced by the growth of human knowledge [...] 2. We cannot predict, by rational or scientific methods, the future growth of our scientific knowledge. [...] 3. We therefore can not predict the future course of human history 4. [...] This means that we must reject the possibility of a theoretical history [...] There can be no scientific theory of historical development serving as basis for historical prediction. 5. The fundamental aim of historicist methods [...] is therefore misconceived."[12] One such fundamental aim turns out to be formulating such historical laws which would allow the prediction of even very distant events, albeit not in complete detail. According to Popper the historical laws that make predictions possible are essentially "historical prophecies."[13] They do not and cannot have justification in objective knowledge. They may be and very often are justified, however, by the "habit of historical prophecy, so widespread among our intellectual leaders" and by the opinion of those who believe that "intellectual leaders are gifted with such powers."[14]

In volume I of *The Open Society*, which is entitled *The Spell of Plato*, Popper analyses both his theory of social life and the philosophers who were the forerunners of historicism and who exerted an influence on the Platonic standards of rationality. According to his opinion, Plato – similar to other Greek

[11] Cf. ibidem, p. 21 ff.

[12] Cf. K. R. Popper, *The Poverty of Historicism*, London 2002, pp. xi–xii.

[13] Cf. ibidem, p. 37.

[14] "But there are sometimes further motives for holding historicist beliefs. The prophets who announce that certain events are bound to happen make propaganda for them, and help to bring them about. The prophets who foresee the upcoming millennium very often express in their predictions a deeply rooted dissatisfaction with the present state of affairs: their fantasies may inspire true comfort in those who cannot cope without such support. It ought to be remembered, however, that such influence can prevent us from solving everyday problems of living in a society [...] If you know that things are bound to happen whatever you do, then you may feel free to give up the fight against them." Cf. K. R. Popper, "Przedmowa do czytelnika polskiego" [A foreword to the Polish reader], op. cit., p 24 ff.

philosophers – was mainly under the influence of Heraclitus, the philosopher who "discovered the idea of change" – "Everything is in flux and nothing is at rest" is the motto of his philosophy.[15] In light of the beliefs of both philosophers all change "must be directed towards the imperfect and the evil, towards corruption." Plato, however, believed that "it is possible for us, by a human, or rather by a superhuman effort, to break through the fatal historical trend and to put an end to the process of decay." This effort is based on reason, which is shared by only few.[16] Moreover, this is where Platonic rationalism stems from, as well as its components, such as: 1. methodological essentialism (according to which "it is the task of pure knowledge or 'science' to describe the true nature of things, i.e., their hidden reality or essence"); 2. descriptive sociologism ("Plato's sociology is an ingenious blend of speculation with acute observation of facts"); 3. A rigorously observed class or rather caste system (in *The Republic* "there are actually only two castes, the military caste – the armed and educated rulers – and the unarmed and uneducated ruled, the human sheep"); 4. totalitarian justice ("I assert that in *The Republic* he used the term 'just' as a synonym for 'that which is in the interest of the best state'"); 5. institutionalism ("Plato's principle of leadership is far removed from pure personalism, since it involves the working of institutions); 6. The concept of the "philosopher king" who is not only "a lover of truth," but also – in situations where it is in the interest of the state – of half-truth, or even untruth ("it is one of the royal privileges of the sovereign to make full use of lies and deceit"). This of course does not constitute a complete list of the components of Platonic rationalism that were analysed and presented by Popper in *The Open Society*. Yet even its abbreviated and simplified picture may bewilder or even shock the contemporary reader. This is acknowledged by the author of *The Open Society* himself, in the summary of the presentation of Plato's "philosopher king."[17]

2. Aristotle

The position of Aristotle (384–322 BC) in European philosophy is as strong as Plato's, and in some respects his influence is even more evident (for instance

[15] Cf. K.R. Popper, *The Open Society and its Enemies*, Princeton 1966, pp. 11–12.

[16] "[...] the prophecy, in the *Statesman*, of the return of the Golden Age, of a new millennium, is the expression of such a belief in the form of a myth. This may be, but he certainly believed in both – in a general historical tendency towards corruption, and in the possibility that we may stop further corruption in the political field by *arresting all political change.*" Cf. ibidem, pp. 20–21.

[17] "I think we must face the fact that behind the sovereignty stands the quest for power. The beautiful portrait of the sovereign is a self-portrait. When we have recovered from the shock of this finding, we may look anew at the awe-inspiring portrait; and if we can fortify ourselves with a small dose of Socratic irony then we may cease to find it so terrifying." Ibidem, p. 157.

with respect to various systematisations and classifications). He was born in Stagira, in a family which had connections to the Macedonian royal court (his father was a personal physician to Amyntas III, the grandfather of Alexander the Great). He was sent to Plato's Academy, where he was educated in the art of rhetoric (even participating in oratorical contests). After the death of Plato he accepted the invitation of Hermias, ruler of Assos, and left the Academy and Athens. After a three-year stay in Assos he went to Mytilene (on the island of Lesbos). Together with his disciple, Teophrastus, he established a philosophical circle which was modelled on Plato's Academy. At the beginning of the year 342 BC he was invited by Philip II, the father of Alexander the Great, who was thirteen years old at the time, to Pella, the capital of Macedonia, which he accepted, becoming tutor to the future ruler. There is no indication that his views on social life had any influence on the politics of this ruler, who was ambitious and ruthless in pursuit of the objectives he had set for himself. In 335 BC, Aristotle returned to Athens and founded his own philosophical school there (near the temple of Apollo Lyceus), which was named peripatetic (Gr. *peripatetikos* – one who walks from place to place), after the custom of having philosophical discussions while walking about. During its twelve years of activity in Athens, the school was highly acclaimed, and in later centuries it became a symbol of the splendour of Greek thought for many philosophers and scholars. After the death of Alexander the Great (he died in mysterious circumstances in 323 BC in Egypt, at the age of 33), anti-Macedonian sentiment flared up in Athens, prompting Aristotle to leave the city. He spent the final year of his life in his mother's estate in Chalcis (on the Euboea island).

Aristotle's literary output is considerable, both in terms of quality and quantity. Diogenes Laertius, in his *Lives and Opinions of Eminent Philosophers*, calculated the number of poems in Aristotle's works and came to a total of 445 270. At the same time he drew attention to a good starting point for the discussion of the Aristotelian concept of rationality of social life: Aristotle divided the whole of philosophy into two parts, namely practical and theoretical philosophy. "The practical is divided into the ethical and political, the latter including considerations affecting not only the state, but also the management of a single house. The theoretical part is subdivided into physics and logic; the latter being not only a single category, but rather a highly accurate instrument for every art."[18] Aristotelian logic, or analytics, as he called it, was meant to be both the most efficient tool for other branches of philosophy (the so-called organon), and also an indispensable introduction to them. On-going debates concern its individual nature, and most notably whether it can be reduced to syllogism, a reduction made by the Medieval Aristotelians. What is important to the present discussion is the fact that, according to this logic, what ought

[18] Cf. Diogenes Laertius, *The Lives and Opinions of Eminent Philosophers*, London 1853, p. 191.

to be done first in all branches of science is to acquire knowledge about first principles (which are treated as axioms), and subsequently deduce other assertions (so-called theorems).

There are several rules in the Aristotelian "philosophy of human affairs," which is broadly referred to as practical philosophy. The most general states that "every action and rational choice is thought to aim at some good."[19] The following rules constitute its immediate complementation: identifying good with happiness and happiness with rational activity, which remains in accordance with virtue, or strictly speaking virtues, as there are many of them, ordered according to a hierarchical list. It seems reasonable at this point to quote more broadly from Aristotle's *Nicomachean Ethics*, as we enter the terrain of the theory of social rationalism of this philosopher directly. He writes: "For living is obviously shared even by plants, while what we are looking for is something unique to a human being. We should therefore rule out life as nourishment and growth. Next would be some sort of sentient life, but this again is clearly shared by the horse, the ox, indeed by every animal. What remains is a life, concerned in some way with action of the element that possesses reason. [...] let us assume that we are talking about the life concerned with action in the sense of activity, because this seems to be a more proper use of the phrase. If the characteristic activity of a human being is activity of the soul in accordance with reason or at least not entirely lacking it; and if we say that the characteristic activity of anything is the same in kind as that of a good thing of the same type [...] and if we take this kind of life to be activity of the soul and actions in accordance with reason, and the characteristic activity of the good person to be to carry this out well and nobly, and a characteristic activity to be accomplished well when it is accomplished in accordance with the appropriate virtue; then if this is so, the human good turns out to be activity of the soul in accordance with virtue, and if there are several virtues, in accordance with the best and most complete."[20]

It is debatable what belongs to the first and what to the second order. What remains unquestionable, however, is the fact that Aristotle equated a human being with the pursuit of such a basic aim in life, which is to achieve happiness with courage, and then courage with virtue, and virtue with rationality. What is implied is that an irrational person is not capable of being happy. For a better understanding of this rule, Aristotle classified virtues and indicated their relation to reason and rationality. The first group are the so-called intellectual virtues pertaining to the most noble part of the soul, i.e., theoretical reasoning –

[19] Aristotle, *Nicomachean Ethics*, Cambridge 2000, p. 3.

[20] Ibidem, pp. 11–12.

they are referred to as *dianoethical*. One of the virtues of this type is wisdom. The other group comprises the so-called ethical virtues – they also pertain to the rational part of the soul, but only in the sense that they are developed by reason in the process of taking control over various extreme urges and feelings – rashness and cowardice, meanness and prodigality, etc. Aristotle also indicated a general rule concerning this activity of reason. It is the doctrine of the so-called golden mean between the extremes. In practice, the rule is to lead to the development of such ethical virtues as good temper, courage, modesty, temperance, righteous indignation, justice, generosity, truthfulness, friendliness, proper ambition, magnanimity, magnificence and prudence (practical wisdom). They are all supposed to display a moral and rational character simultaneously. This means that they are both dependant on reason and have rational grounds. For example, prudence is supposed to be the "golden" (i.e. rationally justified) mean between cleverness and inanity, temperance a rationally justified mean between extravagance and miserliness, generosity a rationally justified mean between prodigality and meanness. It is also important to note that dianoethic virtues are considered superior to ethical virtues (this means, among others, that one cannot be truly courageous without being wise), with reason superior to both. Accordingly, it is not possible to be courageous, which is ethically virtuous, without being rational, or to be rational without courage.

Aristotle's association of ethics with politics is based on naturalistic as well as theistic grounds – the philosopher refers not only to "worldly things," but also to what belongs to the divine world. Briefly speaking, it appears that social life is a necessity: not evidence of the greatness of humans, but of their fundamental weakness. It manifests itself above all in the inability of humans to achieve what they desire most, which is perfect happiness. The latter is destined for gods and gods only, since only they are capable of such activity as "theoretical contemplation." In *Nicomachean Ethics* he wrote that "while the life of the gods is entirely blessed, and that of human beings is so to the extent that it contains something like this sort of activity, none of the other animals are happy, because they have no share in this contemplation. Happiness, then, extends as far as contemplation..."[21]

One may ask the question whether gods in this context are social or asocial beings? Aristotle himself did not deliberate on this, as he limited his ethics to the statement that God is perfection and what is left to humans is to contemplate God, who represents the highest level of rationality, as well as to imitate Him in every possible context, which is possible in social life, among others. Rational justification for such a life is the mentioned imitation of God or the

[21] Ibidem, p. 198.

aim of absolute perfection, which is basically the same thing. This justification undoubtedly made it easier for later Christian theologians to incorporate Aristotle's social thought into the doctrine of the Church.

In *Politics* Aristotle equated social life in communities larger than a village with living in the state: "[w]hen several villages are united in a single community, perfect and large enough to be nearly or quite self-sufficient, the state comes into existence, originating in the bare necessities of life, and continuing in the strive towards a good life. Therefore, if the earlier forms of society are natural, so is the state, for it is their end, and the [completed] nature is the end [...] Hence it is evident that the state is a creation of nature, and that man is by nature a political animal. And he who by nature and not by mere accident is without a state, is either above humanity, or below it; he is the 'tribeless, lawless, hearthless one,' whom Homer denounces – the outcast who is a lover of war; he may be compared to an unprotected piece in the game of draughts [...]."[22] He later added (in defence of both rational human beings and a rational state), that what distinguishes human beings from other living creatures is the fact that "[...] it is characteristic of man that he alone has any sense of good and evil, of just and unjust, and the association of living beings who have this sense makes a family and a state. Thus the state is by nature clearly prior to the family and to the individual, since the whole is of necessity prior to the part [...] the proof that the state is a creation of nature and prior to the individual is that the individual, when isolated, is not self-sufficient, and therefore he is like a part in relation to the whole. But he who is unable to live in society, or who has no need for it because he is sufficient unto himself, must be either a beast or a god."[23]

This complete support for rational human beings living within a rationally organised state is directly reflected in the perception of the functioning of a family as no more than a gear in the great machine that the rational state constitutes. Needless to say, the one cannot function without the other. There is no doubt, however, that according to Aristotle it is not the state which plays an auxiliary role in relation to the family, but the family in relation to the state. In order to aptly fulfil its role, it ought to be organised hierarchically. In *Politics* the role of the master of a family ought to be assumed by the man. To justify this proposal, Aristotle states that a man is by nature stronger and he is guided by reason to a greater extent than a woman. A free woman, however, stands above a slave. The latter is merely "an instrument of action." When further referring to slaves, he wrote that while nature provided them with robust bodies, they received little reason, which means they comprehend very little, and are

[22] Aristotle, *Politics*, trans. B. Jowett, Oxford 1908, p. 28.

[23] Ibidem, p. 29.

driven mainly by their senses and orders coming from those who own them. He would add at the same time that there is very little difference between them and tame animals ("for both with their bodies minister to the needs of life").

In response to the question "What is the task of a social group organised in this manner?" Aristotle indicates not one, but a set of aims situated on different levels, but also complementary to each other. On the most elementary level, which is fulfilling bodily needs, he positions the accumulation of wealth (the study of rational activity in this domain is referred to as chrematistics). It is not expected of people equipped with reason to restrict themselves to mere consumption, or even to accumulation of wealth. In *Politics* Aristotle judges those who "are led to believe that making money is the object of household management, and the whole idea of their lives is that they ought to either increase their money without limit, or at least not lose it. The origin of this disposition in men is that they are intent upon living only, and not upon living well..."[24] And living well is – above all – living wisely. In order to achieve this, one must obviously be equipped with reason and skills enabling one to use it. In light of Aristotle's work quoted above, it is a prerequisite, but not sufficient for acquiring civil rights, as one is also required to be free, take part in courts and citizen's assemblies, which enact the law and rule the state, as well as possess such wealth as enables one to participate in public life. These conditions are not met by slaves or craftsmen, who are also denied citizens' rights by the author of the *Politics.*

In his justification of the idea of a state characterised by such strict hierarchy, Aristotle presents the specific character of three basic systems of government: monarchy, aristocracy and polity, and subsequently indicates their perversions. The first of the forms ("kingship") constitutes a kind of autocracy, the second is the rule of few, the third is the rule of citizens. Of the above-mentioned forms, the perversions are as follows: "of royalty, tyranny; of aristocracy, oligarchy; of constitutional government, democracy. For tyranny is a kind of monarchy which takes to heart the interest of the monarch only; oligarchy sees only the interest of the wealthy; democracy, of the needy – none takes into account the common good of all." What follows, it is irrational by nature.[25] However, until such perversions do not occur, each of the above-mentioned forms of government has its rational justification and may be considered not only in agreement with nature, but also in agreement with dianoethical and ethical virtues, including justice.

[24] Ibidem, p. 44.

[25] Cf. ibidem, p. 115.

However, the level of their compatibility with the above-mentioned values varies. It is the highest in the case of polity, as the general rule of the "golden mean" between such extremities as monarchy and democracy is implemented there to the broadest extent. The implementation of this rule also manifests itself in the fact that in polity the middle class, that is those (male) citizens who are neither extremely rich nor poor, so they find time and pleasure in dealing with public affairs. "And this is the class of citizens which is most secure in a state, for they do not, like the poor, covet their neighbours' goods, nor do others covet theirs, as the poor covet the goods of the rich [...]." Therefore, "the best political community is formed by citizens of the middle class" and "those states are likely to be well-administered, in which the middle class is large."[26]

Aristotle's *Politics* does not discuss the concept of the ideal state. It does, however, present the concept of the best state, also in the sense of being compatible with virtue and reason. It significantly distinguishes this vision of a rational social life form the one proposed by Plato in his *Republic.* After all, it may be suggested that the former was consciously formulated in opposition to the latter. What seems controversial is whether this opposition led Aristotle to break away from what Popper associated with the "closed society." Opinions of experts on these two notions are divided. For example, according to Giovanni Reale "here Aristotle is very close to Plato, which is not commonly acknowledged."[27] Arguments for their similarity are further supported by the focus of both thinkers on what is ideal (spiritual, moral and rational), and also their support for the relatively limited social elite. Although Aristotle did not reduce it to philosophers and the rulers following their advice, it is still small in relation to – as we would contemporarily say – the socially excluded. According to Stagirite this includes not only slaves, but also craftsmen, farmers and women.

Even if the Aristotelian concept of social life does not imply full support for a specific kind of totalitarianism, at least some aspects display such features. The most totalitarian in this Aristotelian optimal state is of course the rule of Reason which in the end proves to be the ultimate conqueror and the most ruthless ruler. It does not allow anyone who does not comprehend and acknowledge of its many mutually complementary arguments to speak.

[26] Ibidem, p. 169.

[27] "[T]here are certain aberrant aspects of the Platonic republic that the Stagirite criticizes and rejects, but not the basic ideal that it expresses." G. Reale, *A History of Ancient Philosophy...*, op. cit., p. 348.

Postscript

The Aristotelian concept of the rationalisation of social life was eagerly commented on in later ages, both by Aristotelians and their critics, including those who believed that it was their lifelong vocation to liberate the thinking man completely from the arguments stemming from it. Some arguments were easier to handle than others. The latter include the Aristotelian arguments justifying the different sorts of discrimination towards slaves, craftsmen, farmers and women. The strongest objection remainshis support of slavery as the basis of rational social life. Needless to say, Aristotle was not an innovator in this matter. On the contrary, he joined an existing school of thought that, in the theory and practice of social life, considered slavery to be in accordance with both nature and reason. He might be accused of not being able to break free of this conviction, which was called a prejudice by his opponents.[28] One might also accuse him of perpetuating and justifying it by the power of his authority.

And yet, it would be difficult to acknowledge him as a "founding father" of such practices which constitute an insult against the basic sense of justice. It seems unlikely that any number of these traders and slave owners read *Politics* or were seeking for justification for their actions in other philosophical works. Even in the 18th century, when the relationship between philosophy, politics and practice grew closer, the topic of slavery was brought up more enthusiastically by its opponents than advocates. The fight against this practice and the views justifying it was not initiated in philosophical circles, but by puritan theologians who were engaged in missionary activity in the so-called New World, i.e., in America. They were American Quakers and Methodists who, first in Pennsylvania and then in other states, publicly denounced slavery by stating that it stood in conflict not only to human nature, but also to divine law.[29] In the second half of the 18th century they gained the support of major American politicians (such as Thomas Jefferson and Benjamin Franklin). This eventually led to first a ban on the slave trade (1807) and later (1863) a proposal abolishing slavery in the United States of America, which was incorporated into the American constitution (the so-called Thirteenth Amendment).

[28] G. Reale writes that Aristotle "embraces a typically Hellenic prejudice according to which the Greek is by nature superior to the barbarian," and continues "which was a prejudice of an absolutely ethnic character, and as such, fundamentally irrational." Cf. ibidem, p. 341.

[29] Gertrude Himmelfarb, when describing the participation of the American puritans in the early stage of the abolitionist movement, notes that in the second half of the 18th century "methodist preachers agreed to free their own slaves and persuaded many of their parishioners to do so as well." Cf. G. Himmelfarb, *The Roads to Modernity. The British, French, and American Enlightenments*, New York 2004, p. 222 ff.

Before it was formulated and written into the US Constitution, it had raised many doubts. For example, T. Jefferson, during the time when he was governor of Virginia (1779–1781), brought about the ban on the slave trade in this state, but at the same time he proposed that former slaves should be provided with weapons and sent as colonists to other states. During her analysis of this difficult time in American history, G. Himmelfarb observes that in those days such a view "did not seem quite as bizarre as it now appears to be" (as it was based on the presumption that there exist "deep-rooted prejudices of whites" and "the memories of blacks of the injuries they had sustained [...] which would always divide the races"), and this was not isolated. ("Madison had endorsed a similar proposal [...] Where the society had sought to transport only freed slaves to Africa, Madison suggested that the policy be extended to all blacks and that the government bear the cost of transportation...")

In the Old World, the initiators of the great debate on slavery, and later of the ban on the slave trade, were puritan clergymen as well as politicians and philanthropists. In Great Britain such leaders of the abolitionist movement included William Wilberforce (he had a significant influence on the British Parliament's ban of the slave trade in 1807), and Thomas Fowell Buxton. Philosophers, politicians and social activists in other countries followed the example of England. Moreover, it ought to be noted that in 1810 the slave trade was abolished in Mexico and Venezuela, in 1811 in Chile, in 1812 in Argentina and several years later also in other South American countries. In the second half of the 19th century and in the 20th century a similar struggle took place in Africa and Asia. The last of these countries where slavery was abolished in the formal-legal sense was Saudi Arabia (in 1962). Of course this had a significant impact on those who derived profit from slavery, but also on those who attempted to providerational justification for it.

Placing craftsmen on a level not much higher than slaves – with the Aristotle's justification that they are "an instrument of action" – also has a long history in European culture. Certainly the author of *Politics* was not its inventor. With the force of his authority, however, he contributed to its reinforcement, and those who attempted to re-evaluate this matter had to deal both with the custom of treating craftsmen as people of a lower social category, and the philosophical grounds for their exclusion from the group enjoying full civil rights.

Around the 13th century three social estates were distinguished in Europe: those who pray, that is the clergy (who constituted the First Estate); those who fight, that is knights and nobility (who constituted the Second Estate); and the third estate, which included either only craftsmen, or also, as for example in France, craftsmen and farmers. Each of these estates had specific duties, and each of them benefited from certain privileges which were granted by the law (fiscal, legal, honorary, etc.). However, the various proportions between duties and privileges (also referred to as freedoms) in each of the estates was uneven. This generated feelings of injustice and in time led to revolutionary changes in the feudal system.

However, its beginnings were much more peaceful. It came about from a re-evaluation of the system which included raising the status of some of the groups in the third estate. The first such attempts occurred towards the end of the 14th and at the beginning of the 15th century, and were connected with appreciating crafts such as painting, sculpture, or architecture. As a matter of fact, this led to considerable and relatively quick success: at the end of the 15th century, people engaged in these activities were promoted from craftsmen to artists, which substantially improved their social position. Paolo Rossi mentions that "in the fourteenth century art was still considered a manual skill. The artist was addressed with the familiar 'thou' as were domestic servants. No affluent citizens and nobles would have considered the artist's status humiliating [...]. In the early years of the century, sculptors and architects in Florence were members of the minor guild of masons and carpenters while painters were classed as associates of the major guild of doctors and druggists [...] in the mid-fifteenth century, commissions or an artisan character no longer appeared in keeping with the dignity of the artist. This was the age when Charles V stooped to pick up the brush dropped by Titian."[30] However, it should be noted that the actual group of people who were promoted form the status of craftsman to acknowledged artist was relatively small and, in short, not very stable. This social position was quite difficult to obtain, but relatively easy to lose. Goldsmithing, which may serve as an example here, was treated at some point of its history as authentic art, but within its present social reception functions rather as a form of craft.

Another attempt to raise the value of craft occurred during the Enlightenment. This is best represented in one of the prominent symbols of that time which was *The Encyclopaedia, or a Systematic Dictionary of the Sciences, Arts and Crafts*, colloquially known as *The Encyclopédie*. The order of its components is not coincidental: science features first, art second and craft third. All of these are to be created and controlled by the human reason or a rational entity, which, according to the editors and authors of this work, is a human being.

Whether this and other attempts finally contributed to disproving the Aristotelian position on the subordinate position of craft and craftsmen is not certain – not only because it is deeply rooted in European culture, but also be-

[30] P. Rossi, *Filozofowie i maszyny* [Men and Maschines], Warsaw 1978, p. 32 ff.

cause the levels of respective types of craft vary, as do craftsmen and the types of services they render. A similar conclusion in relation to the social position of women would probably be met with accusations of male chauvinism. This may serve, among others, as confirmation that the women rights movement has achieved significant success during the two centuries of its struggle against the belief (which operated in European culture long before Aristotle) that the sexes are not equal. One of the initiators of this movement was Mary Wollstonecraft, author of the work *A Vindication of the Rights of Woman*, published in 1792 in England. It is worth recalling this defence, as many of its arguments constitute a direct polemic with Aristotle's support for the privileges of men.

Wollstonecraft does not question the Aristotelian proposition that in general women are guided by reason in their actions to a lesser extent than men. In her opinion, however, this is not a result of female nature, but culture, and, strictly speaking, the way they are brought up and prepared for the social role imposed on them by men. In *A Vindication of the Rights of Woman* she writes that "[w]omen are told from their infancy, and taught by the example of their mothers, that a little knowledge of human weakness, justly termed cunning, softness of temper, *outward* obedience, and scrupulous attention to a puerile kind of property, will obtain for them the protection of man, and should they be beautiful, everything else is needless, for at least twenty years of their lives."[31] She also shares Aristotle's view that reason and virtue are strongly associated with each other. She does not agree, however, that women should aim at other kinds of virtue than men: "To account for, and excuse the tyranny of men, many ingenious arguments have been brought forward to prove, that the two sexes, in the acquirement of virtue, ought to aim at attaining a very different character; or, to speak explicitly, women are not allowed to have sufficient strength of mind to acquire what really deserves the name of virtue."[32] Wollstonecraft considers the conviction that women are incapable of cultivating male virtues (courage) and values irrational and, as a matter of fact, as disabling women to fulfil the social functions of good mother, faithful wife, patriotic citizen, etc. ("To render women truly useful members of society, I argue that they should be led, by having their understandings cultivated on a large scale, to acquire a rational affection for their country, founded on knowledge, because it is obvious that we are little interested about what we do not understand."[33]) The work also includes a passage in which men are accused of sexism. ("I lament that women are systematically degraded by receiving the trivial attentions which men think it manly to pay to the sex, when, in fact, they are insultingly

[31] Cf. M. Wollstonecraft, *A Vindication of the Rights of Woman*, London 1891, p. 14.

[32] Ibidem.

[33] Ibidem, p. 278.

supporting their own superiority.") Following this line of argumentation this precursor of the feminist movement draws the general conclusion that by ignorance women are rendered foolish or vicious at present" and a "revolution in female manners" ought to be effected in order to change this situation.

At present, it may be stated that at least in the West such a revolution has been accomplished. It manifests itself among others in the fact that women have gained the right to vote, access to education, the right to hold public office, including governmental office, on equal terms with men. However, this did not happen overnight, or to the extent that the radical proponents of the feminist movement would have wanted, such as Betty Friedan, the author of the book *The Feminine Mystique.* Here she condemns discrimination towards women in the spheres of the law, the workplace, earnings and maternity (she advocates the right to abortion). It seems reasonable to reiterate at this point that the great struggle for voting rights which took place in 19th century Europe basically concerned only the rights of men. In many European countries women obtained the rights much later (for example in France in 1944, in Italy in 1945, and in Switzerland as late as in 1971). Needless to say this "revolution in female manners" did not result in, and in fact could not have resulted in the elimination of various prejudices and stereotypes regarding the so-called female nature.[34] In any event, this struggle constitutes a continuation of the great polemic with the rationality standards of social life adopted and promoted by Aristotle and the Aristotelians.

[34] For more on the subject cf. U. Johansson, *Transformation of Gendered Work: Dualistic Stereotypes and Paradoxical Reality*, Lund 1997.

Chapter II

Rationality of social life according to the Renaissance philosophers

At the outset of this chapter I present a vision of the rationality of social life which was still being developed within the framework of Christian thought, yet, in the context of the Late Medieval period it would already herald a new era. Leone Battista Alberti is its representative author. In the last part, I delve into another vision, which moves outside of the universe of Christian values and enters the domain characteristic of the later secular culture, as represented by Niccolò Machiavelli.

1. Leone Battista Alberti

Alberti (1404–1472) is mostly remembered as a great architect, responsible for the construction of some notable architectural artefacts, including a triumphal arch in Ferrara which stands to this day. He is also the author of the treatise *On the art of building in ten books* (*De re aedificatoria*, 1452), which became something of a textbook for many Renaissance architects. His *The Family in Renaissance Florence* (*I libra della famiglia*, 1444) remains much less known. The main protagonists of this treatise, which is written in dialogical form, are Adovardo, Giannozzo, Lionardo and Battista. The former two tend to be more defensive of traditionalisms than the others, however, all of them demonstrate some degree of openness towards novelty. The work comprises four books – the first one dominated by the question of raising children, the second by marriage, the third by running the household, and the fourth by sociability. All are permeated by the common motifs of rational time use and rational management. In addition, they are all written from a down-to-earth perspective, their considerations framed in the temporal, earthly perspective.

Expanding on the question of rational time use, the protagonists consider how to spend the relatively short time-span on individual human life efficiently. One of them (Giannozzo) asks another (Lionardo): "And do you know, on the other hand, how they would be merely losing time?" Lionard answers: "Doing nothing, I suppose," to which Giannozzo adds: "Certainly, and also if what could be done by one is occupying two or more, or if, where two or more are needed, one is toiling and sweating all alone; or if one or more are given tasks to which they are ill-suited. Where too many are employed, some time is wasted. Where there are fewer than needed or where the workers are not sufficiently skilled for the job, it is worse than if they did nothing, since they labor in vain and largely upset or spoil the thing that they are set to do. [...] Certainly they should not be allowed to waste their time like this. Each should be ordered to do what he knows how to do and can do."[1]

From a current perspective these statements seem banal. We have become used to the fact that one needs to work, and that those who do not should not count on social recognition. Furthermore, we also expect that in order to work one first needs preparation, and serious effort throughout to reach significant results, and that in performing tasks one is required to co-operate with others, but only with those who prove to be prepared and indispensable. The real trick, however, is not only efficient work and co-operation with others, but also in profitably orienting oneself towards the markets for goods and services. In explaining this to the readers of *The Family in Renaissance Florence*, Alberti writes: "Selling is, in truth, solely mercenary. You serve the needs of the buyer, and he pays you for your labor. You gain your reward by demanding more of others than you paid for the things they buy. Essentially, then, you sell not the commodity but your labor. For the commodity you receive the equivalent in money, and for your work you receive the profit."[2]

The same could be expressed in a more learned manner by means of the categories subsequently introduced by economists, such as "production efficiency," "social division of labour," or Smith's "invisible hand" regulating the behaviour of producers and consumers in the market. In the period under consideration these concepts, of work as something that does not reduce men to beasts of burden but in fact ennobles them and makes them truly human, were not in circulation, or even featured in common ways of thinking about work. By the time that the leading strata of public opinion in Europe started thinking in this way, those privileged by birth or religious rite could only "lower

[1] L. B. Alberti, *The Family in Renaissance Florence*, Columbia, SC 1969, pp. 180–181.

[2] Cf. ibidem, p. 142.

their banners," i.e., the nobility and clergy would slowly be divested of their entitlements.

In *The Family in Renaissance Florence*, one also finds the connection between the social role of money and rational production and behaviour in the market. Alberti wrote that "money appears to be the root of all things, or the hook to acquire them with, or their sustenance. Money, as nobody denies, is the sinews of any kind of work. If a man has plenty of it, he can easily meet all needs and satisfy a great many desires. With money you can have both a house and a farm and all the labor of men. All the crafts work like slaves for anyone with money. A man who lacks money wants for almost anything. [...] But if money fulfils our needs, why trouble our minds with the management of other things?"[3]

This seems somewhat redolent of Franklin's dictum that "time is money," where money is not a passport towards idleness, but rather to further activity and broadening one's sphere of influence and authority. It also includes a certain *votum separatum* countering the typical Medieval way of thinking about time, agency and economic activity. Time for the Medieval man is first and foremost available for implementing divine will, with respect to which human agency must remain subservient, while rational economic management consists basically in making optimal use of all the chances granted by God for salvation and eternal life. Whether those chances are taken advantage of is again not strictly speaking up to the human individual, but depends upon Divine Grace, which is dispersed for free, i.e., irrespective of individual attainments, and according to Divine Mercy.

According to Jacques Le Goff, this idea persists throughout the Middle Ages, but it is more accentuated during the early Middle Ages in the fourth to the tenth centuries and again in the eleventh and twelfth centuries: "The optimistic image of man as a reflection of the divine image, capable of continuing creation on earth and of saving himself, dominated from the twelfth and thirteenth centuries onward."[4] In the light of the first vision, human labour is not a gift, but a curse and includes an element of penance. Those who work a lot must have deserved their fate and there is no possibility for them to be freed from the necessity allotted to them. According to the second vision, labour does not cease to serve eschatological functions, however, it does start to play important social roles, such as the raising of men from poverty as well as the development of the ability to act constructively and co-operate with others. At least up to this point, Alberti's *The Family in Renaissance Florence* seems to fit in well with this later vision.

---

3 Cf. ibidem, pp. 232–233.

4 Cf. J. Le Goff (ed.), *Medieval Callings*, Chicago 1990, p. 4.

His work can be read not in the context of two competing tendencies in the intellectual culture of the time, but rather from the point of view of the social changes which affected Western countries in modern and contemporary periods, i.e., the emergence and functioning of capitalism with its privileging of both the market as the primary regulator of social life, and of the economic agents capable of operating on the market in a rational manner. Such a reading of *The Family in Renaissance Florence* can only be somewhat selective, but it does not require any great effort to find elements of the capitalist or proto-capitalist spirit in this work. These appear, for instance, in passages where Alberti makes a case for the desire for material goods as the prime mover behind all human endeavours: "when one considers getting them, the conclusion seems obvious that it boils down to buying and selling, lending and borrowing." In other words, it boils down to the operations of the so-called market. It is worth noting that the *The Family in Renaissance Florence* not only mentions the capitalist market, but also such forms of capitalist ethos as conscientiousness, prudence and reliability. These come in many different shapes: "great things grow from many small ones;" "add task to task, and you shall diminish the needs;" "add craft to craft, and you shall bring about happiness;" "wealth is desired so as not to feel need, and those who are no longer in any need became too wealthy," etc. All this, according to Max Weber, belonged to the spirit of capitalism, and its specific rationality.[5]

The question emerges as to what exactly Alberti meant by the family in the title of his book. Apparently, he would not have objected to saying that at the core it constitutes a kind of productive enterprise. Being a Christian writer, he attempts to retain in his description some of the sanctity or at least intimacy of family life, for instance in relation to the problems of fidelity or sexual practices. He is not so discreet, however, when it comes to the social functions of the family. He devotes lengthy passages to functions like the cultivation of civic virtues, for instance generosity ("The avaricious irritate me, because they do not make use of their possessions when needed, and because they want wealth too much") or charity, because happiness cannot be obtained without deeds which are good, right and virtuous. He also writes about the

[5] M. Weber explains this in his introductory remarks on the spirit of capitalism: "The impulse to acquire, pursuit of gain, of money, of the greatest possible amount of money, has in itself nothing to do with capitalism [...]. One may say that it has been common to all types and conditions of men at all times and in all the countries of the earth, wherever the objective possibility of this exists or has existed – it should be taught in the kindergarten of cultural history. [...] Capitalism may even be identical to restraint or at least rational tempering of this irrational impulse. But capitalism is identical to the pursuit of profit, and forever renewed profit, by means of continuous, rational, capitalistic enterprise." Cf. M. Weber, *The Protestant Ethics and the Spirit of Capitalism*, New York 1930, p. 17.

division of social roles among men and women; for instance, in one of the dialogues Gionnozzo announces: "Since I find it no easy matter to deal with the needs of the household when I must often be engaged outside with other men in arranging matters of wider consequence, I have found it wise to set aside a certain amount for outside use, for investments and purchases. The rest, which takes care of all the smaller household affairs, I leave to my wife's care."[6]

The dominant motif in the *The Family in Renaissance Florence* does not contradict Christian thinking in any obvious way. It already features in the biblical dictum "if anyone is not willing to work, let him not eat." This tradition can be seen to be in accord with the rule that "one has just as much, as one is personally capable of earning." It would be challenging, however, to make both these maxims consonant with the practice of the Catholic church of the time. Great religious reformers such as Luther or Calvin claimed that these are reconcilable and therefore chose to openly oppose the practices. Alberti was neither as bold in his views on social life, neither was he willing to formulate any such radical demands. In his *The Family in the Renaissance Florence*, clear signals appear nevertheless that not all was well in the common home for all Europeans that the Church of Rome was at the time.

Postscript

An interesting complement to the work of Alberti can be found in the picture of women and family in the Medieval era put forward by Christiane Klapisch-Zuber. This context allows not only for a better understanding of the originality of *The Family in Renaissance Florence*, but also demonstrates the relationship between convictions expressed in this work and contemporaneous social practices. An important part of this sketch consists of an attempt to explore the social rationalisations of family life promoted by the Church of Rome in the conditions of the Late Medieval period. It is developed next to the main thrust of the analysis which aimed to provide a picture of Medieval women, who were captured within "the framework that contemporaries automatically assigned to them, and within the sets of constraints that kinship and family imposed upon the emergence of women as individuals possessing full enjoyment of juridical, moral, and economic personality."[7]

Among others, Klapisch-Zuber emphasises the social dimension of the marital relationship as a form of reaching or reinforcing peace. ("As a gage of

[6] Cf. L. B. Alberti, *The Family in Renaissance Florence*, op. cit., p. 207.

[7] Cf. Ch. Klapisch-Zuber, "Women and the family," in J. Le Goff (ed.), *Medieval Callings*, op. cit., p. 300 ff.

peace and an instrument of concord, [a woman's] role went beyond her individual destiny or her personal aspirations.") This role was not only restricted to women from aristocratic strata, but also those with a lower social standing, including burgher families. In any such relationships, the question of personal love would have to be de-emphasised, as the primary duty was that towards the family ("working to perpetuate the lineage into which she entered by procreating for it, and faithfully assuring it the use of her body and of the goods that she had brought"). Sometimes this would even trump the ecclesiastic ban on marriage among close relatives. One phenomenon that comes to the fore in this context is that of downward social mobility of women ("It has been shown that the matrimonial strategy most current among the knightly class in the eleventh and twelfth centuries and among aristocratic and burgher circles in the fourteenth and fifteenth centuries led fathers to choose daughters-in-law of higher birth"), as well as the transfer of goods (both mobile and immobile) between the families of spouses. These would go in both directions, i.e., not only from the wife's family, but also to it, when the husband's family would be expected to provide compensation for the loss of the daughter.

Matrimony would obviously not always amount to a mere act of trade, yet, in the 14th and 15th centuries the problem of female dowry became so vital that "the married woman in southern France and in Italy (later in Spain as well) was defined by the dowry her family provided. In the north the widow's portion funded by the husband persisted until the early modern era."[8] One consequence of these trade-like arrangements was the diminution of the social position of women, which became expressed among other things in their expropriation ("[d]owering permitted the elimination of women from the inheritance of family wealth"), decrease in their economic function, as well as weakening in legal standing. This might have resulted, and according to the quoted author did, in disparaging male attitudes towards women, which would be exacerbated by frequent instances of infidelity (tolerated with respect to husbands, and sternly condemned and punished when it came to wives). In this context, Alberti's remarks on spouses' treatment of each other as partners appear very progressive.

Klapisch-Zuber does actually mention *The Family in Renaissance Florence*, but finds there not this progressive element, but rather an attempt at rationalisation and elevation of such a model where "a man nearing thirty, an adult, thus brought an adolescent into his house."[9] Within this model, "the man should

---

[8] Cf. ibidem, p. 290.

[9] "Should we be astonished then, that the resurgence of moralising literature and treatises on domestic economy during the late Middle Ages included admonitions directly inspired by Aristotle's *Politics* or Xenophon's *Economics*? Rationalising the practices of their own milieu and

wait to marry until he has reached the fullness of "perfect age;" the women, on the contrary, should be given to the husband young, in order to avoid perversion before marriage, since women "become full of vices when they do not have what nature requires." The double quotation-marked statement comes from Alberti, and constitutes one of the reasons to justify this particular model of family. Klapisch-Zuber provides other apparent reasons, such as the need for high fertility under conditions of high infant-mortality ("a child had only one chance out of two of reaching adulthood") or the instability of relationships in conditions of urban life.

Literary works such as Alberti's did not play a leading regulatory role in the social life at the time, the rationalising momentum notwithstanding. This role still belonged to the Church of Rome. Therefore, its policy – what we would nowadays call pro-family policy – is the prime focus of Klapisch-Zuber's analysis. The Church's raising of marriage to the rank of sacrament boosted its social recognition, but also opened the door for ecclesiastic manipulation with respect to all the vital elements of this union, starting from the procedure of becoming married, and ending with the questions of spousal sexual practices. The Church was frequently forced to deal with pre-existing practices, customs and deeds, such as the acquisitions of women through rape or abductions ("often to force the families to come to an agreement"). Family and financial pressures on forming marriages have already been discussed, but it seems important to note that according to Klapisch-Zuber, the Church actually aimed to constrain them. However, "centuries of pastoral teaching would be needed before the idea of a union accepted without any pressure and founded on individual impulse and reciprocal attraction could become an integral part of people's thinking."

Among the particularly difficult questions, there were those pertaining to sexual intercourse. Different social groups had differing perspectives on the acceptance of marital and extramarital relationships, and furthermore doctrinal reasons which associated the corporal aspects with sin and thus lead the Church towards sanctioning marital sexual intercourse merely to sustain procreation functions. ("Engendering valid heirs was the great challenge that faced families in an epoch in which death struck hard and often.") This resulted in the proliferation of various prohibitions and injunctions intended to constrain sexual intercourse driven by physiological drives: "from the very earliest Middle Ages [...] churchmen established a calendar, in theory very limited, of the times when a couple could have sexual relations without arousing clerical

their times, men like Giovanni Morelli or Leon Battista Alberti in his *Libri della famiglia* took their model from real life." Cf. ibidem, p. 298.

objections," and also the Church showed "continuing vigilance concerning the legitimacy of the practices, the postures, and the time on conjugal relations."[10]

There seems to be no simple and unambiguous way to explain what rationality may underlie these policies. Klapisch-Zuber admits that these rulings on the practices of sexual initiation and experience came to constitute a clear challenge to common sense. Some of them, seem to have been borne out by medical knowledge, such as the prohibitions on intercourse with women in advanced pregnancies or during menstruation (according to Bernardino of Siena "if the children are generated at such time, they will be born monstrous or leprous"). Many of these prohibitions also found justification in popular stereotypes concerning feminine nature, such as the conviction that women are wayward.[11]

2. Niccolò Machiavelli

Machiavelli (1469–1527) found prominence in the history of social thought mostly through his *The Prince* (*Il Principe*) – a work which has caused major controversies ever since its publication, and faced bitter opposition from religious circles. The Church censors considered it anti-Christian and put it on their Index Librorum Prohibitorum in 1559. At the same time it seems important to emphasise that its author did not think of himself as a bad Christian. He was nevertheless aware that not everything about the Church was as it should be. After all, Cesare Borgia, the son of Pope Alexander VI, is one of the positive heroes in *The Prince*. This fact and other circumstances shed light on a number or theses formulated in the work.

It is important to note that the author lived in a period when the western Christendom was going through a deep crisis of power, morality or even common decency, all of which were indicated by the leaders of the protestant resistance. What made Machiavelli different from these leaders was something which could be called Christian conscience. In the process of his intellectual development he would become increasingly convinced that this conscience plays no special role in the contest for power. This conclusion was reinforced

[10] "The degree to which people heeded submission to religious prohibitions is more obvious, and observance of 'prohibited times' – Advent and Lent – when the Church forbade the celebration of marriage and recommended continence (although not making it obligatory) is more directly measurable." Ibidem, p. 300.

[11] "The proper 'use' of wives meant, in fact, that men must constantly be on guard against their demands. Their bodies, so necessary to the survival of lineages, were ruled by an overly inconstant nature. Poorly governed by women's incomplete reason, the body required that its lord, the husband, use it to satisfy his appetites with prudence and regularity." Ibidem, p. 305.

by the dramatic events being played out in Florence of his time, i.e., the city of his birth, political career and great defeat. What provided him especially strong inspiration were the events inspired by the persona of Girolamo Savonarola, a Dominican monk who prophesised an imminent second coming of Christ and called the burghers of the city to rise up. He received support from Florentine Signoria, which emboldened his attacks against the local tyrant-rulers, and even against the pope, which finally lead to the cursing of the rebellious monk and his city supporters. In the end, the Florentines distanced themselves from Savanarola and brought him to court, where he was sentenced to public burning (the sentence was executed on May 28th, 1498). Machiavelli commented in his *The Prince* that "all armed prophets were victorious and the unarmed came to ruin. For [...] people are fickle by nature: it is easy to convince them of something, but difficult cult to hold them in that conviction. Therefore, affairs should be managed in such a way that when they no longer believe, they can be made to believe by force."[12] Savanarola's defeat did nevertheless open the path to high office for Machiavelli, who received the post of the head of the second chancery of Florentine Signoria. The scope of his duties included defence as well as foreign relations. This was connected with his frequent travels to other countries, including France, Germany and Rome, and it was during one of these voyages that he met Cesare Borgia.

In part VII of the *The Prince,* he appears as one of two examples of a successful political career. The other one mentioned is Franzesco Sforza: "Francesco became Duke of Milan from his station as a private citizen through appropriate methods and a great deal of virtue; what he acquired with a thousand hardships he maintained with little effort. On the other hand, Cesare Borgia, called Duke Valentino by the people, acquired the state through the fortune of his father, and when this was lost, he lost it, despite the fact that he did everything a prudent and virtuous man could to root himself securely in those states that the arms and Fortune of others had granted him. For [...] anyone who does not lay his foundations beforehand can do so later only with the greatest of virtue, although this is done with difficulty for the architect and danger to the building. If we therefore consider all the Duke's achievements, we shall see that he laid sturdy foundations for his future power."[13]

Machiavelli describes the activities of Cesare Borgia which first led to him gaining control over the principality of Romania, and later over Urbino. On his way this insightful and virtuous man faced the powerful families of Orsini and Colon, "It was necessary to disturb the political balance of Italy

[12] Cf. N. Machiavelli, *The Prince*, Oxford 2008, p. 22.

[13] Cf. ibidem, pp. 24–25.

and throw the Italian states into turmoil so that he could safely make himself the master of some of them." He achieved this in the following way: "He won over all their followers who were noblemen, making them his own noblemen and giving them huge subsidies, and he honoured them, according to their rank, with military commands and civil appointments. As a result, affection for their factions was wiped from their hearts in a few months, and all of this affection turned towards the Duke. After this, he waited for the opportunity to wipe out the Orsini leaders, having already put to flight those of the Colonna family. A good opportunity arose, and the use he put it to was even better. [...] Having wiped out these leaders, and having reduced their partisans to his allies, the Duke had laid very good foundations for his power."[14]

After the death of his father – Pope Alexander VI – and the short pontifical reign of Pope Pius III, Pope Julius emerged as the new threat to prince Valentino, who "[a]gainst this possibility, [...] thought to secure himself in four ways: first, by wiping out all the bloodlines of those rulers he had despoiled in order to deprive the Pope of that opportunity; second, by gaining the friendship of all the noblemen of Rome [...] in order to hold the Pope in check by this means; third, by making the College of Cardinals as much his own as he could; fourth, by acquiring such a large territory before the Pope died that he would be able to resist an initial attack on his own." The main problem lies not so much in the fact that Machiavelli would publicise such information on these actions, but in that he evaluates them in a positive manner. In the summarising statement he states clearly: "Therefore, having summarised all the Duke's actions, I would not know how to reproach him. On the contrary, I believe I am correct in proposing that he be imitated by all those who have risen to power through the Fortune and with the troops of others."[15]

In later parts of the *Prince*, there are more examples of such rulers, whose actions would come into clear conflict with Christian moral principles, and yet, Machiavelli would evaluate them positively. Although in his descriptions of the actions of those who become princes "through some wicked and nefarious means" he makes the adjustment that "without otherwise entering into the merits of this method," but then immediately adds "consider them sufficient for anyone who finds it necessary to imitate them." Further on, one finds statements that not every crime is reprehensible, and also clear directions concerning "whether cruelty be used badly or well."[16]

[14] Cf. ibidem, p. 26.

[15] Cf. ibidem, p. 29.

[16] "Those cruelties are well used [...] that are carried out in a single stroke, done out of necessity to protect oneself, and then are not continued, but are instead converted into the greatest possible benefits for the subjects. Those cruelties are badly used that, although few at the outset, increase with the passing of time instead of disappearing." Ibidem, pp. 33–34.

Some of the considerations which concerned the ecclesiastic principalities and their rulers must also have made them feel uncomfortable. Already at the outset of these reflections, Machiavelli states that "they are acquired either through virtue or through Fortune, and are maintained without one or the other. They are sustained by the ancient institutions of religion, which are so powerful and of such a quality that they keep their princes in power no matter how they act and live their lives." In the concluding remarks, he indicates the struggles over the posts of cardinals among the great families as the root of all discontent.

The list of such statements and evaluations which could disturb the conscience of the contemporary reader of the *Prince* is obviously much longer. Let me just mention at this point that Machiavelli, in his reflections "of generosity and miserliness" declares that "it would be good to be considered generous. Nevertheless, generosity employed in such a way as to give you a reputation for it will injure you," and while discussing ways of being faithful and sincere he says: "how praiseworthy it is for a prince to keep his word and to live with integrity and not by cunning, everyone knows. Nevertheless, one sees from experience in our times that the princes who have accomplished great deeds are those who have thought little about keeping faith and who have known how to manipulate men's minds cunningly; and in the end they have surpassed those who laid their foundations upon sincerity. Therefore, you must know that there are two modes of fighting: one in accordance with the laws, the other with force. The first is proper to man, the second to beasts. [...] a prince must know how to employ the nature of the one and the other; for the one without the other does not last. Since a prince must know how to make use of the nature of the beast, he should choose from among the beasts the fox and the lion; for the lion cannot defend itself from traps, while the fox cannot protect itself from the wolves. It is therefore necessary to be a fox, in order to recognise the traps, and a lion, in order to frighten the wolves."[17]

Important additions to this vision of the cunning and courageous ruler and the kind of actions which make ruling possible can be found in *Discourses on Livy*. Machiavelli started writing this treatise in 1513, and finished work in 1519. It was republican Rome that assumed the role of the positive heroes, and more specifically its qualities "ordering republics, maintaining states, governing kingdoms, ordering the military and administering war, judging subjects, and increasing empire." On the other hand, the negative role is played by "the weakness into which the present religion has led the world," as well as "the evil that ambitious idleness has done to many Christian provinces and cities."[18]

---

[17] Cf. ibidem, p. 60.

[18] Cf. N. Machiavelli, *Discourses on Livy*, Chicago 1996, p. 6.

In *Discourses*, Machiavelli conducts a detailed analysis of the historical sources of the power of republican Rome, starting at the foundation of the City of Rome and moving on to demonstrate how this ancient republic evolved towards what in of K. R. Popper's terms could be called an open society, or rather an overly open society: "because of the liberality that the Romans practised in giving citizenship to foreigners, the many new men born in Rome began to have so much share in the votes that the government began to vary, departing from the things and the men to which it was accustomed."[19] Before this came to pass, the great Rome and great Romans imposed their significant imprint on the history of humanity.

Discourses is composed of XLIX parts, each of which features such an important imprint. For example, in the first part of the first book, Machiavelli indicates several elements inherent in the foundation of Rome, which later proved beneficial to the growth of its power; among these, he mentioned both the constitution of Rome as a free and independent city, but also its favourable geographic situation in a fertile neighbourhood not far from the sea: "it is a more prudent choice to settle in a fertile place, if that fertility is restrained within proper limits by laws." Rome was indeed blessed with such laws and lawgivers – in the first part of *Discourses* Romulus and Numa are mentioned by name, while in later parts the institutional forces such as the senate, consuls, and people's tribunes are discussed at length.[20]

The analysis of how these law-givers operated leads Machiavelli to the assertion that in general the power of the state is not built upon consensus among the social forces, but upon discord among them. In the title of *Part IV of Book I* it is explicitly stated that "the disunion of the Plebs and the Roman Senate made that Republic free and powerful," and among the justifications for this statement there is the argument that "[t]he desires of free peoples are rarely pernicious to freedom because they arise either from being oppressed or from suspicion chat they may be oppressed." However, no comparably unambiguous answer is provided to the question in the title of part V, which can be phrased as "Where can the guard of freedom be settled more securely – in the people or in the nobility, and which has greater cause for tumult?" where Machiavelli argues that "[w]ith the Lacedemonians, and in our times with the Venetians, it has been put in the hands of the nobles; but with the Romans it

[19] "When Quintus Fabius, who was censor, became aware of this, he put all these new men from whom the disorder derived into four tribes, so that being enclosed they could not corrupt all of Rome." Ibidem, pp. 309–310.

[20] "Remaining mixed, it made a perfect republic, to which perfection it came through checked disunion of the plebs and the Senate, as will be demonstrated at length in the next two chapters." Ibidem, p. 14.

was put in the hands of the plebs. [...] If one considers the reasons for this, there is something to say for every side; but if one examines their endings, one takes the side of the nobles, because the freedom of Sparta and Venice held longer than that of Rome," and these indeed persisted longer, even though in Sparta the government remained in the hands of the few, i.e., the king and a small senate, whereas in Venice the government was in the hands of a relatively large number of Venetian nobles.

These and similar comparative analyses lead Machiavelli towards the formulation of the general thesis that there do not and cannot exist ideal or universal social systems, or to put it somewhat differently, those which are best suited to a particular time and place would for many reasons not be possible under different conditions. Furthermore, "since all things of men are in motion and cannot stay steady, they must either rise or fall: and to many things that reason does not bring you, necessity brings you."[21] This necessity directing our actions amounts to forces which human reason proves incapable of controlling. It could attempt to persuade the people to take such actions which would preclude the most negative consequences. From this point of view, "[a] mong all men praised, the most praised are those who have been heads and orderers of religions. Next are those who have founded either republics or kingdoms. After them are those placed over armies, who have expanded either their kingdom or that of the fatherland. To these literary men are added [...] To any other man, the number of which are infinite, some share or praise is attributed in accordance with his art or occupation. On the other hand, destroyers of religions, squanderers of kingdoms and republics, and enemies of the virtues, of letters, and of every other art that brings utility and honour to the human race, are infamous and detestable, as are the impious, the violent, the ignorant, the worthless, the idle, the cowardly."[22] In the subsequent parts of *Discourses*, Machiavelli explains in detail why the former should be singled out for praise and the latter for condemnation.

These historical considerations abound with references to the contemporaneous situation of Italy which aim to find those responsible for the fragmentation into multiple states and statelets, which fragmentation renders them incapable of facing foreign powers such as France or Spain. The main responsibility is supposed to lie with the Church of Rome. In *Part XII of Book I* Machiavelli argues against the frequent belief that "the well-being of the cities of Italy arises from the Roman church" and formulates the thesis that "because of the wicked examples of that court, this province has lost all devotion and

[21] Cf. ibidem, p. 23.

[22] Ibidem, p. 31.

all religion – which brings with it infinite inconveniences and infinite disorders; for as where there is religion one presupposes every good, so where it is missing one presupposes the contrary."[23] On the other hand, other passages include the praise of such rule and rulers that were facing various threats and clung to power through cunning and foresight as well as force and ruthlessness if the need arose, providing in effect peace and social order to their subjects.

One cannot give a single unambiguous evaluation of the rationality or irrationality of such actions. Within Machiavelli's framework, social rationality is not only a historical category, but also a pragmatic one, i.e., being entangled in various effects – sometimes expected and desired, at other times unexpected and undesired. This depends not so much on the actions of the ruler, but is rather the result of various contingencies, which sometimes prove propitious and sometimes defeat the best of plans and motives.

A good example of this occurs in *Part XXIV of Book II*: "Fortresses are generally more harmful than useful." This consideration starts, as many other parts of *Discourses*, with the appraisal of the wise conduct of the Romans: "When the Romans wished to secure themselves against the peoples of Latium and of the city of Privernum, they did not think of building some fortress, which would be a check to keep them faithful." It moves on to the situation in contemporary Italian states, where some rulers would always build fortresses for others to destroy. Francesco Sforza, the Milanese prince, appears again as the main protagonist in the story, and it is remarked that he "was reputed wise and nonetheless constructed a fortress in Milan, I say that in this he was not wise, and the result has demonstrated that such a fortress led to harm for his heirs, not security." A different course of action was assumed by Cesare Borgia, who declined to build a single fortress in his country, and went as far as "having all the fortresses in that province ruined, since he judged them harmful."[24] There are multiple other examples of the pragmatic rationality of rulers and their rule in *Discourses on Livy*.

Postscript

It goes without saying that Machiavelli associates rationality with diverse modes of social action. Further explanation seems warranted concerning these modes and their respective types of rationality. One of their possible

[23] Ibidem, p. 38.

[24] "Since he was loved by men, out of respect for them he did not want [fortresses]; and he saw he could not defend [fortresses] on the enemy's account, since an army in the field was needed to defend them: so he turned to ruining them." Ibidem, p. 187.

typological orderings was put forward by Max Weber in his project of interpretative sociology, the basic notions which include that of social action. In the light of this sociological perspective, social action is "oriented to the past, present or future behaviour of others." What comes into play are the following types of action: 1. instrumentally rational, 2. value-rational, 3. affectual, 4. traditional.[25] In each of these cases one can speak of rational action, yet, this rationality has so many different meanings that they sometimes complement and at other times contradict each other, and it would require a detailed consideration of a particular instance of action to be able to determine what exactly the complementary and contradictory aspects turn out to be. Instances of such analyses can be found in the works of Machiavelli.

Two exemplary cases are represented by the actions of Francesco Sforza and Cesare Borgia. According to Machiavelli's description, both of them acted instrumentally rational. What is more, they were both oriented to the same goal: gaining power and holding on to it for as long as possible. However, according to M. Weber, "value-rational action may thus have various different relations to instrumentally rational action" and in some cases it can even be considered irrational from the perspective of value-rationality. In Machiavelli's narrative, one would have to consider the destruction of fortresses by Cesare Borgia value-rational, while Francesco Sforza's construction of fortress would have to be seen as irrational as they brought his heirs harm, not security.

These examples serve to demonstrate the complexity of Machiavelli's understanding of rationality in action, as well as the multi-faceted nature of the dictum famously ascribed to him: "the end justifies the means." One should bear in mind that from his point of view it is not every goal that can justify the means employed by the rulers, and certainly the means cannot simply amount to the gaining of power and holding on to it for as long as possible.

[25] M. Weber explains the characteristics of these actions in the following manner: 1. "Strictly traditional behavior, like the reactive type of imitation discussed above, lies very dose to the borderline of what can justifiably be called "meaningfully oriented" action, and indeed often on the other side. [...] Purely affectual behavior also stands on the borderline of what can be considered "meaningfully oriented," and often it, too, goes over the line. [...] The orientation of value-rational action is distinguished from the affectual type by its clearly self-conscious formulation, of the ultimate values governing the action and the consistently planned orientation of its detailed course to these values. Action is instrumentally rational when the end, the means, and the secondary results are all rationally taken into account and weighed. This involves rational consideration of alternative means to the end, of the relations of the end to the secondary consequences, and finally of the relative importance of different possible ends. Determination of action either in affectual or in traditional terms is thus incompatible with this type." Cf. M. Weber, *Economy and Society: an Outline of Interpretative Sociology*, Berkeley 1978, pp. 25–26.

Such thinking and associated actions can only be considered affectual, but not value-rational, nor even traditional. This fact is underscored by the fates of rulers who came into power only to lose it in dramatic style. The discussion as to which ends under which circumstances justifies all the means employed to gain and retain power, and for how long can it serve as such a justification, remains open.

This is a question familiar to many scholars focusing on Machiavelli's legacy. One approach can be found in Ruggiero Romano's *Machiavelli and History*. According to this author, "Machiavelli put forward and developed a new concept of state," or to be more precise "there are two sides to his work: the 'desacralisation of state' means it is stripped of any values it was associated with for centuries, while at the same the state becomes sacralised in a new way." This new sacralisation comes through the reference of those worldly values which remain diametrically opposed to Christian ethics and moral concepts, such as falsehood, hypocrisy, faithlessness and murder.[26]

What appears to be of particular concern in the works of Machiavelli are those actions aimed at creating a state where citizens have the capacity to lead happy lives and rulers can rule relatively undisturbed. From Machiavelli's perspective one should not look for the sources of the requisite values in God, let alone the Church of Rome. The nature of man would mean that such values should be sought, not only in the good, but perhaps rather in its bad aspects. According to Pierre Manent, another scholar of Machiavellian thought, Machiaveli was not only the modern discoverer of the creative power of evil, but also of a specific "alchemy of evil."[27] This obviously involves certain irrational and affective elements, but at the same time there is something definitively rational, in the sense of maintaining peace and social order. These, according to Machiavelli, constitute the dominant social values, and whoever does not understand this or cannot accept this will lose out in the long run.

Among modern rulers it seems easy enough to find those who had some understanding of this lesson and attempted to implement it in practice. The list is actually long and diverse, and to indicate this diversity I would mention two cases here – one taken from the history of papacy and the other from the

[26] Cf. R. Romano, "Machiavelli i historia," [Machiavelli and History]. in idem, *Między dwoma kryzysami. Włochy Renesansu* [Between Two Crises. Italy in the Renaissance], Warsaw 1978, p. 144 ff.

[27] "They do not participate in a good, they are delivered from an evil. They are delivered from primary evil, violence and fear, by another evil, cruel repression; from a second evil, resentment, they are healed by a third evil, fear. This 'homeopathic' approach purges them of hate by letting just the right amount of fear; and fear is always needed. The political order becomes the alchemy of evil, the suppression of fear through fear." P. Manent, *An Intellectual History of Liberalism*, Princeton 1995, p. 19.

history of Prussia. The former was described by Leopold von Ranke in his *History of Papacy* and is associated with the reign of Pope Pius IV (1559–1565). The great achievement of this Pope for the Church of Rome was successfully bringing the prolonged Council of Trento to an end (1563). His way towards High Office remained very much Machiavellian, in that he needed a lot of cunning to attain the rank of Cardinal (he came from a minor, impoverished line of the Medici), and later, while aspiring to becoming pope, he kept emphasising his character traits as radically different to those of his predecessor. Pope Paul IV is presented by Ranke as a stern individual, the restorer of inquisition and zealous defender of older dogmas, while at the same time being a proud person who "made himself difficult to access; even in the smallest matters he liked to make a display of dignity and majesty." In contrast, "Pius was all good-nature and condescension. He was seen on the street daily, mounted or on foot, almost unattended and conversing affably with everybody [...] he would pour forth his feelings in a thousand cordial assurances, emphasising how he hated bad people from the very heart, and his natural love of justice, that he desired to injure no man in the enjoyment of his freedom, but to be kind and friendly to all."[28] After becoming pope, however, he turned out not to have much mercy for opponents – among them the nephews of Paul IV, of whom he "determined to make a terrible example." He would find mercy for his own kin, whom, just as his predecessor, he would honour with high church offices. At the same time, it should be noted that his demonstrations of mild manners were not constraining him from steering the proceedings of the Council of Trento in the direction of such conclusions that imposed high rigour upon the members of the Church of Rome.[29]

The actions of Frederick the Great, King of Prussia, provide another example of Machiavelli's ideas in practice. His youthful treatise, published anonymously in Halle (1739), portrays him as originally in opposition to Machiavelli. He claims there that the fundamental assumptions taken by Machiavelli contradict healthy ethical principles, and that furthermore the his thesis concerning the theory of the state are as evil as they are superficial in the claim that the cunning politician could assume the path of crime and most revolting injustice, which would lead him towards greatest honours. The subjects in this view would constitute mere serfs, whose subjugation to the will of the prince would be as absolute as in the relation of the sheep to the shepherd who can

[28] Cf. L. von Ranke, *The History of the Popes: Their Church and State*, London 1851, pp. 236–237.

[29] L. Ranke writes that "the faithful were again subjected to intolerant church discipline, and in serious cases, to the sword of excommunication." Ibidem, p. 256.

tdispose of them as he pleases.[30] It might be that he perceived Machiavellian elements in the policies of his father, Frederick I, which contributed to his 1731 attempt to escape from Berlin. He was however apprehended and court-martialled on the charge of desertion. His sentence was eventually commuted thanks to the interventions of Prussian ministers as well as other monarchs, but he was forced by his father to take up the job of a lesser bureaucrat and marry the princess Elisabeth Christine Braunschweig-Bevern, on whose looks and sharpness of mind historians have been discreetly indifferent. In 1740, he ascended to the throne after the death of his father, and for some time attempted to project the image of an anti-Machiavellian attitude, seeking the company of the philosophers of the Enlightenment. Some of these Enlightenment ideas he even attempted to implement, for example religious tolerance or mercantile economics. However, when it turned out, that these do not strengthen his position with respect to other European states sufficiently, he engaged military struggle against his major competitors, including Austria, England, Holland and Saxony. In this context he proved to be not only a gifted military leader, but also a skilful politician, capable of first finding agreement with the enemies of his enemies, only to challenge the allies of yesterday after victory. This was for instance the case in his relations with the French, on whom he initially relied for support in the war against the Czechs over the control of Silesia, only to defeat them later in the battle of Rossbach (1757). On his deathbed he may not have had too many friends in Europe, yet, he had an enlarged and strengthened state. He also left *Political Testament*, which included his profession of faith in a strong and ruthless ruler and the efficacy of Machiavellian politics of a style which perhaps allows for tolerance, but not for enemies or those who fail to follow the ruler's policies.[31]

[30] Friederick II, *Antimachiavell ou Examen du Prince de Machiavell*; after: *Filozofia niemieckiego Oświecenia. Wybrane teksty z historii filozofii* [Philosophy of German Enlightenment. History of Philosophy: Selected Sources], Warsaw 1973, p. 399 ff.

[31] Cf. Friederick II, *Die Politischen Testamenten*, München 1941.

Chapter III

Rationality of social life according to the 17th century English philosophers

The two concepts of rationality of social life under consideration in the present chapter demonstrate for the most part the convictions separating the main social actors in 17th century England. These comprise, on the one hand, the proponents of monarchism, i.e., the Tories, and on the other hand the adherents of parliamentarism, i.e., the Whigs. These convictions spanned the realms of philosophy, as well as politics, economics, dynastic and religious concerns, and in this last respect they were especially heated in the strains between the Anglican Church and the Puritans aiming to defend their devotional autonomy. Both concepts of rationality under discussion included designs to bridge these divides.

1. Thomas Hobbes

For a number of reasons, Hobbes (1588–1679) happened to be closer to the Tories than the Whigs. He was brought up in a family closely associated with the Anglican Church (his father was a vicar), and he undertook his studies in Oxford, which, just like Cambridge, was under strict Anglican control at the time. He graduated with honours in 1608, which helped him to obtain the position of private tutor in the house of Lord Devonshire, in whose service he remained for over 60 years. In 1610, he undertook his first voyage to France and Italy, countries he subsequently visited on a number of occasions. These voyages allowed him not only to directly observe social conditions, but also to come into contact with some great foreign scholars and philosophers, such as

M. Mersenne and Galileo. His *Elements of Law, Natural and Politic* (1640) were understood by the English Whigs as praise to absolute monarchy, and in fear of their reprisals Hobbes fled to France, where he published another version of the work under the title *De Cive* (1642). It included accusations levelled at the religious groups responsible for the breaking out of the English Civil War. In 1647, Hobbes fell gravely ill, and after recuperating he started working on the *Leviathan*, the work which brought him both fame and the animosity of numerous opponents.

Leviathian preaches the praise of strong public authority, as the beast is supposed to stand for a state which is "but an Artificiall Man; though of greater stature and strength than the Naturall, for whose protection and defence it was intended; and in which, the Soveraignty is an Artificiall Soul, as giving life and motion to the whole body: The Magistrates, and other Officers of Judicature and Execution [...] Salus Populi (the Peoples Safety) its Businesse; Counsellors, by whom all things needfull for it to know, are suggested unto it, are the Memory; Equity and Lawes, an artificiall Reason and Will; Concord, Health; Sedition, Sicknesse; and Civill War, Death. Lastly, the Pacts and Covenants, by which the parts of this Body Politique were at first made, set together, and united, resemble that Fiat, or the Let Us Make Man, pronounced by God in the Creation."[1]

However, *Leviathian* embodies praise of the natural law of man, implying such a human who strives to satisfy all the natural needs by means of all that is available and by the act of creation. These needs include the desire to know oneself and one's environment, knowing both the immediate and the more distant future, as well as conversing and communicating with other people. In short, such a human is not merely capable of living and acting rationally, but actually understands this rationality as a way of keeping close to one's own nature as well as the nature of things in general. The answer to the general question of how such an individual could and should attain the desired goals is given by Hobbes over the three parts of the book.

In the first part, *Of Man*, he describes and explains among other things modes of creating natural bonds with the environment. The first of these steps should be sensory contact ("For there is no conception in a mans mind, which hath not at first, totally, or by parts, been begotten upon the organs of Sense.") The second should consist in making use of human imagination and memory, while the third has to include analysis of what constitutes the matter of these impressions and imaginations, and distinguishing them from "the Externall Body, or Object, which presseth the organ proper to each Sense,"

[1] T. Hobbes, *Leviathan; Or, The Matter, Form, and Power of a Commonwealth Ecclesiastical and Civil*, London 1886, p. 15.

i.e., all that constitutes conjunctions of the fictions of mind, dreams and all other kinds of visions.

This sensory conception of the origins of both the form and content of human cognition is associated with a naturalist concept of human reason, understanding and knowledge. In this perspective, human reason is "nothing but Reckoning (that is, Adding and Substracting) of the Consequences of generall names agreed upon, for the Marking and Signifying of our thoughts," human understanding is nothing but a conceptual grasping of all that is counted, registered and signified ("When a man Reasoneth, hee does nothing els but conceive a summe total [...] conceiving of the consequence of the names of all the parts, to the name of the whole"), and human knowledge is acquired: "By this it appears that Reason is not as Sense, and Memory, borne with us; nor gotten by Experience onely; as Prudence is; but attayned by Industry; first in apt imposing of Names; and secondly by getting a good and orderly Method in proceeding from the Elements, which are Names, to Assertions made by Connexion of one of them to another; and so to syllogismes, which are the Connexions of one Assertion to another, till we come to a knowledge of all the Consequences of names appertaining to the subject in hand..."[2]

In this part of *Leviathian*, Hobbes also presents a naturalistic understanding of feelings and desires, such as the desire to experience pleasure and avoid pain, a naturalistic view of the intellectual virtues ("by Vertues intellectuall are always understood such abilityes of the mind, as men praise, value, and desire should be in themselves"), a naturalistic take on "power, worth and dignity," as well as a naturalistic conception of religion and religiosity. The latter are supposed to be based, firstly, on the desire to know the reasons behind things and states of affairs; secondly, on the natural human proclivity towards thinking that every thing has a beginning; thirdly, on the natural tendency to fall back on authority whenever one's own reason is at a loss; and fourthly, on the human "caution of the Future." In fact, there are many more reasons one could list, but all of them boil down to the conclusion that *natural religion* can not only be rationally understood and explained, but also that particular stages of its rationalisation can be demonstrated – from polytheistic pagan beliefs, to the assumption of one God eternal, infinite and almighty.

These considerations of natural religion are concluded with critical remarks towards the Church of Rome. Hobbes would oppose the lack of virtue among its shepherds ("insomuch, as the fayling of Vertue in the Pastors, maketh Faith faile in the People") and also the introduction of Aristotelian philosophy and doctrine into religion by the scholastics. This was supposed

[2] Cf. ibidem, p. 33.

to be "from whence there arose so many contradictions, and absurdities, as brought the Clergy into a reputation both of Ignorance, and of Fraudulent intention; and enclined people to revolt from them, either against the will of their own Princes, as in France, and Holland; or with their will, as in England."

Other reasons crucital to this social mutiny were the papal interdicts, which were beneficial to the papacy and its spiritual subjects, but not to sovereign rulers such as Henry VIII of England, who therefore had to negate such religious jurisdiction over their own subjects. "For who is there that does not see, to whose benefit it conduceth, to have it believed, that a King hath not his Authority from Christ, unlesse a Bishop crown him? That a King, if he be a Priest, cannot Marry? That whether a Prince be born in lawfull Marriage, or not, must be judged by Authority from Rome? That Subjects may be freed from their Alleageance, if by the Court of Rome, the King be judged an Heretique? That a King [...] may be deposed by a Pope (as Pope Zachary,) for no cause; and his Kingdome given to one of his Subjects? That the Clergy, and Regulars, in what Country soever, shall be exempt from the Jurisdiction of their King, in cases criminall? Or who does not see, to whose profit redound the Fees of private Masses, and Vales of Purgatory; with other signes of private interest, enough to mortifie the most lively Faith..."[3] It goes without saying that anyone not under the spell of scholastic speculations, and thus using their own natural reason, would see just that. In the third part of the Leviathian, *Of a Christian Common-wealth*, there are multiple indications concerning the ways in which such reason could and should cope with social conditions, which it does not want to accept for whatever reason.

According to the assumptions in the first part of the book, every human is endowned with reason in equal measure. It is this equality that brings about prudence ("For Prudence, is but Experience; which equall time, equally bestowes on all men, in those things they equally apply themselves unto"), the equality of "hope in the attaining of our End," the equality of fear of the force of other people, and the equality of the feelings which make people live in peace. These feelings include fear of death: "Desire of such things as are necessary to commodious living; and a Hope by their Industry to obtain them. And Reason suggesteth convenient Articles of Peace, upon which men may be drawn to agreement. These Articles, are they, which otherwise are called

[3] "[...] as the fayling of Vertue in the Pastors, maketh Faith faile in the People: and partly from bringing of the Philosophy, and doctrine of Aristotle into Religion, by the Schoole-men; from whence there arose so many contradictions, and absurdities, as brought the Clergy into a reputation both of Ignorance, and of Fraudulent intention; and inclined people to revolt from them, either against the will of their own Princes, as in France, and Holland; or with their will, as in England." Ibidem, p. 120.

the Lawes of Nature." The first of these laws is "the Liberty each man hath, to use his own power, as he will himselfe, for the preservation of his own Nature." The second is the readiness ("when others are so too") to resign from this prerogative, so far as "for Peace, and defence of himselfe he shall think it necessary, to lay down this right to all things."[4]

Hobbes considered these two laws of nature necessary but not sufficient conditions for the conclusion and implementation of beneficial contracts between all those, who want and know how to use their natural reason. Other conditions include abiding by the agreed contracts (otherwise they are "[words alone, if they be of the time to come, and contain a bare promise"), gratitude (which Hobbes associated mainly with "That a man which receiveth Benefit from another of meer Grace, Endeavour that he which giveth it, have no reasonable cause to repent him of his good will"), the right of compliance ("That every man strive to accommodate himselfe to the rest"), as well as the ease of forgiveness. In all, Hobbes mentions eighteen such laws of nature. So as to make their understanding and implementation easier in the practical actions of common men, he distills them into the formula: "Do not that to another, which thou wouldest not have done to thy selfe."

This formula plays a key role in the vision of a rationally organised state presented in the second part of *Leviathan*. This state is based on the aforementioned laws of nature. However, these laws are constantly threatened by elements, over which the state has to exercise control. One of these elements includes: "our naturall Passions, that carry us to Partiality, Pride, Revenge, and the like. And Covenants, without the Sword, are but Words, and of no strength to secure a man at all." Somewhat later, Hobbes adds that "[t]he only way to erect such a Common Power, as may be able to defend them from the invasion of Forraigners, and the injuries of one another, and thereby to secure them in such sort, as that by their owne industrie, and by the fruites of the Earth, they may nourish themselves and live contentedly; is, to conferre all their power and strength upon one Man, or upon one Assembly of men, that may reduce all their Wills, by plurality of voices, unto one Will: which is as much as to say, to appoint one man, or Assembly of men, to beare their Person [...] This done, the Multitude so united in one Person, is called a common-wealth."[5] This form of state was called "Leviathian" in the title of the book, as under all conditions this state has "the use of so much Power and Strength conferred on him, that by terror thereof, he is enabled to forme the wills of them all," and those who called it into being remain its subjects.

---

[4] Cf. ibidem, p. 113 ff.

[5] Cf. ibidem, p. 147 ff.

According to Hobbes, there exist two distinct ways of bringing about this state of affairs, i.e., by force or spontaneity. This second way happens when "men agree amongst themselves, to submit to some Man, or Assembly of men, voluntarily, on confidence to be protected by him against all others. This latter may be called a Politicall Common-wealth, or Common-wealth by Institution; and the former a Common-wealth by Acquisition." Of the first Hobbes provides a careful analysis of methods of state creation, and distinguishes several types of states. When it comes to states established by institution, these include monarchy, democracy and aristocracy, and in states created through acquisition one can distinguish those where rule is hereditary and those where it has to be obtained through military conquest.[6] The way in which power is obtained has consequences not only for the manner of its execution, but also for the rights of the governing and the governed – including the existence of freedoms or lack thereof – the origination of particular forms of private and public associations, and even for the method of nurturing and growing the community of state. Considering all the different consequences that the manner of obtaining power might have, Hobbes concluded that there are pros and cons to all of them, while on the whole the forcible gaining of power seems to have more obvious disadvantages compared to situations where people agree to delegate power out of free will.

In the general conclusion to these analyses and postulates based on them, Hobbes recognises that they all stem from the rules of innate reason and refer to the reason of both the governing and the governed. However, he writes that "considering how different this Doctrine is, from the Practise of the greatest part of the world, especially of these Western parts, that have received their Morall learning from Rome, and Athens; and how much depth of Morall Philosophy is required, in them that have the Administration of the Soveraign Power; I am at the point of believing this my labour, as uselesse, and the Common-wealth of Plato [...]. But when I consider again, that the Science of Naturall Justice, is the onely Science necessary for Soveraigns, and their principall Ministers; and that they need not be charged with the Sciences Mathematicall (as by Plato they are), further, than by good Lawes to encourage men to the study of them; and that neither Plato, nor any other Philosopher hitherto, hath put into order, and sufficiently, or probably proved all the Theoremes of Morall doctrine, that men may learn thereby, both how

[6] "The right of Dominion by Generation is that which the Parent hath over his Children, and is called paternal." While the rights of conquest apply "when the Vanquished, to avoyd the present stroke of death, covenanteth either in expresse words, or by other sufficient signes of the Will, that so long as his life, and the liberty of his body is allowed him, the Victor shall have the use thereof, at his pleasure." Ibidem, p. 80.

to govern, and how to obey; I recover some hope, that one time or other, this writing of mine, may fall into the hands of a Soveraign, who will consider it himselfe [...] without the help of any interested, or envious Interpreter..."[7] This undoubtedly amounts to the support for a strong ruler, one who is not only capable of using the arguments of force, but also the force of arguments, including philosophical (moral), political, religious and many other kinds of arguments. If the subject is not capable of understanding and accepting, so much the worse for such an unruly imbecile subject. For the sovereign does wield a sword, which he is able and allowed to use. His subjects know this, or at least are supposed to, and the fear of the sovereign remains one of the most vital pillars of peace and social order.

Postscript

Comparing Hobbesian rationality standards with those of earlier thinkers allows for a better understanding of their originality. This point is emphasised by Pierre Manent's study *Hobbes and the New Political Art*. He demonstrates the novelty of Hobbes's views, arising from the clash of two traditions – the old Aristotelian praise of civic freedom, and the newer medieval doctrine put forward by the Fathers of the Church, and especially Saint Augustine, which emphasised civic duty. In Hobbes's days, the former doctrine remained popular in English universities, while the latter dominated in Puritan circles.[8] According to P. Manent, both traditions "conspired to foment the spirit of disobedience" of the 17th century English social groups who inspired the destructive Civil War.

The author of the *Leviathan* attempts to persuade the reader that it was actually civic disobedience which lead to the tragic chain of events disrupting English society – hence his glorification of obedience to such political power which is able to impose obedience on subjects, even if this is done by brute force. The trick lies in not being compelled to use such brutal tactics, as this is a strategy available to all individuals living in the state of nature, by recourse to their most primitive powers. The art of wielding power consists in such actions which keep the subjects in awe of the potential for the use of force, and

[7] Cf. ibidem, p. 328 ff.

[8] "The secular cause is found in the influence of the universities, which educate the elite; the religious cause is found in the influence of the Presbyterians, or Puritans, who are by and large made up of the people. The universities' influence stems from classical studies, from Greek and Roman models glorifying 'freedom'. The Puritan influence stems from religious conception, attributing the right and duty to obey individual inspiration, and the right and duty to 'dogmatise' to everyone who shares it." Cf. P. Manent, "Hobbes and the New Political Art," in *An Intellectual History of Liberalism*, trans. R. Balinski, Princeton 1996, p. 39 ff.

afraid of all the extreme consequences (including death) that those who refuse obedience must face. Fear of death seems to Hobbes to be morally superior to actual killing, which constitutes a major innovation in that "the Greek idea of a benevolent nature [...] is completely ruined."[9]

However, P. Manent goes much further in emphasising the novelty of Hobbesian social thought, as claims that "Hobbes's thought is thus the common matrix of modern democracy and liberalism. It founds the democratic idea because it develops the notion of sovereignty established on each subject's consent. It founds the liberal idea because it develops the notion of the law as device external to individuals." According to this author, such an account involves some contradiction when it comes to positive claims: "They have a common 'negative matrix': they agree that man has no ends inscribed in his nature, and that the element of human action is not the good or goods."[10] Action is concerned with doing lesser evil, but in the case of such a ruler as Leviathan, it is a lesser evil in the overall social scale. This constitutes the highest reason and legitimation of all actions – also those traditionally reserved for God and his earthly successors, as everything which is human remains within the scope of power of Leviathan, and this includes religion. This conclusion no doubt appears disputable, and is conducive to deeper reflection on the ideas of Hobbes.

Adopting this expansive Hobbesian view of rationality standards might be seen as framing them within the struggle between the Anglican Church and the Puritans over culture – not only religious, but also political, including the culture of spiritual reign – or, to put it more bluntly, over settling the question of who should rule.[11] While the Anglicans were in agreement with the Puritans that the supreme power over the soul is wielded by God, there are significant differences between them when it comes to questions of how spiritual rule should be implemented on Earth. The Anglicans believed that the supreme earthly representative of God is the king of England, and would

---

9 Cf. ibidem, p. 24.

10 Cf. ibidem, p. 33.

11 "[...] Puritanism was not a uniform current, and had already split into a number of factions in the 16th century. The most affluent among the puritans – among both the burghers and gentry – aimed to impose a strict Calvinist structure onto the Church [...]. These were known as Presbyterians, as the primary role within their Church organisation was played by the leaders of religious communities known as presbyters [...]. A more radical faction of the puritan movement can be found among the independents, who proclaimed the complete autonomy of every community from regal and ecclesiastic powers. They were demanding complete independence of religious adherence and were opposed to any obligatory ceremonial forms; they also allowed every member of the congregation to assume the right of preaching." Cf. H. Zins, *Historia Anglii* [The History of England], Wroclaw – Warsaw – Cracow 2001, p. 177.

actively oppose anyone claiming otherwise. For the Puritans the crucial answers to such questions hinged upon the acceptance of such crucial doctrines as the fall of man ("Man, by his fall into a state of sin, hath wholly lost all ability of will to any spiritual good accompanying salvation") and double predestination (divine distinction between those to be damned and those to undergo salvation), enlightening some and blinding others ("As for those wicked and ungodly men, whom God as a righteous judge, for former sins doth blind and harden, from them he not only with-holdeth His grace, whereby they might have been enlightened in their understandings and wrought upon in their hearts, but sometimes he also withdraweth the gifts...")[12]

According to Max Weber, whose reconstruction of the Puritan doctrine is presented here, the question "Am I one of the elect?" must sooner or later have arisen for every believer and have forced all other interests to the background."[13] Various answers were given to this question, but Weber was interested mostly in those which directly contributed to the formation of the capitalist work ethos and professional ethics. Examples include those which feature in Richard Baxter's *Christiana Directory*, which included the commendation of labour as a means of one's own worthlessness," or in Robert Barcley's *Apology* and John Fox's missionary work (both of them were Quaker leaders), or among the Baptists (Hanserd Knollys) and the Methodist movement (John Wesley). In effect, Puritanism as a social-religious movement "carried the ethos of the rational organisation of labour," and led to the reinforcement of other forms of capitalist rationality, such as rational planning, saving, credit and time allocation. Instead of the "loss of time through sociability, idle talk, luxury, even more sleep than is necessary for health," one was supposed to work towards divine and personal glory. At the same time wealth is multiplied, which in itself serves as indisputable proof of one's rational mobility, resourcefulness and foresight, as well as proof that God is on our side.[14]

In assessing how Puritan ethics are related to politics, Weber points especially to the associated ethos of individual freedom, i.e., the right of every

[12] Cf. M. Weber, *Protestant Ethics and the Spirit of Capitalism*, New York 1930, p. 101.

[13] By way of justification, Weber points to the *Westminster confession*, which put claimed that "even the chosen one often has to struggle long and hard to attain the certitude which consciousness of having done his duty gives him and of which a true believer will never be entirely deprived." Ibidem, p. 220.

[14] M. Weber refers to passages from Baxter's *Christian Directory* ("the most complete compendium of Puritan ethics"), which include statements such as: "Keep up a high esteem of time and be more careful every day that you lose none of your time, than you are that you lose none of your gold and silver. And if vain recreation, dressings, feastings, idle talk, unprofitable company, or sleep be any of temptations to rob you of any of your time, accordingly heighten your watchfulness." Cf. ibidem, p. 261.

man to chose his own path of rational life on Earth, as well as the right to shape the institutional frames of this life. The Puritans would consider all those who did not accept these rights enemies, just as they would oppose enemies of God, true Christian faith and a state whose primary task and vocation is standing guard to these freedoms.

Hobbes's name does not feature in the *Protestant Ethics*, and yet it seems indisputable that the Hobbesian standards of rationality of social life, including religious life, are not questioned there. The problem lies not so much in the fact that this kind of rationality is deprived of the much sought-after ultimate or at least sufficient reason (*ration sufficiere*), as that, within this framework, such a place can be held by the reason of state, which cannot be strong without subjects' subservience to authority. Whoever fails to understand this has to be aware of potentially harsh consequences and cannot depend on help from any of the secular or ecclesiastic institutions, or social groups, nor even can they hope to find explanation or justification for such insubordination in the Holy Scripture or their own conscience. This is where the strong emphasis on obedience to authority in the *Leviathan* comes from. Among other things, it presupposes the faith that those at the top of the hierarchy are well aware of their socially sanctioned rights and duties, including the fact that they would lose the legitimacy to rule if they fail to properly discharge the latter or if they abuse the former.

This faith seems to constitute one of the weaker links in this concept of rationality of social life. Such conclusion can be reached, for instance, upon reading George Macaulay Trevelyan's *Social History of England.* It features descriptions of the 17th century rulers of England – not always so wise as to match their designs to resources, and thus to join the ranks of the losers – as well as historic descriptions of social groups which were on the ascendant, and changed the English monarchy step by step into one that reigned but did not rule at the turn of the 17th and 18th centuries. Generally speaking, it was the parliament-based cabinet thatassumed all the prerogatives of political rule. One possible justification for Hobbes's alignment with the monarchists could be that in the period when he was writing *Leviathan* the balance of force between the proponents of strong royal power (the "round heads") and the supporters of parliamentary domination (the "cavaliers") was still even. Who would have the upper hand in the end was still an open question, and the lines dividing the supporters of the two respective camps were not yet fixed.[15]

---

[15] "To speak in general terms, Royalism was strongest where the economic and social changes of the previous hundred years had been least felt. The King and the Church were best loved in rural regions and market towns furthest from capital, and least connected with overseas commerce. Parliamentary and Puritan sympathy was strongest where recent economic change

2. John Locke

Locke (1632–1704) did not have such indisputable connections to Puritanism, yet his biography does show some. He encountered the beliefs of this social-religious movement in his family home (his father was a lawyer sympathetic to the Puritans), and later during his studies in Oxford (1652–1660). For a short period he became a lecturer there, but was convinced to leave his post in 1661. A major turn in his life occurred when he met Lord Anthony Ashley (later Earl of Shaftesbury), a politician in favour of constitutional monarchy, civic freedoms and religious toleration.[16] On his advice, he first came back to teaching at Oxford, and later moved to France (1675). After returning to England (1679), he was again associated with Shaftesbury, who was at the time holding the office of the Secretary of the Privy Council. The failed attempt to prevent the succession to the throne of James II (brother of Charles II) forced Locke to seek refuge in the Netherlands together with his protector. It was during his stay in this country that he published his *Letter Concerning Toleration* (1689).

In the first sentence of the treatise Locke proclaimed toleration among Christians to be the "chief characteristical mark of the true church,"[17] and he adds that whoever is "destitute of charity, meekness, and good-will in general towards all mankind [...] is certainly yet short of being a true Christian himself." This constituted a *votum separatum*, not only against members of the Anglican Church, who denied the Puritans the right to public expression of faith, but also against those extreme varieties of Puritanism, which considered only their own religion to be truly Christian. In justification of this position, Locke quoted the Gospels, but also referred to such church practices as imposing faith upon people by force, which warranted the question whether they were really meant to contribute to the glory of God and salvation of soul, or were perhaps merely serving the interests of those who "under pretence of religion, may not seek impunity for their libertinism and licentiousness." The question was largely rhetorical for both Locke and the Puritans. It was mainly posed in the *Letter Concerning Toleration* to provide strong justification for the radical postulate "I esteem it above all things necessary to distinguish exactly the busi-

---

had gone furthest, as in London [...] in the sea ports [...] and in the newer type of manufacturing towns or districts like Taunton, Birmingham and the clothing Dales on both sides of the Pennies." Cf. G. M. Trevelyan, *English Social History: From Chaucer to Victoria*, London 1942, p. 241.

[16] Cf. A. A. C. Shaftesbury, *Life, Unpublished Letters, and Philosophical Regimen*, New York 1900.

[17] Cf. J. Locke, *Four Letters on Toleration*, London 1870, p. 2.

ness of civil government from that of religion, and to settle the just bounds that lie between the one and the other."[18] He explains at the same time that "The commonwealth seems to me to be a society of men constituted only for procuring, preserving, and advancing their own civil interests. Civil interests I call life, liberty, health, and indolence of body; and the possession of outward things, such as money, lands, houses, furniture, and the like."

The Church aspired to command over all these earthly goods, and frequently proved successful in these attempts. In Locke's view, this is unacceptable: "Let us now consider what a church is. A church then I take to be a voluntary society of men, joining themselves together of their own accord, in order to the public worshipping of God, in such a manner as they may judge acceptable to him, and effectual to the salvation of their souls. I say, it is a free and voluntary society. Nobody is born a member of any church..."[19] At the same time, every man is born a free individual and "[n]o member of a religious society can be tied with any other bonds but what proceed from the certain expectation of eternal life." If the individual somehow becomes enslaved, he immediately strives to drop his chains, and would ultimately be successful. In this way, Locke combines the idea of tolerance with the idea of freedom, and these in turn with the idea of rationality – both individual and collective, i.e., when the individual as citizen is able and willing to co-exist with others, acting both in the interest of his individual goods but also in the interest of the public good, the state should not constrain those efforts, but should help facilitate them.

These forms of life, coexistence and action, are supposed to be founded not only on innate freedom and reason, but also on human work. In the final parts of the *Letter Concerning Toleration*, those who have lived a happy and prosperous life thanks to hard work are praised, while those who "rather injuriously prey upon the fruits of other men's labours, than take pains to provide for themselves" are sternly censored. The demand is expressed for a state which protects the former. This is the reason and legitimation for the rule of those entrusted with public office: "This is the original, this is the use, and these are the bounds of the legislative, which is the supreme power in every commonwealth. I mean that provision may be made for the security of each man's private possessions; for the peace, riches, and public commodities of the whole people; and, as much as possible, for the increase of their inward strength, against foreign invasions."[20]

---

[18] "If this be not done, there can be no end put to the controversies that will be I always arising between those that have, or at least pretend to have, on the one side, a concernment for the interest of men's souls, and on the other side, a care of the commonwealth." Ibidem, p. 5.

[19] Cf. ibidem, p. 7.

[20] Cf. ibidem, p. 28.

In *Two Treatises on Government*, Locke treats the separation of Church and State as a foregone conclusion which does not require any further explanation. On the other hand, he finds it necessary to explore the question of how to organise the functioning of secular political power rationally. In the first treatise, issue is taken with Robert Filmer, author of *Patriarcha, or hhe Natural Power of Kings*: "The False Principles and Foundation of Sir Robert Filmer, And His Followers, are Detected and Overthrown." According to Locke, this doctrine is false by virtue of relying on the assumption that "all government is absolute monarchy" and "no man is born free." From such claims follow conclusions equating paternal with royal authority, as well as the claim that the latter comes directly from divine sources and therefore God is the only Lord to whom kings are accountable. Furthermore, from such a conception of power follows that "since men had nothing else left them, they might in slavery have such undeniable proofs of its necessity, that their consciences might be convinced, and oblige them to submit peaceably to that absolute dominion, which their governors had a right to exercise over them."[21] This absolute dominion was supposed to apply only in the temporal domain. In short, the treatise of sir Robert Filmer is nothing but an attempt to defend the absolute monarchy in England.

In the second treatise, "An Essay Concerning the True Original Extent and End of Civil Government," he puts the foundation for public authority not in the Holy Scriptures and the teachings of the Church, but in the state of nature, i.e., "a state of perfect freedom to order their actions, and dispose of their possessions and persons, as they think fit." This also happens to be a state of equality "wherein all the power and jurisdiction is reciprocal, no one having more than another." From these two states he derives "great maxims of justice and charity" as well as the principle of fundamental reasonableness: no one ought to harm another in his life, health, liberty, or possessions," which, to put it in more general terms means "the peace and preservation of all mankind."[22]

In the state of nature "there is no superiority or jurisdiction of one over another, what any may do in prosecution of that law, every one must needs have a right to do." However, some individuals cannot realise this in their own conduct, and they should be considered criminals by the force of the law. "In transgressing the law of nature, the offender declares himself to live by

[21] J. Locke, *Two Treatises on Government*, London 1823, p. 11.

[22] "Every one, as he is bound to preserve himself, and not to quit his station wilfully, so by the like reason, when his own preservation comes not in competition, ought he, as much as he can, to preserve the rest of mankind and may not, unless it be to do justice on an offender, take away, or impair the life, or what tends to the preservation of the life, the liberty, health, limb, or goods of another." Cf. ibidem, p. 101.

another rule than that of reason and common equity, which is that measure God has set to the actions of men, for their mutual security..."[23] In this way, Locke associates rationality with justice, and irrationality with criminality, and both of these with the right to punish whoever violates natural law, as well as demand of the criminals that they compensate the injured parties. The reference to divine creation is not supposed to decrease the power and legitimacy of this law, but rather to strengthen it.

In the state of nature, it is often difficult or even impossible to enforce all the right laws, such as when "ill-nature, passion and revenge will carry them too far in punishing others; and hence nothing but confusion and disorder will follow." The means of counterbalancing these difficulties comes in the form of the civic government and political society, which, according to Locke, amounts to a form of government, which is created by rational, free, equal and just people, and a society in which those people call into office the governing powers and can discard them if they are acting irrationally, which is to say when they do not properly execute their duties.

In enumerating the duties of those granted political power, Locke points in the first instance to the establishment of such laws that secure the citizenry from any state of war, or a "state of enmity and destruction."[24] Secondly, he mentions the securing of citizens' property, including control over one's own person. ("Every man has a property in his own person: this nobody has any right to but himself.") Locke explains in detail what the basis of such a prerogative is, namely, both human labour and divine decree, but he also spells out its proper scale. ("The measure of property nature has well set by the extent of men's labour and the conveniences of life.") Thirdly, he mentions the establishment of such laws which guarantee civic freedoms ("where there is no law, there is no freedom.")[25] This relatively short list of the main duties that the public authority is expected to assume is supplemented by paternalistic power, which cannot stem only from the fact of having fathered a child, but has to involve the duty of care for the child. This power is necessarily limited in time ("The bonds of this subjection are like the swaddling clothes they are wrapt up in, and supported by, in the weakness of their infancy: age and rea-

[23] Cf. ibidem, p. 193.

[24] "To avoid this state of war [...] is one great reason of men's putting themselves into society, and quitting the state of nature" Cf. ibidem, p. 204.

[25] "[...] but freedom is [...] a liberty to dispose and order as he lists, his person, actions, possessions, and his whole property, within the allowance of those laws under which he is, and therein not to be subject to the arbitrary will of another, but freely follow his own." (ibidem, p. 234). It also involves following the voice of reason: "Thus we are born free, as we are born rational." (ibidem, p. 237).

son, as they grow up, loosen them, till at length they drop quite off, and leave a man at his own free disposal") and does not pertain to their life and property.

These considerations of paternal authority serve not only as an attempt to show the necessarily fluid boundary dividing the public and private realms, but also introduce the reasons why humans abandoned the initially solitary life for life in groups, finally leading to the formation of political society. Locke sees the hand of omnipotent God playing a role in this, as under strong obligations of necessity, convenience, and inclination He made human society dependent on Him, and equipped humanity with understanding and language to continue and enjoy it. Whatever use of their reason and speech people make, however, is entirely up to them.

In the panoramic view of social life sketched in the subsequent parts of the treatise, starting with the origins of political societies and ending with his contemporary society, Locke considers some of the uses that people make of their divinely endowed abilities to be in accordance with their purpose. Often, this is not the case. As an example of the former, one could mention the spontaneous formation of families ("Conjugal society is made by a voluntary compact between man and woman"), while not forming families or forming them under coercive circumstances is an example of the latter. These would also include situations where the husband becomes some sort of master of life and death over the wife, children, domestics or slaves.

In a broader social dimension, the considerations above also apply to the absolute ruler or any absolute power.[26] In the chapters *Of Conquest, Of Usurpation*, as well as *Of Tyranny* he presents actions where the power of the sword takes the upper hand over the powers of reason. ("The conqueror, it is true, usually, by the force he has over them, compels them, with a sword at their breasts, to stoop to his conditions, and submit to such a government as he pleases to afford them.") In such actions one can perhaps find some form of rationality, but not social rationality, which equal, free and rational individuals could accept. This social rationality is mostly presented in chapters IX to XV, which balance out some earlier assumptions and postulates, and include vital expansions to Locke's understanding of the model of social rationality.

These are mostly concerned with the divisions and hierarchical arrangements of political powers, including the legislative, the executive and the federative. Legislative power, which Locke calls the legislative, is supposed to be both the first (called into being prior to all others) and the highest power.

---

[26] "For if it be asked, what security, what fence is there, in such a state, against the violence and oppression of this absolute ruler? the very question can scarce be borne. They are ready to tell you, that it deserves death only to ask after safety." Ibidem, p. 267.

("This legislative is not only the supreme power of the commonwealth, but sacred and unalterable in the hands where the community have once placed it.") It is brought into being by the people, and can be dismissed by the people, whenever they consider the authorities to have breached the trust vested in them. Other conditions for the socially rational functioning of the legislative include: 1. Continuous operation within a given time-period; 2. Abstaining from legislating arbitrary decrees; 3. "The supreme power cannot take from any man any part of his property without his own consent;" 4. "The legislative cannot transfer the power of making laws to any other hands;" 5. "[It] must not raise Taxes on the property of the people, without the consent of the people."

While the legislative power can be divided into executive and federative powers, the two should be held in the same hands: "both of them requiring the force of the society for their exercise, it is almost impracticable to place the force of the commonwealth in distinct, and not subordinate hands; or that the executive and federative power should be placed in persons, that might act separately, whereby the force of the public would be under different commands: which would be apt some time or other to cause disorder and ruin."[27] One could nevertheless indicate significantly different social duties of all these powers. According to Locke, the duty of the executive consists in "comprehending the execution of the municipal laws of the society within itself, upon all that are parts of it," while the federative power is responsible for "the management of the security and interest of the public without, with all those that it may receive benefit or damage from, yet they are always almost united."

In the chapter "Of Prerogative," Locke presents situations where the executive and federative powers can "do several things, of their own free choice, where the law was silent." This can take place when "in some governments the law-making power is not always in being, and is usually too numerous, and so too slow, for the dispatch requisite to execution" or if " the law was silent, and sometimes too against the direct letter of the law, for the public good, and their acquiescing in it when so done." What remains of crucial importance, however, is for the rulers to be of a strong and good character and that they understand their social duties and prerogatives correctly.[28] In general, Locke still takes it to be the rule that power has to be exercised within rationally legislated and executed laws, some exceptions notwithstanding.

[27] Cf. ibidem, p. 316.

[28] "And therefore he that will look into the history of England, will find, that prerogative was always largest in the hands of our wisest and best princes; because the people, observing the whole tendency of their actions to be the public good, contested not what was done without law to that end..." Ibidem, p. 332.

All these considerations on "true original extent and end of civil government" are concluded in the chapter *Of the Dissolution of Government.* Locke begins with a critique of solutions which involve foreign troops, and moves on to the analysis of situations where change is brought about by domestic forces. Among the latter cases, he distinguishes situations where there is rational justification for such actions from those where such justification is too weak to gain social acceptance. This second situation can occur "when he who has the supreme executive power neglects and abandons that charge, so that the laws already made can no longer be put in execution." More complicated concerns are involved in the rationally justified dissolution of the government. This can take place, for instance, when 1. The legislative undergoes a change, 2. "[T]he prince hinders the legislative from assembling in its due time, or from acting freely, pursuant to those ends for which it was constituted, the legislative is altered;" 3. "When, by the arbitrary power of the prince, the electors, or ways of election are altered, without the consent, and contrary to the common interest of the people;" 4. When legislators act contrary to the purposes for which they were elected; and some other special cases. In Locke's view, civic society is the proper arbiter of whether or not the public authority has lost the legitimacy to govern, or, to be more precise it is this collective wisdom within which certain specific social tasks are undertaken by the enlightened monarch, the enlightened gentry and the enlightened people.

Postscript

There are crucial differences between the models of social order described by Hobbes and Locke. The former sided with a rationally executed absolute power, while the latter believed in a power rationally executed and divided. These differences stem from their respective assumptions concerning human nature, where Hobbes was convinced of the natural human proclivity towards evil rather than good, while Locke reckoned that man is inclined to do good by nature. These tendencies were supposedly especially visible in the state of nature, i.e., a period where either no power structure existed or it was not rationally divided, executed and sanctioned by established laws. Both philosophers agreed that the state of nature could not exit in perpetuity. However, according to Hobbes it could not go on because it led to the state of internecine and universal warfare, whereas Locke thought that the state of nature had to come to an end because of the emergence of a criminal minority, which adhered to a set of norms and rules different from those of the rational majority and, yet, proved successful in their imposition.

These significantly different perspectives on human life in the state of nature and the reasons for its demise underlie the differences in their views on the role of public authority. In the Hobbesian view, political power is in the first instance responsible for preventing harm being done and punishing all those who cannot or do not want to control their natural urges and abilities. On the other hand, Locke sees the chief role of public authority in the creation of the best possible environment for putting those urges and desires to good use. This is why in the former author's writing so much space is devoted to questions of criminality and punishing the guilty, while the latter philosopher has little to say on these issues. It is also significant that one includes judicial powers among the core elements of public authority, while the other does not, which leads to differences in understanding positive laws. According to Hobbes, these comprise both the right to live in peace and the criminal law guarding this right, while Locke adds the right to life, as well as the right to work and enjoy the fruits of work, right to private property and its protection from others, the right to adhere to any religious creed the citizen finds proper, but also such civic freedoms which allow for creating, controlling, and dismissing public authorities. These differences in the two philosophers' understanding of positive laws make Locke's model of social life more akin to the later liberal doctrines than that of Hobbes.

This opinion appears to be shared by Pierre Manent in his *Intellectual History of Liberalism*. He admits that the social views of Locke "are of course of great importance for the elaboration of the liberal doctrine." Yet, he indicates two crucial simplifications. The first concerns the primacy of political and philosophical over economic questions, as in Locke's theory "the world of economy alone is not sufficient; it needs the political institution for guaranteeing its existence." The other simplification relates to the subservience of the executive to the legislative, which Manent takes to be socially ambiguous, as "[t]he legislative, as the more direct expression of individuals in civil society, is the supreme power. Our political institutions founded on the idea of representation naturally attribute supreme power to the legislative power. Simultaneously, executive power embodying the difference between the state and civil society, or between man's political and natural conditions, finds in its de jure inferiority a de facto principle of action."[29] According to P. Mannent, the first simplification was later corrected by subsequent generations of political economists, while the second remains to this day the temptation for the legislative to become the dominant power in the state.

[29] Cf. P. Manent, *An Intellectual History of Liberalism*, Princeton 1995, p. 51 ff.

Chapter IV

Rationality of social life according to the Enlightenment lawyers

The words and deeds of Enlightenment lawyers had a crucial impact on the events that played out as the Great French Revolution. They first demonstrated their power by forcing the meeting of the Estates-General, whose proceedings they steered in such a way that the third estate became de facto dominant thanks to their ability to co-opt some members of the nobility and clergy to their cause.[1] The lawyers subsequently assumed key positions in both the legislative and executive bodies, and brought about a relatively swift collapse of the *ancien régime* with its laws; at the same time, a new regime emerged on the basis of laws that they considered more rational and better suited to social needs, of which they considered themselves representatives. Their successes seem to have been even greater in the long run, as the ideas they fought for in the late 18th century would slowly become commonplace in the countries of western Europe. In short, these countries would increasingly rely on legal systems that were both rational and comprehensible from the point of view of the common citizen. The standards of this rationality are obviously of an Enlightenment pedigree. In the present context, I will consider two of those lawyers, Charles Montesquieu and Cesare Beccaria, whose impact was crucial to the formulation of these standards, while bearing in mind that they were only two among many other influential lawyers.

[1] Jan Baszkiewicz refers to the first stage of the Great French Revolution as "the revolution of attorneys": "it merits the name not only because almost half of the 578 deputies of the Third Estate were lawyers, of whome many were attorneys (for example Robespierre, Mounier, Barnave, Merlin de Douai, Le Chapelier, Lanjuinais), but also because the political conflict was initially focused on formal legal questions, such as the proper way of verifying the mandates of deputies: together or separately." Cf. J. Baszkiewicz, *Historia Francji* [The History of France], Wroclaw – Warsaw – Cracow 1974, p. 332.

1. Charles Montesquieu

From a contemporary point of view, many of the claims made by Montesquieu (1689–1755) might seem self-evident – not only to lawyers but also to regular citizens whose dealings with the law are restricted to the practical domain. Yet, at the time when he was presenting them, an entirely different system of laws appeared to be self-evident. Montesquieu had to deal with them not only as a subject of the King of France, but also as a practising lawyer. He came from an old line of French nobility, whose centuries of service to the crown were mostly rendered by sword rather than intellectual means. Nevertheless, his family decided to educate him, first at home and later in Collège de Juilly, which was run by French Oratorians (he graduated in 1705). He continued his education in the Law Faculty of the University of Bordeaux. After graduation he initially practised law in Paris, but after the death of his father (1713) he was compelled to move back to Bordeaux. In 1715, he married an affluent Protestant, and in 1716 inherited from his uncle the property in Brède (Aquitaine) as well as the seat of the deputy speaker of the regional parliament in Bordeaux (at the time French parliaments were not legislative but judicial institutions). All this allowed his family to lead a life of secure material setting, and he started to devote his time to the natural sciences (he was interested in physics, geology and biology) as well as philosophy.

His literary debut – the *Persian Letters* (1721) – already brought him much recognition and granted a place among the Enlightened philosophers. They constituted something in between the two genres in vogue at the time: the travel journal and the philosophical tale. The protagonist – the Persian noblemen Usbek – is a ruler forced to seek refuge in exile from the schemes of his enemies. He finds safe haven in France, and spends time studying his new surroundings. These observations lead to a picture of France and the French as well as the citizens of some other countries that is satirical and at times also critical. Usbek is often perplexed by the customs, practices, prejudices and public institutions he encounters. In *Letter XXIX*, one learns that at the helm of such a curious religion as Christianity appears to be one finds the pope: "an old idol, kept venerable by custom. Formerly he was feared by princes [...]. He is, however, no longer dreaded. He declares himself to be the successor of one of the first Christians, called Saint Peter: and it is certainly a rich succession, for he possesses immense treasures, and a large territory owns his sway."[2] One can also learn that there is little tolerance for the heretics in Spain and

[2] Cf. Montesquieu, *Persian Letters*, trans. J. Davidson, London 1891, p. 92.

Portugal: "Happy the man, who, when he falls into the hands of these people, has been accustomed to finger little balls of wood while saying his prayers [...] Without that, the poor devil is in a wretched plight. Although he should swear like a Pagan that he is orthodox, they may very likely decline to admit his plea, and burn him for a heretic." It goes without saying that the enlightened reader understood well enough that the criticism of such religious practices was not merely restricted to the particular countries named in the letters.

Apart from the anti-clerical motifs, there is also a clear anti-monarchical current in the letters, related to the reign of Louis XIV: "the king is a great magician, for his dominion extends to the minds of his subjects; he makes them think what he wishes," and on top of that makes people believe "his touch is a sovereign cure for all sorts of diseases." What is more, this strange king "has a minister who is only eighteen years old, and a mistress who is fourscore," "although he flies from the noise of the cities, and is inclined to be reticent, from morning till night he is engaged in getting himself talked about." It goes without saying that all this was considered irrational or contrary to common sense by Montesquieu, which boils down to more or less the same thing, as his standards of rationality prove largely based on common-sense foundations.

The publishing success of the *Persian Letters* allowed Montesquieu to break away from the tedious judicial duties of Bordeaux parliament and to become a well-received guest in the royal court and Parisian literary circles. In 1728, thanks to the support of the society meeting in the salon of Madame de Lambert, he was admitted into the Académie Française. In those years, he would travel frequently in Europe – for instance, he visited Vienna and London as well as Italian cities such as Rome, Florence and Napoli. During these travels he would collect literature and observations useful to the compiling of his further works. In 1734, he published *Considerations on the Causes of the Grandeur and Decadence of the Romans*, where he sketched the vision of Roman history as progressing from the barbarian phase when Romans would subjugate other peoples, later creating a new civilisation, up to their ultimate decline. In 1748, he published *The Spirit of the Laws*, the work which solidified his position as a great theorist of constitutional and criminal law, and subsequently contributed to the rise of the ideology of the Great French Revolution.

In Montesquieu's design, the book was not expected to be so revolutionary, and in the introduction he would already emphasise that "I write not to censure anything established in any country whatsoever," but so as to "persuade those who command to increase their knowledge in what they ought to prescribe."[3] There are many pages in the book which clearly hail the traditional order – such

[3] Cf. Montesquieu, *The Spirit of Laws*, trans. M. Richter, Indianapolis 1900, p. xxxii.

as the declared attachment to the monarchic rule, the Catholic church or the social structure based on estates. On the other hand, there are passages in the book which clearly present him as a supporter of such reforms, which would lead to the creation of democratic social structures. ("When the body of the people is possessed of the supreme power, it is called democracy.") It is difficult to find passages where clear revolutionary demands are expressed, but then this depends largely on what one would seek in the book. The proponents of radical change were looking for the revolutionary spirit, and proved successful in finding it, but when the revolutionary dust settled, the author came to be perceived as the advocate of a sort of legalism that attempted to build bridges between tradition and modernity.

The effort to reconcile these two worlds remains an important element in *The Spirit of Laws.* Its most important endeavour is to demonstrate the nature of the laws and their foundations, as well as specifying their roles in making social life more rational, just and happy. The work starts by pointing this out in the first paragraph: "Laws, in their most general sense, are the necessary relations arising from the nature of things." In subsequent passages a distinction is made between the so-called natural laws ("they derive their force entirely from our frame and existence") and positive laws legislated by nations, such as political and civil laws. From a general point of view, Montesquieu writes "Law in general is human reason, inasmuch as it governs all the inhabitants of the earth: the political and civil laws of each nation ought to be only the particular cases in which human reason is applied."[4] In this way, he combined the question of the rationality of laws, i.e., their establishment by reason, with that of their validity, i.e., being in force. One should also note that different kinds of rationality and validity can be distinguished.

Montesquieu explains this using the example of the three types of government – the republican (which he subdivides into the democratic and the aristocratic), monarchic, and despotic types. Each of these represents a specific kind of rationality distinguished both by its nature and force, as in democracy: "As most citizens have sufficient ability to choose, though unqualified to be chosen, so the people, though capable of calling others to an account for their administration, are incapable of conducting the administration themselves"), but also by its mode of operation, for example in the republic virtue is constitutive, while honour plays this role in the monarchic, and fear in the despotic.

After considering these three forms of government, Montesquieu comes to the conclusion that the least rational is the despotic, while moderate monarchic government represents the highest degree of rationality. To justify

[4] Cf. ibidem, p. 6.

this claim he wrote "In despotic states, the nature of government requires the most passive obedience; and once the prince's will is made known, it ought infallibly to produce its effect," whereas in the moderate monarchic states power is limited by the very foundation from which it springs, which is to say "by honour, through which a monarch, reigns over the prince and his people," as well as by the reason for moderation: "in a monarchy the prince receives instruction, at the same time that his ministers have greater abilities, and are more versed in public affairs, than the ministers of a despotic government."

In the *Spirit of Laws*, no open criticism of the contemporaneous French monarchy is put forward, yet Montesquieu makes some remarks on monarchs that proved deficient in virtue and honour, or perhaps failed to grasp their meaning properly. What strange kind of virtue could it have been that found expression in the courtly life, filled with "Ambition in idleness; meanness mixed with pride; a desire of riches without industry; aversion to truth; flattery, perfidy, violation of engagements, contempt of civil duties, fear of the prince's virtue, hope from his weakness, but, above all, a perpetual ridicule cast upon virtue," and what strange honour guides the monarch who "calls to the state his capital, the capital to his court, and the court to his own person," and the court to genuflect before the monarch and focus on thinking and speaking exactly as he expects them to. While such actions cannot be treated as utterly irrational, their type of rationality is not one that could be praised by the enlightened person.

This motif is not developed any further in the subsequent parts of the *Spirit of Laws*. Montesquieu tends to focus rather on questions concerning the proper form the laws legislated by the people should take so as to be rational and helpful in realising social aims. It seems clear from his arguments that laws cannot in fact be thought of as truly arbitrary, given all the multiple determinants that appear to shape them. He mentions among them the "physical conditions of the country," including the climate, soil quality, size and population of the country. After those, he indicates the cultural conditions: "the degree of liberty which the constitution will bear; to the religion of the inhabitants, to their inclinations, riches, numbers, commerce, manners, and customs."

Montesquieu devotes a lot of attention to the correlations between the laws and the more general qualities of spirit, desires and climate – almost the entire third part of Book I focusses on such considerations. In general, he singles out three climactic zones – cold, warm, and moderate. In the first of these, inhabitants tend to be stronger than those living in the other two: "This superiority of strength must produce various effects; for instance, a greater boldness, that is, more courage; a greater sense of superiority, that is, less desire of revenge; a greater opinion of security, that is, more frankness, less suspicion, policy, and cunning. In short, this must be productive of very different tempers." On the other hand, people living in the warm zone are supposed to be "like old men, timorous – put a man into a close, warm place, and [...] he will feel a great faintness. If under this circumstance you propose a bold enterprise to him, I believe you will find him very little disposed towards it; his present weakness will throw him into despondency; he will be afraid of everything, being in a state of total incapacity." The other differences between the three zones are related to degree of sensitivity ("In cold countries they have very little sensibility for pleasure; in temperate countries, they have more; in warm countries, their sensibility is exquisite"), resistance to pain, and even "that the soul is most sensibly moved by whatever relates to the union of the two sexes." ("In northern climates scarcely has the animal part of love a power of making itself felt [...] In warmer climates it is liked for its own sake, it is the only cause of happiness, it is life itself.")

From a present point of view, accounts of culture strictly dependent upon nature might seem somewhat amusing. When it comes to the question of social rationality, however, Montesquieu's position is clear and consequently justified. It boils down to the conviction that this rationality has its roots neither in the divine, nor even in the human mind, but rather in nature itself. While nature remains heterogeneous, there cannot be any single social rationality, and those that appear in different times and places must necessarily be susceptible to change, so far as the external conditions change. It is this part of the *Spirit of Laws* which pertains to social rationality in what its author considers to be its broadest available understanding.

One might also speak of social rationality in a narrower sense, as legislated by the rational law-givers and those governing powers that stand on its guard. One key element of this kind of rationality consists in the division of those powers which later came to be known as *constitutional.* It is introduced in Book XI *Of the laws which establish political liberty with regard to the constitution*, where Montesquieu writes: "In every government there are three types of power: the legislative; the executive in respect to things dependent on the law of nations; and the executive in regard to matters that depend on the civil law." These powers are instituted precisely to ensure the political freedom of the citizens: "The political liberty of the subject is a tranquillity of mind arising from the opinion each person has of his safety. In order to have this liberty, it is requisite the government be so constituted as one man need not be afraid of another. When the legislative and executive powers are united in the same person, or in the same body of magistrates, there can be no liberty; because apprehensions may arise, lest the same monarch or senate should enact tyrannical laws, to execute them in a tyrannical manner. Again, there is no liberty, if the judiciary power be not separated from the legislative and executive. Were it joined with the legislative, the life and liberty of the subject would be exposed to arbitrary control; for the judge would be then the legislator. Were it joined to the executive power, the judge might behave with violence and oppression. There would be an end of everything, were the same man or the same body, whether of the nobles or of the people, to exercise those three powers..." This last institution only occurs in the despotic system, which proves the worst for the totality of citizens. In the subsequent parts of the treatise, Montesquieu attempts to demonstrate that citizens can never feel secure when one particular governing body assumes both of these powers.

In the following book he takes up the question of "political liberty in relation to the subject" (the previous one dealing with political liberty "with regard to the constitution"). It follows from his argumentation that it can take two principal shapes, either passive (the citizen being secured from the exploits of any of the branches of government) or active (when the citizen has influence on the creation of laws). The citizen's political freedom is directly related to his personal freedom. Personal freedom generally amounts to the capacity for "free exercise of the will," which includes freedom to think, speak and write ("a citizen in this state will say and write whatever the laws do not expressly forbid to be said or written"), as well as freedom of conscience, i.e., being free to choose whatever religion the particular citizen considers to be in line with their reason, conscience, customs and habits. Nowadays, all this constitutes elementary civic competence, but at a time when western civic society was still in its infancy, such statements were far from self-evident.

Montesquieu's views concerning criminal law follow a similar pattern. He assumes it to be a general rule that the punishment has to be adequate to the nature of the crime, of which he would distinguish four kinds: "Those of the first species are prejudicial to religion, the second to morals, the third to the public tranquillity, and the fourth to the security of the subject." The first concerns acts that are sacrilegious and their penalisation which should be based on "depriving people of the advantages conferred by religion in expelling them out of the temples, in a temporary or perpetual exclusion from the society of the faithful, in shunning their presence, in execrations, commination, and conjurations."[5] When it comes to crimes against morals, these are actions that involve "the violation of public or private continence [...] directing the manner

[5] Montesquieu provides specific examples of such crimes against religion which can be seen as an affront to common sense, for instance when "Aaron was detected, as he was poring over a book of Solomon's, the reading of which was sufficient to conjure up whole legions of devil)," or to quote another example: "The history of Constantinople informs us that in consequence of a revelation made to a bishop of a miracle having ceased because of the magic practices of a certain person, both that person and his son were put to death."

in which the pleasure annexed to the conjunction of the sexes is to be enjoyed." These should be punished by "privation of such advantages as society has attached to the purity of morals, fines, shame, necessity of concealment, public infamy, expulsion from home and society." The crimes of the third kind are those which "disturb the public tranquillity" and they should be punished by "imprisonment, exile, and other like chastisements, proper for reclaiming turbulent spirits, and obliging them to conform to the established order." According to Montesquieu, threatening the security of citizens amounts to the gravest of crimes, which should be punished by "retaliation, by which the society refuses security to a member, who has actually or intentionally deprived another of his security"; in other words, whenever someone "violated the security of the subject so far as to deprive, or attempt to deprive, another man of his life," then they deserve to die, while for those whose crimes are against property "it would be much better, and perhaps more natural, that crimes committed against the security of property should be punished with the loss of property," and when it comes to such individuals that do not have property of their own, "instead of a pecuniary, to substitute a corporal, punishment." In this classification crimes against religion assume a worse than secondary importance and they are seen to be merely ecclesiastic punishments. This means that they are seen as relating not to the citizenry in general, and are only a problem for those who belong to the particular religious community and may feel offended by such crimes. This is not yet pushing religious life out of the public and into the private sphere, but it does constitute an important step in such a direction. Further steps of this nature were indeed made during the Great Revolution, and subsequently in the second half of the 19th and early 20th century, and they found expression in the formal division of church and state.

Postscript

At this point it seems worth exploring the relationship between the ideas of *Spirit of Laws* and the *Declaration of the Rights of Man and of the Citizen* proclaimed by the National Constituent Assembly on August the 26th, 1789. In spite of ample criticism, the Declaration did in fact shape the general direction of the French legislators and became the foundation for all the subsequent constitutions, both in the period of the Great Revolution (in 1793 and in 1795) as well as later (in 1848, 1948, and 1950). On many public buildings in contemporary France, one can find the key message of the Declaration, expressed in the slogan: "Liberty, Equality, Fraternity." In my view, this message is very much like that of *Spirit of Laws*.

In the commentary to the Declaration (and 27 other projects introduced in the National Assembly in 1789), Christine Fauré mentions that it was "proclaimed in great haste, in result of turbulent events shaking the country, and accompanied by many quarrels and contradictions" among the deputies. Under such increasing contradictions new committees would be called into existence: "and so on July 7th the Constitutional Committee was called into being, comprising thirty cells, a week later – on July 14th – another Constitutional Committee of eight members, which was superseded on August 12th by a five-member Committee. On the assumption that the decrease in the number of members would simplify the task and guarantee its completion, and acting on the pressures of time and environment [...] it was decided that the edited document would come under a vote of the General Assembly. Each of the chapters is based on the initial draft, and they were put to the vote by Sieyès." Before voting on the motion, one of the deputies (Bouche) demanded that the assembly declares "The Declaration of the Rights of Man and Citizen to be incomplete" and that "if need arises of new amendments then their drafts would be put to the vote of the Assembly before the Constitution." A motion to that effect passed.[6]

These circumstances do explain to some degree the concise form (only 17 short paragraphs) and rather general nature of some of the provisions. In the commentary to the document quoted above it is remarked that "the question of religion was reduced to its social correlates" and that it appeared in a maximally reduced form in the preamble (which states that "the National Assembly recognizes and proclaims, in the presence and under the auspices of the Supreme Being"), and in Article X. ("No one shall be disquieted on account of his opinions, including his religious views, provided their manifestation does not disturb the public order established by law.") This does not make it possible to tell what the actual attitude to the Christian religion and religiosity was among the Enlightenment legislators. This was only later manifested by their actions, including the confiscation of a major part of the possessions of the Catholic Church, as well as the liquidation of most monasteries. At that stage of the revolution it would have been unwise and pointless to argue that the less religion and religiosity there would be in French society, the more rationality it would contain. It seems to me that these ideas have a lot in common with the proposals put forward by Montesquieu, especially when one considers not so much the general declarations, but the concrete suggestions, for instance, in the sphere of criminal law.

[6] Cf. Ch. Fauré (ed.), *Les déclarations des droits de l'homme de 1789*, Paris 1988, p. 15 ff.

The declaration devotes by far the most extensive attention to civic freedom, which is already mentioned in the first sentence of the first article of the Declaration: "Men are born and remain free and equal in rights." In subsequent articles, the question of equality is de-emphasised, while the question of freedom receives primary focus. In Article 2 we read: "The aim of all political association is the preservation of the natural and imprescriptible rights of man;" Article 4 states that "Liberty consists in the freedom to do everything which injures no one else" and "These limits can only be determined by law;" Article 6 details a basic civic freedom as the right to participate in the legislative process ("personally, or through his representative"); Article 7 explains both the rules of restricting freedom and taking it away ("No person shall be accused, arrested, or imprisoned except in the cases and according to the forms prescribed by law"), it also makes a distinction between freedom and lawlessness whenever. ("Any one soliciting, transmitting, executing, or causing to be executed, any arbitrary order, shall be punished.") In the aforementioned Article 10 the fundamental freedom to express one's own beliefs is discussed (the religious question assumes a secondary role in this respect). In Article 11, the statement further highlights this freedom in that "The free communication of ideas and opinions is one of the most precious of the rights of man." Article 13 discusses the civic duty of taxation ("for the maintenance of the public forces and for the cost of administration"), however Article 14 immediately adds that "All the citizens have a right to decide, either personally or by their representatives, as to the necessity of the public contribution; to grant this freely; to know to what uses it is put; and to fix the proportion, the mode of assessment and of collection and the duration of the taxes."[7]

In the articles expressly mentioned above and in many others one can clearly make out the influence of Montesquieu's *Spirit of Laws*, with its principles of passive and active freedoms (with clear emphasis on the latter) as well as the division of powers (for example Article 16 says that "A society in which the observance of the law is not assured, nor the separation of powers defined, has no constitution at all"). The bearing of this on social rationality appears abundantly clear, as the authors of the Declaration shared the conviction that it is reasonable and rationally justified to allow the citizen to maintain the largest possible freedom to think, speak, write, print and act, which should work to the better of the particular man and citizen, as well as the society at large. Subsequent events, including waves of revolutionary terror, served as major correctives on this faith in the natural abilities of man to rationally coexist with others, yet the document itself entered the general canon of modern western culture.[8]

[7] Cf. ibidem, p. 11 ff.

[8] It was already pointed out by Émile Faguet that the *Declaration* constitutes principally an act of faith in Man, cf. E. Fauget, *Liberalizm* [Liberalism], Lwów (n.d.), p. 34 ff.

It is worth noting that the problems of private property and its protection, mentioned in passing in *Spirit of Laws*, became a priority in the 1789 *Declaration of the Rights of Man and of the Citizen*. In a commentary to the Declaration and other drafts considered by the National Constituent Assembly in July and August of 1789, Christine Fauré writes that these questions proved highly controversial, and that while the Deputies were not divided on the question of whether or not to protect private property, but by the consideration of how far such protection should go, and which groups should enjoy these protections, for instance, whether it should be granted to women, children or foreigners residing in France.[9] In the end, a general formulation was agreed upon (Article 17): "Since property is an inviolable and sacred right, no one shall be deprived thereof except where public necessity, legally determined, shall clearly demand it, and then only on condition that the owner shall have been previously and equitably indemnified." Private property is also explicitly mentioned in Article 2 (where this right is counted among the four basic civic rights), and indirectly in Articles 13 and 14 (pertaining to the imposition and payment of taxes). It can therefore be said that. from the point of view of the Enlightenment lawyers (and politicians), one cannot speak of social rationality without addressing the fundamental problem of the protection for private property acquired in accordance with the law.

2. Cesare Beccaria

Beccaria (1783–1794) was among the most important intellectual heirs of Montesquieu in the 18th century. While he did not gain comparable international fame, he was a well-known at the time, and his *Essay on Crimes and Punishments* (1764) was translated into multiple languages (for example French, English, German) during his lifetime. The life and activity of Beccaria revolved around Milan, one of the major centres, next to Naples, of the Italian Enlightenment. He obtained academic law credentials, studying in Padua, and his dissertation proves that he was thoroughly oriented in the ideas and demands of the Enlightenment. To some extent he owed this to contacts with the circle of Milanese philosophers assembled around the journal "Il Caffe." In fact, it was in fact its founder, Pietro Verri, who suggested writing the *Essay on Crimes and Punishments*.[10]

While comparably short (it includes only 47 short chapter-paragraphs), this text is very impressive. Both in terms of the range of covered questions, and the high degree of intellectual independence exhibited by the author. In the introduction, Beccaria pays homage to the "immortal" Montesquieu and

[9] Cf. Ch. Fauré (ed.), *Les déclarations des droits...*, op. cit., p. 25 ff.

[10] Cf. V. Titone, *La storiografia dell'illuminismo in Italia*, Milano 1969, p. 63 ff.

declares the wish to "follow the steps of that great man," while also expressing the hope that the "studious part of mankind," to whom the treatise was addressed "will easily distinguish the superstructure from the foundation."[11] In the message "To the Reader" opening the treatise, Beccaria discusses his differences with the received legal order. This stands in contrast to the author of the *Spirit of Laws* who treated them with some deference and indicated natural and cultural justifications for their origins and social existence. On the other hand, according to Beccaria, they are an "inheritance" from the "laws of an ancient conquering race, codified twelve hundred years ago by a prince ruling at Constantinople, and since jumbled together with the customs of the Lombards." He writes further of the "silent war" waged between rational people and those who are used to enforcing cruel and unjust criminal law. He emphasises that "the cruelty of punishments, and the irregularity of proceedings in criminal cases, so principal a part of the legislation, and so much neglected throughout Europe, has hardly ever been called into question. Errors, accumulated through many centuries, have never yet been exposed by ascending to general principles; nor has the force of acknowledged truths been ever opposed to the unbounded licentiousness of ill-directed power, which has continually produced so many authorised examples of the most unfeeling barbarity. Surely, the groans of the weak, sacrificed to the cruel ignorance, and the indolence of the powerful; the barbarous torments lavished, and multiplied with useless severity, for crimes either not proved, or in their nature impossible, the filth and horrors of prison, increased in the most cruel tormentor of the miserable, uncertainty ought to have roused the attention of those, whose business is to direct the opinions of mankind."

One general conclusion stemming from this introduction is that modern nations need rationality and justice, which cannot be achieved without some degree of understanding for those on a collision course with the law, even if forced onto it by the basic necessities of life. In Beccaria's opinion, this is the blueprint of thinking to which Enlightened law-givers and policy-makers should adhere. Beccaria develops and specifies this general thesis, that there is a connection between rationality and just lenience in the criminal code, as well as understanding on the part of justices and rulers. These concretisations are accompanied by considerations of the general nature of positive laws, i.e., their origin, social function, diversity, etc.

[11] "I shall be happy, if, with him, I can obtain the secret thanks of the obscura, and peaceful disciples of reason, and philosophy, and excite the tender emotion, in which sensible minds sympathise with him, who pleads the cause of humanity." Cf. C. Beccaria, *An Essay on Crimes and Punishments*, London 1983, p. 4.

In § I, Beccaria states that "laws are the conditions, under which men, naturally independent, united themselves in society." In § II we read that "every act of authority of one man over another, for which there is not an absolute necessity, is tyrannical. It is upon this then that the sovereign's right to punish crimes is founded; that is, upon the necessity of defending the public liberty, entrusted to his care, from the usurpation of individuals." To this he adds that, without this, law would be "transferred from individuals to nations." This leads him to conclude (formulated in § III) that "the laws only can determine the punishment of crimes and the authority of making penal laws can only reside with the legislator, who represents the whole society united by the social compact." ("This obligation, which descends from the throne to the cottage, and equally binds the highest and the lowest of mankind, signifies nothing more, than that it is in the interest of all, that conventions, which are useful to the greatest number, should be punctually observed.") In the conclusion of § III he adds that "if it can only be proved, that the severity of punishments, though not immediately contrary to the public good, or to the end for which they are intended, vis. to prevent crimes, be useless; then such severity would be contrary to those beneficial virtues, which are the consequence of enlightened reason." In § IV and § V he opposes the adherence to the spirit of the law rather than its letter ("there is nothing more dangerous than the common axiom: *the spirit of the laws is to be considered*," "the spirit of the laws will then be the result of good, or bad logic of the judge; and this will depend on his good or bad digestion; on the violence of his passions; on the rank and conditions of the accused, or on his connections with the judge; and on all those little circumstances, which change the appearance of objects in the fluctuating mind of man"), and shows clear preference for written and printed laws ("this will put a stop to the fatal liberty of explaining, the source of arbitrary and venal decisions"). In § VI he considers the "proportions between crimes and punishments" ("a scale of crimes may be formed, of which the first degree should consist of those, which immediately tend to the dissolution of society, and the last, of the smallest possible injustice done to a private member of society"), and in the subsequent chapter he suggests such a hierarchy, where he considers the gravest crimes which involve "injury done to society," and comprise three types: "Some crimes are immediately destructive of society, or its representative; others attack the private security of the life property, or honour of individuals, and a third class consists of such actions as are contrary to the laws which relate to the general good of the community."

When it comes to other paragraphs devoted to more general considerations, § XI ("Of Crimes, which disturb the public Tranquillity") merits further attention, as it poses a series of fundamental questions, such as "What are in general the proper punishments for crimes? Is the punishment of death really useful, or necessary for the safety, or good order of society? Are the tortures and torments consistent with justice, or do they answer the end proposed by the laws? Which is the best method of preventing crimes?" The question of using torture with respect to the accused is covered at length in § XVI, which states among other things that "no man can be judged criminal until he be found guilty," and that any confessions induced by torture or the threat of torture has no merit. ("This infamous test of truth is a remaining monument of that ancient and savage legislation, in which trials by fire, by boiling water, or the uncertainty of combats, were called the *judgements of God*.")

§ XXVII ("Of the Mildness of Punishments") and § XXVIII ("Of the Punishment of Death") serve as a sort of summary of the opening 26 paragraphs. In the former, the general rule is formulated that the efficacy of punishment is not determined by its severity, but by the certainty of facing responsibility for the crimes committed: "The certainty of a small punishment will make a stronger impression, than the fear of one more severe if attended with the hopes of escaping; for it is the nature of mankind to be terrified at the approach of the smallest inevitable evil, whilst hope [...] hath the power of dispelling the apprehension of the greater; especially if supported by examples of impunity [...]. If punishments be very severe, men are naturally led to the perpetration of other crimes, to avoid the punishment due to the first. The countries and times most notorious for severity of punishments, were always those in which the most bloody and inhuman actions and the most atrocious crimes were committed; for the hand of the legislator and the assassins were directed by the same spirit of ferocity; which on the throne dictated laws of iron to slaves and savages, and in private instigated the subject to sacrifice one tyrant to make room for another."[12]

Beccaria is typically seen as subscribing to the demand of removing capital punishment from the books of law, and in § XXVIII described the problem in the following way: "The useless profusion of punishments which has never made men better, induces me to enquire, whether the punishment of death be really just or useful in a well-governed state?" However, he does not give an unambiguous answer to this question, as he singles out two situations where capital punishment can be seen as necessary: firstly, in cases where, in spite of incarceration the criminal "though deprived of his liberty, [...] has such power and connections as may endanger the security of the nation," and secondly, when imposing the death penalty would be the only means of deterring others from committing crimes. In the same paragraph he nevertheless states that

[12] Cf. ibidem, pp. 74–75.

"if the experience of all ages be not sufficient to prove that the punishment of death has never prevented determined men from injuring society; if the example of the Romans; if twenty years reign of Elisabeth, empress of Russia, in which she gave fathers of their country an example more illustrious than many conquests bought with blood." To this he also adds that "it is not the intenseness of the pain that has the greatest effect on the mind, but its continuance, for our sensibility is more easily and more powerfully affected by weak but repeated impressions, than by a violent but momentary impulse." It seems thus safe to assume that he not only considered the death penalty to be barbaric, but also inefficient.[13]

Beccaria's treatise also includes a general theory of social life, at the foundation of which lies the belief that life consists of a constant struggle between human passions, which are the more difficult to control, the larger the state is. "It is impossible to prevent entirely all the disorders which the passions of mankind cause to society. These disorders increase in proportion to the number of people, and the opposition of private interests. If we consult history, we shall find they are increasing, in every state, with the extent of dominion."[14] This would result in great chaos, should there be no social laws or seats of power legislating and executing. What counts in the end, of course, is for those laws and powers to be rational, which means among other things that they should be generally valid and of a beneficial character with respect to the majority of citizens.

Postscript

An important addendum to the work of Beccaria and his conception of social rationality could be constructed via a survey of subsequent liberalisations of criminal codes in many countries, which includes the abolition of capital punishment as well as the prohibition of torture. Equally important would be studying the ever stronger correlation between the leniency of laws and other regulators of social life – such as the rule of tolerance, or the notion of subsidiarity. Even without going into the legal and social details of these processes. one can confidently assert that they exerted a major influence on what Karl R. Popper called the "open society." Although most Western societies now belong to this category, multiple social problems are associated with this openness; contemporary France may serve as a case study in this respect.

[13] Stefano Rodotà, the author of the introduction to the referenced edition of *On Crimes and Punishments* thinks there are no grounds for considering him to be "absolutely opposed to capital punishment."

[14] Ibidem, pp. 21–22.

One of the chief characteristics of contemporary France is the multicultural composition of the country. This came about through a number of waves of immigration waves in the 20th century. In the 1920s and 30s these immigrants came from Central and Eastern Europe (for example from Poland and Russia), while in the 50s and 60s there was a major wave of migrants from the former French colonies in Africa and Asia. All this led, according to Michael Walzer, to France becoming "the classic nation-state and, at the same time, Europe's leading immigrant society," where the French nation exhibits "extraordinary assimilative powers."[15] This picture may have been accurate in the closing days of the previous century, especially if one were to consider multiculturalism and migrations from the American perspective, or. more accurately, the pre-9/11 American perspective. The terrorist attacks in New York, and later also in the UK and Spain, brought certain changes to this way of thinking (not only in the US) and forced an apparent stall in the established assimilatory capacities of western societies.[16]

This can also be seen in France. Although it has so far not been affected by Islamic fundamentalist terror to the same degree as the other western countries mentioned, it became the site of disturbances calling into question these assimilatory capacities in the street riots of October 2005. The majority of the participants were children or grandchildren of immigrants from the 50s and 60s, who inherited not only the culture of their predecessors but also their inability to find their way in a new social environment, and therefore poverty and deep frustration. This raises new arguments for both the old and the new enemies of open societies, such as those assembled under the banner of the French National Front. The riots also raise doubts as to the general rules of contemporary social life, including the leniency of laws and the actions of the powers and institutions expected to guard the laws. While any forceful intervention of riot police against these rebellious youth contradicts this rule, one cannot on the other hand tolerate actions such as the arson of cars or looting of shops. It is not at all clear what responsible politicians, or for that matter common Europeans, should be doing in the face of such events.

---

[15] Cf. M. Walzer, *On Toleration*, Yale 1997, p. 51 ff.

[16] These attacks have indeed resulted in publications severely critical of the politics of "openness" within Western societies – such as the book *The Rage and the Pride* published by popular Italian journalist Oriana Fallaci.

Chapter V

Rationality of social life according to the Enlightenment economists

It was also among the economists of the Enlightenment period that Reason – in its various conceptualisations – would be called upon as supreme justice, witness and adjudicator. However, the problem remained that it would frequently prove difficult to determine the exact range of its possible applications (if they were to be limited in at all), and it was also questionable to what extent Reason could be considered unbiased when it came to judging Reason itself. Enlightenment economists attempted to deal with this challenge. Their preferred approach assumed the supremacy of 1. Practical, i.e., pragmatic, over theoretical, i.e., contemplative, Reason, 2. Collective over individual Reason, as well as 3. Reason that proves able and willing to adjust plans and capabilities to the changing realities of social life. The epitome of these superior qualities came in the form of the enlightened homo oeconomicus – a human individual engaging in rational economic activities within a rationally organised economy. What constituted the yardstick of this rationality was not only the calculus of costs and profits, but also a way of using profits which would further perpetuate the accumulation of wealth. Such an approach to rationality became opposed both to the economical orientation towards consumption, and to the excess of thrift. Among the British enlightenment economists, thinking about rationality would either be anticipating or directly founding the capitalist ethos, but in the case of the French economists, the situation appears to be more complex. To some extent, their efforts were aimed at preserving the received order of the world of feudal social structures and feudal agricultural economics, whose crisis they hoped could be coped with by way of applying some rational reforms. Among the former it was the mercantilists who were most prominent, while the latter were dominated by the physiocrats.

1. François Quesnay

The economic theories of the physiocrats do not attract as much contemporary attention as they were generating in the 18th century, and even the main figures are rarely mentioned outside the context of academic lectures on the history of economics. In their heyday, however, they were seen not only as constituting the cutting edge of rational economic thinking, but many of them were either important public figures themselves or sometimes crucial advisors capable of influencing key political and economic policy decisions. This is certainly true in the case of Quesnay (1694–1774), who served as the personal doctor to the King of France (the monarch was reportedly referring to him as *mon penseur* – my thinker), but was also intellectually associated with the circles of the French encyclopaedists. To *Encyclopaedia or a Systematic Dictionary of the Sciences, Arts and Crafts* he contributed the following entries: "Evidence" (*Evidence*), "Farmers" (*Les Fermiers*), "Grains" (*Les Grains*), as well as "Taxes" (*Impots*). These did not spur wider discussions, but wide general interest was certainly aroused by his *Economic Tables* and *Maxims.*

His general views of man and the world – both natural and social – were expressed in the encyclopaedic article "Evidence." In the light of this exposition, man is a being capable of rational thinking and acting, but this rationality deserves recognition only if it is combined with reasonableness, which allows admittance to the realm of culture permeated by human and divine intelligence. These types of intelligence are supposed to make it possible for the thinking man (*l'homme raisonnable*) to reach certain basic truths, including the then commonly acknowledged truth that humans stand higher than animals but lower than God in the hierarchy of beings. They are also supposed to include the supposedly less obvious truth that humans are capable of analysing the different motives of human action and acting in accordance with such precepts, which led not only to the achievement of true freedom but also true morality, i.e., one that is not entangled in refined affectations, and reminds every man of his duties towards God, towards himself, and towards others, and makes it possible to see the impropriety of moral evil and the wrongness of crimes.[1]

After rendering in this encyclopaedic entry to God what belongs to God, Quesney moves in the other entries to the specifically human capacity (or lack thereof) for rational economic action. In the entry "Farmers" he analyses and evaluates the efficiency of economic management of French farmers, i.e., "those who lease country property and work it for profit. They produce the

---

[1] Entry: "Evidence" I quote after: F. Quesnay, *Pisma wybrane* [Selected Writings], Cracow 1928, p. 18 ff.

kind of wealth and resources most essential to the support of the state..."[2] Most employ double plot rotation and use oxen, while a minority employ triple plot rotation and use horses. It is this minority that acts more rationally, which is measured by Quesnay through a detailed balance of expenses and profits. On the side of the profits one can find such socially important items as: 1. "The wealthy farmer puts the peasant to work and supports him; 2. "The peasant in turn provides the citizen who is poor with all the necessary produce;" 3. Invigoration of trade; 4. Boosting the profits of owners and the state, etc.

In the entry "Grains," Quesney states that "The principal articles of commerce in France are grains, wines and spirits, salt, hemp and flax, wool, and some other products obtained from livestock," but that the country should focus on the agricultural production for which it has perfect conditions, and when accompanied by proper and responsible state policy it could also have adequately prepared producers, leading to an adequate supply of grain to satisfy social demand. This proper and responsible state policy would comprise rational internal policy – especially support for the most efficient economic arrangements in agriculture and for the trade arrangements between the countryside and the cities – as well as a rational external policy – including a managed trade in grain which would ban exports in such conditions when the grain supply proves inadequate to satisfy demand. By way of summary of the entire entry, Quesney proposes economic rules of government, which constitute a sort of physiocratic manifesto.[3] What transpires from these rules is a vision of the state where the dominant position is held by the most effective agricultural producers, and where the government supervises their ways of management, trade and co-operation with those that supply them with the necessary capital means and tools.

---

[2] F. Quesnay, "Farmers [abridged]," *The Encyclopedia of Diderot & d'Alembert Collaborative Translation Project*, trans. N.S. Hoyt and T. Cassirer, MPublishing, Ann Arbor 2005; In France, this relatively large social group of farmers leasing their lands was subjected to various feudal and senioral duties. "The feudal rights stemmed from the hierarchy of land possession: the rent (set a long time back and rather low) served as a symbol of subservience to the territorial lord; *champart*, a payment in kind, which was universally hated for being rather high and proportional to the harvest; significant dues to be paid in case of selling the farm (no less than 10%). The senioral rights were a relic of the historical power of the lord over the peasant, which was than already largely superseded by the state. These included legal duties, various occasional donatives, fees and labour services; monopolies – mills, bread ovens, wine-presses; the right to hunt and keep doves." Cf. J. Baszkiewicz, *Historia Francji* [The History of France], Wroclaw 1974.

[3] He states that 1. "[I]ndustrial work does not increase the wealth of a nation;" 2. "Industrial work contributes to the population and to the growth of wealth;" 3. "Industrial work that employs men to the detriment of farming the land is harmful to the population and to the growth of wealth;" 4. "The wealth of farmers gives rise to the wealth of farming;" 5. "Industrial work contributes to the augmentation of revenues from landed property, and the revenues from landed property support industrial work..." F. Quesnay, "Grains [abridged]," *The Encyclopedia of Diderot & d'Alembert...*, op. cit.

In the entry *Taxes*, Quesney not only criticises the apparently largely irrational system of taxation instituted in France at the time, but also proposes a scheme, which according to his views would lead to growing wealth for the producers (in agriculture and industry) and traders, as well as those who engage in neither of these activities but obtain some income from land and property rents or other real estate that they own. In the first section (under the title *Money Wealth*, where Quesnay calls into question the fundamental assumption of the mercantilists, i.e., the assumption that the wealth of the nation is not measured by the value of commodities produced, but by reference to their value expressed in money). He opposes this assumption, because in his view all the great fortunes that, on the surface, seem to represent the wealth of the state, in fact point to its decadence and ruin – by wasting huge productive resources they work to the detriment of farming, trade and industry. The remedy for this malady, as well as other economic and fiscal malformations, should base the calculus of income on the profits of landed estates, and especially on the profits gained through the production and trade in the basic food commodity of the time – grain. Any rational fiscal policy of the state should nevertheless also consider other factors than just the profits generated by productive activities, including: 1. The cost of gathering taxes (taxes based on foodstuffs and commodities require the hiring of many tax collectors, which often generates sizable costs), 2. Time required to produce and merchandise the particular goods (for instance, production and merchandising of wines takes longer than the production of grain), 3. Costs involved in the import of foreign goods such as salt, tobacco, or "colonial goods" (which even at a high level of taxation are supposed to create losses for the sovereign and the nation), as well as many other circumstances which remain outside the control of consumers, producers and tax authorities. The general conclusion stemming from this configuration is that neither the realm of taxation, nor those of production and distribution of goods can be completely rationalised. They can however be optimised when it comes to all of these dimensions.

Quesnay's *Economic Table* comprises a short instruction for the behaviour of the three principal social agents, i.e producers, owners and the sterile classes. Only the former two are considered economic agents. This instruction involves a simulation of investments and incomes across the classes, leading to some generalising conclusions. He claims, for instance, that the entire nation, and not only the owners and lords, share an interest in taxation being based on land ownership, as any other form of taxation would oppose the natural order, by being detrimental to economic reproduction.[4]

[4] Cf. F. Quesnay, *Rozbiór tablicy ekonomicznej* [Tableau Economique], in idem, *Pisma wybrane* [Selected Writings], op. cit., p. 97 ff.

These considerations are supplemented by seven remarks, an important additions to the assumptions and postulates put forward in the first part of the *Economic Table*. Among other things, they contain a clear *votum separatum* against consumptionism and a society focused on consumption – he considers expense on consumption to be irretrievably wasted; in the third remark Quesney takes objection to militarism and militant societies by pointing to the Roman Empire, which was able to conquer multiple nations but proved incapable of governing itself; in the fifth remark another objection is raised towards economies oriented only towards internal trade, with the reservation that there is no kingdom furnishing all necessary goods on its own, in the seventh remark criticism is levied at mercantile monetarism, and the confusion of the mass of money in circulation with the wealth of the nation. It goes without saying that Quesnay considers all these features either irrational or barely rational.

Quesnay's *General Maxims* comprise a set of such postulated policy directions, whose complete implementation would make social life not only more rational, but also more just and happy. There are thirty of them in total, and they relate to various spheres of social life, including both the governing and the governed, the producers of material good as well as their consumers, the traders of domestic goods as well as the importers of goods, etc. They should all co-operate together, and what should facilitate that co-operation is "Let the sovereign authority be unrivalled and superior to all individuals of society, and to all unjust enterprises of particular interests; for the domination and subjection of certain forces is the safeguard and lawful interest of all." This is also explicitly mentioned in Maxim I, starting with an admonition to the "unity of authority."[5] Maxim II advises: "Let the Nation be instructed as to General Natural Laws, which make a Government more Perfect", as without enlightenment there can be no way of rationalising the social activities key to social action. Maxim III calls for the recognition of "Earth, Agriculture, Sole Source of Riches," and of agriculture as the key sphere of generating wealth. Maxim IV advises that the owners of land should have their property rights guaranteed. ("For the security of property is the substructure upon which the economic order of society rests. Without the certainty of the security and safety of property the land would remain unfilled. There would be neither proprietors nor tenants to make the necessary outlay in cultivating the land, if the title to the land and its products were not assured to them who made the necessary outlay towards improvement and cultivation.") Maxim V calls for the introduction of such taxation which "be not destructive nor disproportionate

[5] Cf. F. Quesnay, "General Maxims of the Economical Government of in an Agricultural Kingdom," in O. J. Thatcher (ed.), *The Library of Original Sources*, vol. VI: *Advance in Knowledge 1650–1800*, reprinted from the 1901 edition, 2004.

to the revenue of the nation." ("Otherwise the tax would degenerate to spoliation and promptly cause the state to ruin and decay.") These initial maxims and some of the following points constitute general rules of social life of the entire nation and are addressed to the nation as a whole.

Quesnay also formulates various maxims addressed to members of government as well as social and professional groups. Such a character is assumed, for instance, in Maxim VI (it advises farmers to undertake such investments which would allow them to achieve the highest possible national income), and by Maxim VIII, addressed to the "economic government." ("Let the economic government favour productive expenditures and the commerce of the land's products and let fruitless expenditure attend to itself.") Maxim XXII is addressed to the affluent parts of society: "Let the luxury of decoration not be entertained to the detriment of land culture"), and Maxim XXX to the government and in particular the finance minister. Maxim XXX advises: "Let the state avoid loans formed of the funds of financiers, for they burden a state with devouring debts, occasion commerce or traffic of the finances, through the agency of negotiable paper, and where the rebate or discount augments more and more the unfruitful pecuniary fortunes."

These thirty maxims are supplemented by further remarks containing specific explanations and justifications of the need for rational economic activity in an "agricultural kingdom." These articulate clearly that, for instance, all economic agents should be granted the largest possible freedom of activity. What this means for the government is that it should not create or reinforce any monopolies, while for the farmers, industrialists, traders, bankers and other active participants of economic life it means that they should be granted freedom of action and co-operation in the creation of the wealth of the state and citizens. In the remarks to Maxim XIII, Quesnay mentions the need for free decision-making when it comes to the production and distribution of agricultural produce, i.e., free and easy internal and external trade. This postulate is known as the rule of laissez-faire, from the French *laissez faire, laissez passer* (leave us the freedom of action, leave us the freedom of movement), which later became a kind of rallying call for many different proponents of the free market.

Postscript

The social views of Quesnay evolved throughout the two decades he devoted to the study of economics – starting from an attempt to apply a "medical" way of thinking, and leading towards the conclusion that the functioning of various social groups differs in many ways from the functioning of a human organism.

The realities of social life became his preoccupation fairly late in his life – towards the end of the 1740s – his earlier concerns revolving around medical questions. He had in fact published a treatise of healing entitled *Observations sur les effets de la saignée* (*Observations on the Effects of Blood-Letting*). The first of his works devoted to economics and rural development – under the title *Essai sur l'économie animal* (*An Essay on the Animal Economy*) was still written in the mode of a medical dissertation and was addressed mainly to the breeders of animals. What exerted an important influence on his way of thinking was his entrance into the Parisian socjety of philosophers and free-thinkers such as René Louis Voyer d'Argenson, Jean Vincent de Gornay (to whom is attributed the phrase *laissez faire, laissez passer*), or Honoré Gabriel Riqueti de Mirabeau. The latter became a populariser of the physiocratic ideas of Quesnay, also promoting him in literary circles and the salons.[6] Yhe appearance of the theme of liberty in Quesnay's thinking could also be attributed to him.

Concerns with liberty became especially visible in the ideas of Anne Robert Jacques Turgot (1727–1781), who belonged to the younger generation of physiocrats. He was a theorist of rational economic management and its practitioner, as holder of the office of Deputy Attorney-General and later adviser to the Parliament of Paris.[7] While executing these functions he became known as a canny lawyer and politician, as well as mediator in the conflicts between the Parliament and King's Council.[8] His efforts were acknowledged in the court of Louis XV. In 1761, the king entrusted him with the post of intendant of the region Limoges. (Turgot successfully held the office for thirteen years) and later appointed him minister of finance (he held this

---

[6] H. G. R. de Mirabeau (1749–1791) mostly derived his high standing in these circles from the authorship of the literary-philosophical tract. *L'Ami des hommes* (*Friend of Humanity*). His place in history was for the most part earned through his key role in the French National Assembly from the first period of the revolution. Initially he belonged, alongside La Fayette, Rochefoucauld-Liancourt and Condorcet, to the party of patriots which was opposed to the monarchy, yet later would side with the court. Jan Baszkiewicz wrote that Mirabeau "was a great publicist and orator who desired to become the head of the government, however, the Constitutional Assembly closed this way for him by decreeing in the fall of 1789 that no member of parliament can become a minister." Cf. J. Baszkiewicz, *Historia Francji* [The History of France], op. cit., p. 339 ff.

[7] Parliaments within the French system at the time were not legislative bodies but rather arms of the judiciary. At the dawn of the 1789 revolution there were eight of these, with the Parliament of Paris being the most prominent, with jurisdiction over nearly a half of the country.

[8] "The Parliament of Paris was perceived as a representative of the nation, an heir of the Frankish gatherings and the Estates-General. The rights accepting legislation, control over administrative bodies and co-determination of taxation were all ascribed to it. This was an expansive ideology, from which it proved necessary to back down." J. Baszkiewicz, *Historia Francji* [The History of France], op. cit., p. 279.

office in the years 1774–1776.) In this capacity he attempted an ambitious reform of public administration, which involved the elimination of some offices. Encountering determined opposition from various interest groups, he resigned from office.

He presented his views on social life – including economics and economic activity – in a number of publications (his collected works from the years 1913–1933 comprise 5 volumes). He offered a synthetic overview of the main tenets of his thinking in *Reflections on the formation and the distribution of riches* (*Réflexions sur la formation et la distribution des richesses*). These were written in a convention similar to Quesnay's general maxims, i.e., in the form of points discussing general as well as specific questions. The advised course of action is broadly based on the same assumptions that he shared with other physiocrats. Some of those were directly spelt out, as in point 5, which declares the "pre-eminence of the Husbandman who produces over the Artisan who works up materials, the Husbandman is the first mover in the circulation of labours; it is he who causes the land to produce the wages of all the Artisans."[9] Further on, in point 8, he introduces the division of society into two classes, "the farmers and the artisans, stating at the same time that only the former can be called the productive one, or the Cultivators; the second stipendiary, or the Artisans."

In several subsequent points, he questions economic management based on slave labour. He presents it as not only transgressing basic human rights, but also ineffective as progress sets in. He contrasts it with an economy based on the labour of free farmers, free in the possessing land or at least in their capacity for cultivating it. After listing four principal ways of possessing land, he distinguished a further fifth form in point 26 – "farming or the letting out of land," of which writes that it is "the most advantageous of all, but it presupposes a country already rich." He considers this form capable of calculating the incomes and inputs of the different classes.

In the light of Turgot's reflections, rational economic management can be enhanced by both good environmental conditions (such as fertile soil or advantageous climate) and cultural conditions, including the received wealth of farmers and their capacity for multiplying it through the use of appropriate fertilisers, agricultural techniques as well as the system of land use. In point 27 of the instructions for rational management he points out the system of land-leases in northern France as opposed to the system of métayers in southern France, which leads him to the conclusion that the former lands are "incomparably richer and better cultivated." This obviously stems from a superior system of land-use. Similarly, he analyses the effects of various

[9] Cf. A. R. J. Turgot, *Reflections on the Formation and Distribution of Riches*, London 1911, p. 8.

means of measuring the value of goods, including the use of gold and silver, on trade. While Turgot sticks to the conviction that the land is the first and primary source of wealth, he admits that in those countries which at the time were mostly reliant on trade (such as England and Holland), gold and silver seem to be the best means of exchange. In many fragments of his *Reflections* one can find the general suggestion that future would belong to those nations, which can not only rationally manage their land-resources, but also rationally use money in agriculture, industry, trade and banking.[10] In his view, rationality is not innate to any single nation, but it rather represents an end-product of development strewn with trials and errors, failures and successes.

Turgot devoted his *Reflections of Universal History* to the historical development of this social rationality. He presents an optimistic vision of humanity advancing through the ages in the direction of superior excellence – not only in economy and management, but also in everyday behaviour and the building of proper social relationships. In these reflections he states that the succession of human generations means that "being endowed with a more developed reason and more liberty of action, man's relations with his fellows are much more numerous and varied. Possessor of the treasure-house of signs, which he has had the ability to multiply almost to infinity, he can assure himself of the possession of all his acquired ideas, communicate them to other men, and transmit them to his successors as a heritage which is always being augmented. A continual combination of this progress with the passions, and with the events they have caused, constitutes the history of the human race, in which each man is no more than one part of an immense whole which has, like him, its infancy and its advancement."[11] In the long history of human development there were always better and worse times, and in some periods Reason seemed to have been in complete decline. Yet Turgot seems unwilling to believe that there were any prolonged periods when humanity did not make any progress at all, and even the middle ages – which he calls the ages of ignorance – were supposed to contribute to the great achievements of later centuries."[12] How this contribution came about is a separate question, as in the *Reflections* beneficial changes often turn out to be the unintended consequences of social designs, for instance when Christian priests argued for the abolishment of slavery, thus bringing about great social and moral change.

[10] In point 73 he questions the rationality of those scholastic thinkers who condemn commercial lending, as in his view: "A loan is a reciprocal contract, free between the two parties, which they make only because it is advantageous to them." Ibidem, p. 62.

[11] Cf. A. R. J. Turgot, "Discours sur l'histoire universelle," in *Oeuvres*, vol. II, Paris 1844, p. 597 ff.

[12] Cf. ibidem, p. 608 ff.

2. Adam Smith

Smith (1723–1790) is considered to be the spiritual father of mercantilism, as well as the foundational figure of modern economics. He was born in Edinburgh, and received his education at the University of Glasgow, where he subsequently became a lecturer in logic and moral philosophy. Among his teachers was Francis Hutchenson – a celebrated philosopher at the time, while David Hume for instance belonged to his close circle of friends. Smith would in his youthful treatise *Theory of Moral Sentiments* (1759) already present man as a being in a close relationship with nature from which he gains – usually in an unconscious manner – everything that is necessary for life. It is in this work that the notion of the market's "invisible hand" appears, making even those sentiments that from a Christian point of view may seem reprehensible, such as greed, available for a rational utilisation of the maximisation of wealth and the enhancement of public good.

The most important of Smith's contributions remains *An Inquiry into the Nature and Causes of the Wealth of Nations* (called the *Inquiry* henceforth), published in 1776. He reiterates the "invisible hand" thesis and provides a broad justification for it. However, it is not the invisible hand that becomes the main focus of the book, but rather the human activity without which it could not conceivably operate. This activity amounts to the continuous labour of every nation: "The annual labour of every nation is the fund which originally supplies it with all the necessaries and conveniences of life which it annually consumes, and which consist always either in the immediate produce of that labour, or in what is purchased with that produce from other nations."[13] What counts here is not merely the individual efforts of particular producers of things both necessary and useful in life, but the labour of the entire collectives which constitute nations. It is the economical co-operation and competition between these collectives that constitutes one of the sources of the wealth of some nations and the poverty of others. This thesis is further developed and justified by Smith in the various parts of his vast treatise.

It seems important to focus on a couple of generalisations presented in the initial parts of the *Inquiry*. One of them is the thesis that the product of labour "bears a greater or smaller proportion to the number of those who are to consume it [...]. But this proportion must in every nation be regulated by two different circumstances; first, by the skill, dexterity, and judgment with which its labour is generally applied; and, secondly, by the proportion between the

[13] A. Smith, *An Inquiry into the Nature and Causes of the Wealth of Nations*, vol. 1, New York 1909, p. 4.

number of those who are employed in useful labour, and that of those who are not so employed [...] The abundance or scantiness of this supply too seems to depend more upon the former of those two circumstances than upon the latter."

Further in the text one encounters the reference to "the savage nations of hunters and fishers," among which "every individual who is able to work, is more or less employed in useful labour, and endeavours to provide, as well as he can, the necessaries and conveniences of life, for himself, or such of his family or tribe as are either too old, or too young, or too infirm to go a hunting and fishing." In spite of this, these nations do not really seem capable of much because they are "so miserably poor that, from mere want, they are frequently reduced, or, at least, think themselves reduced, to the necessity sometimes of directly destroying, and sometimes of abandoning their infants, their old people, and those afflicted with lingering diseases, to perish with hunger, or to be devoured by wild beasts. Among civilised and thriving nations, on the contrary, though a great number of people do not labour at all [...] yet the produce of the whole labour of the society is so great, that all are often abundantly supplied, and a workman, even of the lowest and poorest order, if he is frugal and industrious, may enjoy a greater share of the necessaries and conveniences of life than it is possible for any savage to acquire."

This constitutes indisputable praise of the civilised society, or perhaps, more specifically, of a society which has developed its productive forces to such a degree that it is not merely capable of satisfying the life-needs of the workers, but also of those who, for various reasons, cannot work, but still have needs. In subsequent parts of the *Inquiry*, Smith attempts to demonstrate that the wealth of nations might be dependent on the socially rational behaviour of both these categories, but it is the former that constitutes the primary force behind the generation of wealth.

In the first three chapters of Book I, Smith analyses and demonstrates the "Causes of Improvement in the productive Power of Labour and of the Order according to which its Produce is naturally distributed among the different Ranks of the People." When it comes to the most significant reasons, he emphasises the rational division of labour, which involves many workers with different and mutually complementing abilities in the process of production – for instance in the work of a pin-maker where "One man draws out the wire, another straights it, a third cuts it, a fourth points it, a fifth grinds it at the top for receiving the head.[14] There seem to exist a number of mutually

[14] "This separation too is generally carried furthest in those countries which enjoy the highest degree of industry and improvement; what is the work of one man in a rude state of society, being generally that of several in an improved one. In every improved society, the farmer is generally nothing but a farmer; the manufacturer, nothing but a manufacturer. The

complementing measures of this rationality. First among them is the ability to adjust the division of labour to the place and character of production – these processes look very different in big and small industries, let alone when it comes to the agricultural economy. ("The nature of agriculture, indeed, does not admit of so many subdivisions of labour, nor of so complete a separation of one business from another, as manufactures.") The second of these measures is the greater magnitude of output generated by the same number of workers involved in production, while the third boils down to "the saving of the time which is commonly lost in passing from one species of work to another." The third principle is "the invention of a great number of machines which facilitate and abridge labour, and enable one man to do the work of many."

When it comes to the sources of rationality and rationalisation within the processes of production, Smith would typically answer that at least in the early stages of social development "this division of labour, from which so many advantages are derived, is not originally the effect of any human wisdom [...] It is the necessary [...] propensity to truck, barter, and exchange one thing for another." On the other hand, he indicates the boundaries of rationality and rationalisation of social relations as being specified by the extent of the market ("when the market is very small, no person can have any encouragement to dedicate himself entirely to one employment"), which in turn depends upon the size of the social environment (it is for instance larger in urban than rural settings). Other conditions, such as geographic location, the roads or means of transportation are also mentioned.

In Chapter IV of Book I, it is money which plays the role of protagonist. Money is presented not only as a product of the national human propensity to trade and exchange, but also as a rational way of handling the surpluses of one's own labour. It is far more rational than the direct barter exchange of goods, for which there might not always be a social need. Smith considers the emergence of money to be the effect of multiple efforts undertaken historically by various societies and the sum-total of their failures, for instance "there is at this day a village in Scotland where it is not uncommon, I am told, for a workman to carry nails instead of money to the baker's shop or the ale-house. In all countries, however, men seem at last to have been determined by irresistible reasons to give the preference, for this employment, to metals above every other commodity." The arguments which speak for the choice of a metal-based money include the possibility of 1. Being "kept with as little loss as any other commodity," 2. Being "divided into any number of parts, as by fusion those parts can easily

labour too which is necessary to produce any one complete manufacture, is almost always divided among a great number of hands." Ibidem, p. 11.

be reunited again," as well as 3. The ability to re-mint it into new quantities. Further reasons and rationalisations can be mentioned in relation to 1. When different metals are chosen as the basis for trade and measure of value ("Iron was the common instrument of commerce among the ancient Spartans; copper among the ancient Romans; and gold and silver among all rich and commercial nations"); 2. Minting these metals into different form (from bars to coins); as well as 3. Naming ("first public stamps of this kind that were affixed to the current metals, seem in many cases to have been intended to ascertain [...] the goodness or fineness of the metal"). In summary of these historical analyses the thesis is advanced that it is the exchange value of money that serves as the main rationale for the functioning of social life in civilised societies.

In the subsequent parts of Book I, Smith presents an analysis of such basic economic categories as 1. The real and nominal price of commodities; 2. Wages of labour (with the indication of what causes its inflation or decrease); 3. Capital profits (also including the analysis of the reason for their fluctuation); as well as 4. The rent of the land. Putting it in somewhat anachronistic terms, one could say that Smith is moving from the micro- to the macro-economic, only to come back to the micro-level in his generalisations. These point to the conclusion that the economy constitutes such an interrelated system, where the seeding of a proverbial flower on the plot of one farmer may perhaps influence his output, which in turn could have an effect – through several other links in the chain – on the overall wealth or penury of the entire nation. Rational organisation of the national economy consists exactly in making sure that trivial causes or bad luck do not result in such penury.

Organising economic activity comes easier to those who possess capital in trade or industry, than in the case of those whose capital is in land. This is because it is the former "who commonly employ the largest capitals, and who by their wealth draw to themselves the greatest share of the public consideration", but also because "during their whole lives they are engaged in plans and projects, they have frequently more acuteness of understanding than the greater part of country gentlemen."[15] This is one of the general conclusions of the chapter devoted to the rents appearing at the end of Book I.

In the next four books of the *Inquiry*, Smith presents a number of specific and general questions related to rational management or attempts at rationalisation, which should lead to an increase rather than diminishing of the wealth of the nation. The diversity and variety of questions he tackles makes his remarks potentially useful not only to the businessman, trader, banker, or farmer, but also to the politician or preacher.

---

[15] Cf. ibidem, pp. 218–219.

Books II, III and IV are still especially addressed to businessmen and bankers. The last presents the principles of a system based on trade, i.e., a mercantile one. What lies at the foundation of this system is the assumption that money, that is, gold and silver, constitutes the means of trade and measure of value. In short, the main objective of action within this system is not only to gain money and then to be able to estimate the value of "all other commodities by the quantity of money which they will exchange for."[16] It remains crucial that 1. The exchange should have as broad a character as possible, and specifically that it not be restricted to one nation ("if a nation could be separated from all the world, it would be of no consequence how much, or how little money circulated in it"); 2. That there be no strict prohibitions stifling trade (such as the ban on exporting gold and silver to other countries), 3. That the balances of payment between countries be mutually beneficial, 4. That the parliaments and governments support the interests of their producers, merchants and traders ("it can very seldom be reasonable to tax the industry of the great body of the people, in order to support that of some particular class of manufacturers").[17] Smith expounds further upon these as well as other principles of a mercantile economy in the further chapters of this Book.[18]

All these explanations are complemented by concluding remarks on the mercantile system, including the generalising statement that the creators of the entire mercantile system are not politicians, and not even economic theorists, but the producers, among whom the greatest impact had been coming from the manufacturers and merchants; this in fact may not always be for the greater good of the rational management of the economy and the other groups of rationally acting producers (such as the agricultural producers).

Remarks on the functioning of farmers in the then contemporary economy already appear in the earlier parts of the *Inquiry*. However, in the last Chapter of Book IV, entitled "Of the Agricultural Systems or of the Systems of Political Economy Which Represent the Produce of Land as Either the Sole or

[16] "The great affair, we always find, is to get money. When that is obtained, there is no difficulty in making any subsequent purchase. In consequence of its being the measure of value, we estimate that of all other commodities by the quantity of money which they will exchange for." Cf. A. Smith, *An Inquiry into the Nature and Causes of the Wealth of Nations*, vol. 1, op. cit., p. 325.

[17] Cf. ibidem, p. 405.

[18] It is perhaps worth noting that Chapter II mentions the possible restriction on imports of goods which can otherwise be produced domestically; Chapter III introduces the considerations of a limit of imports from such countries with which the trade balance is considered to be strongly negative, Chapter IV discusses the reimbursement of duties, Chapter V talks of export premiums, Chapter VI of trade treaties, Chapters VII and VIII in turn mention the colonies and motivations for setting them up.

the Principal Source of the Revenue and Wealth of Every Country" we find a detailed polemic with the ideas of the French physiocrats, and especially with Quesnay, whom he considered to have been an ingenious and deep thinker. One should also note that this is not a polemic against the actual managing of the French economy of the time, but rather against the ideas presented by the physiocrats, which Smith considers to be theoretical speculation.

In the opening remarks of this section, a critical point is made which is important to the understanding of the "capital error" of the physiocratic system and of the mistakes which some of the proponents of the mercantile economy are prone to make. Smith claims that the physiocratic system is in its nature a system of restrictions and restraints, or, to be more precise, of such restrictions and restraints upon the liberal plan of "equality, liberty, and justice" which do not allow every man to pursue his own interest in his own way. While some such restrictions may be necessary, it is crucial for them to be rational, unlike those introduced by "Mr. Colbert, the famous minister of Louis XIV," whose economic policies resulted in the growth of industry and trade, accompanied by a decline in agricultural production and the standards of life of those who derive their income from agriculture.[19] However, according to Smith, the crucial error of the economic system proposed by Quesnay is not the introduction of restraints, but the conclusion that it is the farmers who are the productive class, while the artisans, industrialists and merchants were supposed to be a barren and unproductive one.

To refute this physiocratic conviction, a detailed analysis is presented of the way in which artisans, industrialists and merchants function within the economy. This leads to the conclusion that these classes are economically dynamic and contribute to the wealth of the nation. The general thesis that trade is the most progressive part of the economic system is reiterated, com-

[19] "Mr. Colbert, the famous minister of Louis XIV, was a man of probity, of great industry and knowledge of detail; of great experience and acuteness in the examination of public accounts, and of abilities, in short, every way fitted for introducing method and good order into the collection and expenditure of the public revenue. That minister had unfortunately embraced all the prejudices of the mercantile system, in its nature and essence a system of restraint and regulation, and such as could scarce fail to be agreeable to a laborious and plodding man of business, who had been accustomed to regulate the different departments of public offices, and to establish the necessary checks and controls for confining each to its proper sphere. [...] He was not only disposed, like other European ministers, to encourage more the industry of the towns than that of the country; but, in order to support the industry of the towns, he was willing even to depress and keep down that of the country. In order to render provisions cheap to the inhabitants of the towns, and thereby to encourage manufactures and foreign commerce, he prohibited altogether the exportation of corn, and thus excluded the inhabitants of the country from every foreign market for by far the most important part of the produce of their industry." Ibidem, p. 447.

plemented by the statement that "the greatest and most important branch of the commerce of every nation, it has already been observed, is that which is carried on between the inhabitants of the town and those of the country [...]. Whatever [...] tends to diminish in any country the number of artificers and manufacturers, tends to diminish the home market, the most important of all markets, for the rude produce of the land, and thereby still further to discourage agriculture."[20]

The closing sections of the chapter feature general remarks on the role of the state in a rationally organised and manager economy. In general, the state is considered to be a part of the system of political economy within which civic freedoms are cultivated. The duties of a rationally constituted state are: 1. "[T]he duty of protecting the society from the violence and invasion of other independent societies;" 2. "[T]he duty of protecting, as far as possible, every member of the society from the injustice or oppression of every other member of it, or the duty of establishing an exact administration of justice;" 3. "[T]he duty of erecting and maintaining certain public works, and certain public institutions, which it can never be for the interest of any individual, or small number of individuals to erect and maintain."

In the final chapter, entitled "Of the Revenue of the Sovereign of the Commonwealth," Smith gives a detailed analysis of the structure of public income, expenditure and debt, with the view to justify their necessity and analysing the capacity to raise, control and pay back. It seems clear that the more rational the actions of the sovereign and his subjects, the higher would be the income and the more rational their utilisation, while public debt should then be lower and more manageable. This is especially the case when the citizens are not lazy and quarrelsome, and do not seek the opportunity to satisfy their living needs on the battlefields and in the courts, but on their own fields, workshops, in industry or trade, and all other workplaces.

In Part III of the Book, Smith develops an account of the functioning of public works and institutions, arrangements that are publicly funded and maintained so that trade can be maintained more easily, such as roads, bridges, canals or harbours. The cost of their building and maintenance must of course be borne by users paying specified fees, which should be diversified in relation to some criteria, such as demanding a higher toll from luxurious than from regular wagons. In this section he also analyses the expenditure on institutions for the education of the youth and formulates the general thesis that they should be supported by "revenue sufficient for defraying their own expense. The fee or honorary, which the scholar pays to the master, naturally

[20] Cf. ibidem, p. 650.

constitutes a revenue of this kind."[21] Many other such specific policy designs for public institutions feature in this book.

It also includes examples of solutions and social projects which, according to his standards, prove neither rational nor provide any hope for rationalisation in the future. One of these is the project of extending the British Empire to include the conquests of the East-India company. Smith concludes *An Inquiry into the Nature and Causes of the Wealth of Nations* with the postulate that "If any of the provinces of the British empire cannot be made to contribute towards the support of the whole empire, it is surely time that Great Britain should free herself from the expense of defending those provinces in time of war, and of supporting any part of their civil or military establishment in time of peace; and endeavour to accommodate her future views and designs to the real mediocrity of her circumstances." History shows that more than two hundred years of political and economic travails were needed for the government to accept this truth.

Postscript

The vision of rational economic management presented in the *Inquiry* was very well received in the circles of enlightened thinkers immediately after publication. Thomas Robert Malthus (1766–1834) was one of the impressed, but he was influenced not only by the works of Smith, but also by other thinkers, including D. Hume, J.-J. Rousseau and W. Godwin.[22] He approached their ideas with some criticism, focussing not so much on their radicalism as on their propensity for speculation, divorced from the realities of concrete societies. This conclusion can be drawn from the reading of his *Essay on the Principle of Population as it affects the Future Improvement of Society, with Remarks on the Speculations of Mr. Godwin, and other Writers* (1789). In this treatise, Malthus

[21] Cf. ibidem, p. 344.

[22] William Godwin (1756–1836) is counted with Richard Price (1723–1791), Joseph Priestley (1733–1804) and Thomas Paine (1737–1809) as the most radical figures of the British enlightenment, and Gertrude Himmelfarb refers to them as "radical dissidents": "It might even be said that these radicals belong more to the history of the French and American Enlightenments than to the British. Paine spent much of his adult life in America and France, and was a member not of the British Parliament but of the French National Convention. Even after his imprisonment during the Terror and the withdrawal of his French citizenship, he remained in France, returning finally not to England but to America, where he died. Priestly was awarded an honorary seat in the National Assembly but chose to live in America rather than France, he too died in America. Price and Goodwin did live out their lives in England, as ardent sympathisers of the French Revolution." Cf. G. Himmelfarb, *The Roads to Modernity. The British, French, and American Enlightenments*, New York 2004, p. 94 ff.

formulates the thesis that the poor are poor largely because of their own fault, due to the lack of control over fertility leading to progeny far too numerous for their material means. Furthermore, he was convinced that this social group proves incapable of reining in their sexual desires and birth-control. On this foundation he develops the *principle of population*, in the light of which the population growth would always outpace the growth in agricultural productivity. If this does not lead to a great famine, this is only due to the population being kept in check by wars, epidemics, and other natural calamities. This is undoubtedly a very pessimistic assessment of the rationality of human action and the regulating principles of social life. Malthus would subsequently make his criticism somewhat milder, by focusing more on those strata, which are capable of understanding the social needs better than the poor multitudes, or at least can act in a way that contributes to the satisfaction of some of their basic needs. In the treatise *Principles of Political Economy Considered with a View to Their Practical Application* (1820), Malthus sketched such a vision of the state, where the poor-yet-able-to-work multitudes are organised by way of activities such as public works, while the rich strata are induced to invest not only in production, but also in consumption that would boost the economy.

David Ricardo (1772–1823) was another continuator of the social views of Smith. However, he obtained his knowledge concerning rational economic management not at universities, but initially in the family company, and later on at the London Stock Exchange, where he worked as a stockbroker for a number of years. This work experience gave him not only practical knowledge, but also substantial wealth, giving him the opportunity to retire into writing for the rest of his life. In 1809, he published the treatise *The High Prince of Bullion*, while in 1817 *The Principles of Political Economy and Taxation* came out and saw three editions during his lifetime. The last of these was amended by the addition of the chapter "On Machines," in which he leans towards the conclusion that the mechanisation of production leads to an increase in the profits of businessmen, but at the same time causes an increase in the rate of unemployment, the intensification of competition and a decline in the material conditions of the working class. In general, however, he was not opposed to the introduction of machines into industry, while he remained doubtful of such mechanisation which only took the business profits into account. In fact, the rate of profit constitutes the axial concern throughout his reflections in the *Principles*. He would for instance outline production schemes where one would not only take into consideration the cost factors, such as materials or wages, but also time factors (the number of hours required to complete a given task) as well as market multipliers (such as the price of agricultural products, the price of rents, as well as other economic variables. In a manner similar to Smith, he was looking for a relatively stable measure of the value of commodities. In contrast to him, however, he did not see it in gold or silver, but rather – much like the physiocrats – in grain. Still, he would not treat these costs as a constant, but as a market variable dependent on the competition between producers, conditions of the climate and soil, as well as fluctuations in population.

Another context for the exploration of the standards of rationality of social life assumed and postulated by Smith is facilitated by contemporary interpretations of his seminal contribution. These could find layers that the author himself may not have been aware of. One example of such a new reading of *An Inquiry into the Nature and Causes of the Wealth of Nations* features in Karen McCreadie's book *Adam Smith's The Wealth of Nations*, Smith is presented as the father of classical economics, on par with Darwin in the field of biology, but also, and perhaps to an even greater degree, as the founding father of the idea of contemporary capitalism. This is not the capitalism of the ruthless kind, oriented exclusively towards profit, but capitalism with a more human face, capable of appreciating not only profit but also social costs. In total, McCreadie indicates 52 such issues, which have clear if sometimes somewhat ironic connections to the contemporary world. These include points which introduce important corrections to the later combination of protestant ethics with the spirit of capitalism as postulated by Max Weber, and the evaluation of the latter as the expression of the highest form of social rationality.

At the onset of her considerations, McCreadie points to the prominence of key questions in the *Wealth of Nations*, such as, firstly, increase in productivity through improvements in the productivity of every worker, secondly, in the implementation of time-saving schemes, and thirdly, in the invention of a multiplicity of machines. In the generalising conclusion of this list, the author states that: "Every idea that makes or saves the business money is implemented and the inventor wins the cash prize." This obviously comes about as a by-product of rational thinking, and the actions not only of the rationaliser himself, but also of his entire social environment, which facilitated the economic activity. In a similar vein, when it comes to the sources of inventions, McCreadie considers them to be motivated by need, but also by the existence of a great many intellectual innovators as well as those that simply wanted to lead a more convenient life: "They say that necessity is the mother of invention. Adam Smith believed that laziness, or at least self-interest was the father."

In the third part of the book, McCreadie emphasises the importance of intuition, which all too many defenders of rationality were keen to denigrate or ignore. Not Smith, however, who treats it as the source or precondition of success, not only in thinking, but also in practical action and pursuit of material profits ("financial legends and famous inventors often confess the importance of intuition in their success"). These and many other views expressed by Smith, are not, in McCreadie's opinion, an expression of protestant ethics (as Weber would have it) but rather of the extraordinary intelligence of the author of the *Inquiry* – intelligence embodied in the exceptional capacity to observe, analyse, generalise and predict the social consequences of human behaviour in the economic arena. To which extent this presentation expressed McGreadie's personal views as opposed to Smith's original output remains a point of some contention – and McCreadie appears to be keenly aware of this. What her enterprise is about, in the end, is not to conserve the historical achievements of Smith, but to demonstrate the guidance it provides to solving contemporary social problems through inspiration.

Chapter VI

Rationality of social life according to the French socialists

Since the socialists and socialism came into existence in the first decades of the 19th century, the difficulties in situating them on the political scene and determining their role in social life have been significant.[1] This is mainly because socialism was and to a large extent still remains an ideology so inconsistent that it has often been difficult even for socialists themselves, to decide whether they are dealing with "insiders" or "outsiders."[2] Allies as well as opponents have also experienced these difficulties. The latter often chose the easiest way out of the situation, by referring to socialists as all those who either identified themselves with this option or at least voiced opinions which resembled socialist slogans and postulates. As a consequence not only those who identified themselves with socialism, but also those who could admit to anything but to being socialist, were labelled *socialist* and went down in history as such. Examples include the Fourierists, Owenites and Saint-simonists. Those who participated in these ideological groups, the so-called utopian socialism, even though they dissociated themselves from it on many occasions, or even mocked socialists, are also associated with socialism. To the group of critics and detractors belong among

[1] The term *socialism* was first used by the Saint-simonist Pierre Leroux in the year 1834 to describe those who "criticise and condemn individualism." Cf. J. B. Duroselle, *Les débuts de catholicisme sociale en France (1822–1870)*, Paris 1951.

[2] This ideology I understand – largely following Karl Mannheim – as a set of variously complementary general notions, postulates and social slogans, which express various needs of different social groups and justify the need to undertake such actions that could lead to fulfilling these requirements. Cf. K. Mannheim, *Ideology and Utopia. An Introduction to the Sociology of Knowledge*, London 1954.

others Karl Marx and Friedrich Engels, the ideological founding fathers of communism. In their programmatic document, *The Communist Manifesto*, they identified reactionary socialism, further divided into (a) Feudal ("half lamentation, half lampoon; half echo of the past, half menace of the future"); (b) Petty bourgeois ("dissected with great acuteness the contradictions in the conditions of modern production"); (c) German, i.e., "true" ("a weapon for fighting the German bourgeoisie, it, at the same time, directly represented a reactionary interest"); (d) "[C]onservative, or bourgeois" socialism (its representatives "desire the existing state of society minus its revolutionary and disintegrating elements"), and (e) Critical-utopian socialism (its representatives "sink into the category of the reactionary conservative Socialists depicted above, differing from these only by more systematic pedantry").[3] The authors of this document left no doubt that they do not see eye to eye with "these gentlemen."[4] The communists and their concepts of rationality and rationalisation of social life will be discussed more broadly in the next part of this book. At this point, I would like to highlight that they should under no circumstance be associated with socialists and West-European socialism, because as a matter of fact there were more points of difference than similarity. This manifested itself not only in their social theories, or the programmes of their parties, but also, or even above all, in their actions.

Although it is not possible to arrange socialism according to a single uncontroversial criterion, it is possible to indicate the general ideas, postulates and most eminent motives, which socialists would generally endorse. Among the oldest, which originated among the first socialists, are: (a) The notion of voluntary associations into collectives; (b) The notion of benefiting from the co-operatively developed goods according to the labour contributed; (c) A postulate to make work universal for all those who are capable of working; (d) A postulate of improvement of humankind through work; (e) Motives for self-limitation of those who have more than they have to satisfy the basic needs; and (f) Motivating for a preference for the moral aspects of life instead of material aspects. Towards the end of the 19th and at the beginning of the 20th century further postulates were added, such as: (a) Limitation of private

[3] Cf. "The Communist Manifesto," in K. Marx, F. Engels, *Manifesto of the Communist Party*, Peking 1970, pp. 61–73.

[4] In the foreword to the English edition of the *Manifesto* (1888), Friedrich Engels explained to all those who had doubts on this matter: "By Socialists, in 1847, were understood, on the one hand the adherents of the various Utopian systems: Owenites in England, Fourierists in France [...]; on the other hand, the most multifarious social quacks who, by all manner of tinkering, professed to redress, without any danger to capital and profit, all sorts of social grievances, in both cases men outside the working-class movement, and looking rather to the 'educated' classes for support." Ibidem, p. 12.

property; (b) Subjecting the economy to the control of the state, including production and distribution of material goods; (c) Social security for the weakest social groups. Several further basic socialist oppositions may be added to this list, such as anti-individualism (aimed at, among others, liberal ideology), anti-capitalism (aimed above all at its laissez-faire version), or anti-traditionalism (aimed above all at those who defend the feudal system of social relations).

Individual socialists have often differed significantly in their interpretationgs and implementations of these ideas, postulates, and motives. It is justified to distinguish within socialism its right and left wing and to differentiate between manifestations in various places and at various times. In my deliberations I limit myself to the French socialism of the 19th century and the beginnings of the 20th century. I am convinced, however, that referring to socialists from other countries may contribute considerably to the discussion of the socialist standards of social rationality.

1. Pierre-Joseph Proudhon

In the memory of laters generation Proudhon (1809–1865) appears mainly as the author of the dissertation *The Philosophy of Poverty*. In leftist circles Karl Marx advertised the work in a way by satirising it in his *The Poverty of Philosophy* (needless to say, the philosophy of Proudhon). His dissertations, with their provoking titles (*What is Property?*, *What is the third State?*, *Warning to Proprietors*) brought him considerable publicity. They were interpreted as open exhortation encouraging disadvantaged social groups to rebel and caused their author to bebrought to trial.

Proudhon knew from experience the situation of the sectors of French society that worked hard but were not paid well. He was born in Besançon (in the south of France) into a family supporting itself with farm and casual work (trade in wood, for instance). His family was so poor that for some time they could not afford to send their son to school, and when at the age of 11 he began his education, he had to suspend it to work at a local printing press. In later years he would often change his place of residence in search of a better paid job (he worked, among others, in Paris, Marseille and Lyon). His financial situation improved after he received a bursary from the French Academy in 1838. In the years 1840–1842 he wrote and published the aforementioned controversial writings, and in the years 1844–1847 he worked at the printing press of the Gauthier brothers in Lyon. He would often go to Paris during this time, where he established contact with groups like the Young Hegelians who came to France in exile, including Karl Marx. The latter even offered him a chance to co-operate in establishing international structures of the socialist movement. Proudhon, however, refused to participate in this enterprise, as at that time he was working on his dissertation *The System of Economic Contradictions, or The Philosophy of Poverty* (he published it in 1846).

In January 1848 he settled in Paris, and a month later participated in the February Revolution. This led to the overthrowing of king Louis Philippe as well as the conservative social powers that supported him. In historical accounts the rule of this monarch is sometimes referred to as "bourgeoisie monarchy."[5] In June of 1884 the outbreak was ultimately supressed by the National Guard under the command of general L.-E. Cavaignaca. At the time Proudhon served as a deputy to the French Constituent Assembly. There he supported the republican faction, but dissociated himself from the most radical representatives (such as L. Blanc, or L. A. Blanqui). The motto that he identified with at the time was "equality, association and fraternity." He joined (not for long) the social powers supporting prince Louis-Napoléon in his attempts to become the president; France had a republican government at the time (which in historical accounts is referred to as the French Second Republic). When the election was won by the prince-president, however, it soon transpired that this underestimated and ridiculed aristocrat (L. A. Thiers, leader of the Party of resistance, referred to him as an idiot) was capable of misleading not only the socialist left, but also the liberal right in his gamble for power in France. On December 2nd, 1851, the prince-president initiated a coup d'etat and declared himself Emperor of the French Napoleon III, and France the Second French Empire (he considered the empire of Napoleon Bonaparte to be the first one). This lasted until 1870, and ended with military defeat in the war against Prussia.

Even prior to the coup, Proudhon perceived Louis-Napoléon as a threat to the French Republic, and openly stood up against him both in the Constituent Assembly and in articles published in such periodicals as "Le Peuple" and "Voix du Peuple." These attacks were considered serious enough by the authorities of the time to deprive him of his parliamentary immunity and later to bring him to trial and sentence him to three years in prison. While in prison he wrote *The Confessions of a Revolutionary*, and when he was released a three-volume dissertation, *Of Justice in the Revolution and the State.* After publishing it (in 1858) he was sued once again (on suspicion of "offence to public and religious morality"). This resulted in a high fine and three years in prison. Before serving this sentence he took flight to Brussels, where he resided until 1862, living off modest royalties from writing articles. At the time he wrote

[5] Guido de Ruggiero writes that "[t]he *bourgeois* would make political rights the privilege of two hundred and fifty thousand individuals" (the population of France of that time was 35 million). Cf. G. de Ruggiero, *The History of European Liberalism*, Boston 1959, p. 177 ff.

two longer dissertations – *War and Peace* and *The Principle of Federation*. After his return to Paris he became involved in the activities of the French labour movement, where his main contribution was advice and ideas for improving the social position of the "working classes" (he presented these in the dissertation *Of the Political Capacity of the Working Class*).

Proudhon's views on society undoubtedly situate him within the circle of socialists. However, whether he was more aligned to the left or the right depends to a large extent on whether the period of time up to 1848 is taken into consideration, or only the last years of his life. Generally speaking, during the first period he associated himself more with the left, and during later years more with the right. However, due to the multitude of topics that he raised and various, often contradictory, proposals that he advanced, as well as his involvement in events of the time, it is in the case of this author easier to formulate specific statements than general ones; it is advisable to limit the analysis to individual works, as only thus can we find some degree of coherence.[6]

He was the most radical in his convictions when he was publishing his works on private property and formulating "warnings to proprietors." At this time he was without doubt a revolutionary. In the title of the first chapter of one of his texts he defines the "method pursued in this work" as "the idea of a revolution," and in the same chapter he writes: "If I were asked to answer the following question: *What is slavery?* And I should answer in one word, *It is murder*, my meaning would be understood at once. No extended argument would be required to show that the power to take from a man his thought, his will, his personality, is a power of life and death; and that to enslave a man is to kill him. Why, then, to this other question: *What is property?* may I not likewise answer, *It is robbery!*"[7]

There is of course a certain logic to this, but it is – let me state it clearly – the logic of someone who perceives the world in only two colours – black and white. The owners of different types of goods are contrasted to those who do not, as they have been robbed and forced to engaged in inhumane and destructive labour. According to this logic, this is deeply unjust and unjustifiable; and those who do justify it – beginning with the Roman legislators and ending with the Napoleonic Code – are scoundrels, swindlers and thieves of the whatever they possess. For some of these "scoundrels" Proudhon pro-

[6] Leszek Kołakowski also points to this fact in his vast study devoted to the main currents of Marxism. In his opinion, Proudhon "is noteworthy among the early socialists for the many directions in which his influence extended, a fact largely due to the incoherence of his writings and the contradictions they contain." Cf. L. Kołakowski, *Main Currents of Marxism. Its Rise Growth and Dissolution,* vol. 1: *The Founders*, Oxford 1978, p. 203 ff.

[7] Cf. P.-J. Proudhon, *What is Property?*, Princeton 1876, p. 11.

vides first and second names, and in each case he arrives at the conclusion that their arguments are intellectually dubious and their morality suspicious. What remains indisputable is that there is no such thing, or at least there ought to be no such thing, as ownership of goods without work performed. The social rights of those who work hard he classifies as basic and imprescriptible – the right to access land, air and natural resources. In his opinion, those who state otherwise ought to claim their rights in front of the highest courts of justice, which are human reason and a basic sense of social justice. In a pamphlet called *What is Property?* Proudhon conducts a dialogue with all those accused of theft, reproaching them for their sins, such as "taking advantage of a legal privilege" or appealing to such unjustifiable arguments as limitations, agreements or established customs.

In the dissertation *Of Justice in the Revolution and the Church*, neither the revolutionary radicalism of Proudhon is to be found, nor its binary logic, the main argument justifying his accusation against owners responsible for all social misfortunes based on the tragic fate of the "working classes." His general thesis comes down to a constatation that there is no justice to be found either in revolution, or the Church. The new element in this vast work is, in addition to anti-revolutionism, programmatic anticlericalism. In earlier work this appeared only occasionally. However, it is not the Church that is recognised as the main cause of social misfortunes, but revolution; and heformulates arguments to encourage all social powers to prevent them.

These are directed, above all, at those who are responsible for introducing deep contradictions into the fabric of society. In the past, contradictions were present between free citizens and slaves, later between landowners and landless peasants, and even later between capitalists and the "working classes." Proudhon points out that in each case not only the interest of the privileged minority are put first, but also "only the interests of a social group are considered legitimate, taking into account only the immunity and dignity of a group [...]. In such a system individuals do not exist before the law; they are nothing alone; they cannot demand its rights, it has nothing but duties." Further on he adds: this is what "a communist system is like, propagated by Lycurgus, Plato, the founders of religious orders and by most of the contemporary socialists."[8]

Proudhon accuses various communist authors of provoking revolution. He presents a similar critique of the forces which "switched to the hypothesis of unrestricted freedom," taking advantage of the failures of communism: "The advocates of this theory claim that essentially there is no such thing as

[8] Cf. P.-J. Proudhon, "O sprawiedliwości w rewolucji i w Kościele" [Of Justice in the Revolution and the Church], *Wybór pism* [Selected Writings], vol. 2, Warsaw 1974, p. 22 ff.

a conflict of interests; because human nature is common to all and one group needs another, the interest is identical, and thus easy to satisfy; only ignorance of the laws of economics brought about this antagonism, which must vanish the moment we become more enlightened and return to liberty and nature. Briefly speaking, one might reach the conclusion that the discords between people stem mainly from the fact that the authorities interfere with business that does not concern them, out of mania of embracing everything with legal provisions, and out of legality. One must only allow the liberty enlightened by science to act, and order is bound to prevail. Such theory is professed by modern economists, the propagators of free trade, the propagators of the rule of *laissez faire, laissez passer* – 'let do and let pass,' etc." These critical remarks are aimed not only the French Physiocrats, but also at the British and French Mercantilists, like Adam Smith, David Ricardo, Thomas R. Malthus, or Jean Baptiste Say.

Proudhon did not claim that their theories were completely false. His claim was rather that "the only contribution that these theories make to the general knowledge are elements, that is the first draft of economics as a science" and that "they remain in contradiction to each other, and half of them are inapplicable." He contrasted socialists with "political economists," as he referred to them. He wrote about the latter that "they make out a bill to their opponents for the inequality of conditions, for a profligate trade, where monopoly and competition in a monstrous unity give rise to perpetual excess and misery; [...] briefly speaking, they demonstrate distinctly that the system based on property is a terrible delusion against which humanity has vehemently protested for the last four thousand years." Socialists and "political economists" constitute two opposing sides, because while "political economists are ready to sanction egoism, socialism valued above all the principle of shared property. [...] the former consider themselves to be the defenders of religion, authority and other modern principles recognising property [...], the latter reject authority and religion and rely solely on science; however, some sort of religiousness, not completely liberal, and a frivolous disregard for the facts most obviously constitute a distinctive feature of their beliefs."[9] In his opinion this was a weakness of socialism as its social science ought to be "a rational and systematic science" ("not concerned with what society was and will be, but with what it is in the course of its life, that is in all of its subsequent expressions"), and thus there is no room left for religion, or religiousness, or disregard for the facts.

This type of science must, like any other "rational and systematic science," have its primary notions and general assumptions, from which one may deduce

[9] Cf. ibidem, p. 193 ff.

a number of detailed conclusions. Proudhon suggests that *organisation of labour* ought to be considered such a primary notion. In his opinion "it is as clear and rational as the following terms: *organisation of manufacturing plants*, *organisation of the army*, organisation of charity, organisation of war." The following expressions constitute its more or less direct complements "supply, demand, quantity, ratio, price, guarantee." In subsequent chapters of the dissertation *Of Justice* he adds to the list such notions as: *value* ("it is a cornerstone of economic structure"), *utility* ("it is a precondition of exchange"), or *division of labour* ("is the way in which the equality of states and intelligence can materialise").

He presents the thesis that a human being is humanised through labour as one of the general assumptions of his social science. Rational organisation of labour is based not only on the assumption that it contributes (as "political economists" have proven) to increasing the "opulence of the nations," but also on the assumption that "it does not relegate the worker to a subordinate position, it does not make intelligence useless, wealth harmful and equality impossible." This is the case when "an individual is engaged in one and only activity throughout his or her whole life;" "the proficiency and pace of work is then definitely higher than in other cases; at the same time, however, one becomes less capable of performing any other work, either physical, or intellectual; one's other abilities fade; and as a consequence one degenerates as an individual."

Proudhon notes the existence of the phenomenon of dehumanisation through badly organised labour, but also presents proposals to ensure that all those who work, including ordinary workers, will be able not only to acquire an income which is adequate to the amount of work they contributed, but also to develop intellectually and morally. In the chapter devoted to division of labour he presents his conception of a rationally organised enterprise, in which workers are employed sequentially in all branches of production and master "operations which make up the speciality of a given enterprise." In other parts of this dissertation, he presents his visions of rationally organised political power (it is to intervene into the lives of citizens only when "unreasonable luxury" comes into existence, or an equally "unreasonable asceticism"), and rationally organised education (it is to educate during the time of work and through work, that is in individual places of employment).

Postscript

In many respects Proudhon's social views stood in opposition to the liberalism of the time, especially the liberalism promoted by the so-called "political economists." In his works, however, statements also appear which indicate that he was not so different from liberals and liberalism. This seems worth noting, as in they later facilitated the co-operation of socialists and liberals in essential social matters. In several countries of the West they formed coalition governments, for instance the government of the Popular Front of the 1930s in France (the front was a coalition of socialists, communists and radical liberals), or the long rule of the social-liberal coalition in Germany in the 1970s and 1980s.

As a rule, liberals have attached great importance to human and civil liberties. However, they are not indifferent to socialists such as Proudhon. He was the most radical in his defence of these liberties in *The System of Economic Contradictions or the Philosophy of Misery*, where he states that a man is inherently a free being, and liberty is "a force, energy; or spontaneity indifferent in itself to every action, and consequently equally susceptible to any determination."[10] He encounters obstacles in the process of expression and implementation of these liberties, but he is capable of overcoming them. This does not mean that he creates a trouble-free reality for himself. It means that he has paved the way to new obstacles: sometimes better ones, sometimes worse ones, but in each case different to the ones he dealt with before. These constant obstacles on his road to the ideal land of freedom did not discourage him from undertaking new tasks and challenge. On the contrary, it motivated him to face them and prompted him to find new techniques of solving what he called "human antinomy."[11] This confirms – apart from everything else – the faith of a man who wants to act and is capable of achieving at least some of his life-long aims.

The liberals of course also had faith, and still do, in their fellow man – in his ability to act constructively and to co-operate with others, to construct something new and to take control of himself as well as close and distant members of the community. They also believe that as time passes and people gain further experience these abilities are improved and allow for raising the constructions higher and to bring the control closer to perfection. Without all this, the liberties on which they debated and wrote, and for which they fought at the barricades would neither be required, nor even possible.[12] And yet Proudhon also believed in all this. In his dissertation *Of Justice* he wrote: "we have a firm belief in progress, just as we believe in liberty and Justice. [...]

[10] Cf. P.-J. Proudhon, *The Evolution of Capitalism. A System of Economical Contradictions, or The Philosophy of Misery*, Champaign 2004, p. 128.

[11] In order to explain this category he wrote: "An antinomy is made up of two terms, necessary to each other but always opposed and tending to mutual destruction." He also added: "wherever an antinomy appears there is a promise of a resolution of its terms, and consequently an announcement of a coming change." Ibidem, chapter II.

[12] Further on the question of faith of liberals, cf. Z. Drozdowicz, *Liberalizm europejski* [European Liberalism], Poznan 2005.

An atrocious claim that mankind has always been the same, equally stupid, wicked and vile since the first day of its existence, outrages us as a blasphemy; to no lesser extent than negation of freedom and a moral scepticism."[13] To the question "What is the place of Justice in the conception of a rational social life?" Proudhon replied in a similar way to the liberals, that there is no rationality without justice and no justice without rationality, because both belong, or at least should belong to the most elementary components of life and human co-existence.[14]

However, the above-mentioned work also includes statements which indicate the author's unrestricted belief in humanity's capacity for rational action and the creation of just social relations. In "Section Nine – Progress and Fall" he concluded the critique of the so-called "progressives" (the "apostles" of the idea of progress), and in particular the great hopes that they placed in the development of technology and mechanisation of labour. He did not question the idea that technology and mechanisation contribute to the intensification of the process of producing goods, and to a greater integration of the people who participate in this process. At the same time he indicated, however, that that an increased production of goods too rarely implies a more fair division of these goods. Too often this results only in greater profit for the most privileged. Moreover, he claimed that it also too often results in lower quality of the products produced, and the integration of the workers which accompanied the mechanisation leads to enslavement of people by machines. However, he did not oppose the machines. On the contrary, he believed that their emergence was inevitable (they were to constitute a "reverse formula of the division of labour").

He was also not opposed to getting rich as such, or even to some people getting richer than others. On the contrary, he asserted that the spirit of getting rich is inherent to human nature and that each society must have its aristocracy and its pariahs. However, he was against the idea of labour as end in itself, the cult of machines as the new deity and the fact that people were becoming unemployed because of machines. He was also opposed to getting rich without measure, to narrow specialisation, routinisation and monotony of labour in great plants, or to the relegation of people to the position of supplements of machines. It seems that many of liberals would identify themselves with these convictions, especially the so-called "political economists."

[13] Cf. P.-J. Proudhon, "O sprawiedliwości w rewolucji i w Kościele" [Of Justice in the Revolution and the Church], op. cit., p. 326.

[14] While defining his idea of Justice he wrote that "it does not contain antinomy: it is absolute and indefeasible as all law is and just as all laws are, it is transparent. It causes all facts of social life, which are indefinite or contradictory by nature to become susceptible to definition and arrangement." Cf. ibidem, section two, chapter VII.

2. Jean Auguste Marie Jaurès

Jaurès (1859–1914) was one of the most eminent representatives of socialism at the turn of the 19th and 20th centuries – not only in France but also in the so-called Second International (where he belonged to the group which supported parliamentary democracy).[15] He was born in Castres (in Provence) into a modest bourgeois family. He was first educated at a local secondary school and later in the École Normale Supérieur in Paris, where he studied philosophy. After graduating he worked first as a teacher at the lycèe of Albi and later as a lecturer of philosophy at the University of Toulouse. After being elected a deputy in the department of Tarn he sat for four years in the Chamber of Deputies, where he belonged to the group of centrists. In the elections of 1889 he did not succeed, but in 1893 he became a deputy once more (from the mining department of Carnaux; this time he joined the fraction of independent socialists, under the leadership of Alexandre Millerand (they advocated an evolutionary way to at the socialist system). In the same year he defended a doctorate thesis at the Sorbonne on the topic of the sources of German socialism. There he presented the thesis that "socialism originated in the German mind"; and figures such as Luther, Kant, Fichte and Hegel contributed to its formation, and the turning point was when "Marx introduced the Hegelian dialectic to his mind and made a connection between the economic movement in England and this socialist dialectic."[16] In 1895 he got engaged in the so-called "Dreyfus Affair" (the defence of an artillery officer of Jewish background, who was accused of being a German spy and sentenced to be deported from France for life). This affair polarised French public opinion into a minority supporting a judicial review (including the republican Left) and a majority claiming that the punishment for the "traitor" ought to be sustained. During the later investigation it transpired that the main proof of this treason had been fabricated by major Esterhazy, but he was found not guilty in the subsequent trial.

[15] In order to emphasise his eminent position among the socialists of the time, Leszek Kołakowski wrote that "Jaurès made conscious efforts to combine the most varied philosophical and political traditions into a single vision of the world, believing as he did in the essential unity of intellectual and moral trends that presented themselves in the apparent diversity at different stages of history." A few lines further, he adds: "His political and philosophical opponents accused him of glossing over social and doctrinal differences..." Cf. L. Kołakowski, *Main Currents of Marxism. Its Rise Growth and Dissolution*, vol. 2: *The Golden Age*, Oxford 1978, p. 115 ff.

[16] Cf. J. A. M. Jaurès, "U źródeł socjalizmu niemieckiego" [The origins of German socialism], in *Wybór pism* [Selected Writings], Warsaw 1970, p. 67 ff.

The 1898 elections revealed that the majority of French society of the time put their faith in politicians who claimed that the "plot of Jews, Masons and Protestants" accounted for the problems of France. Millerand's Independent Socialists, including Jaurès, found themselves among the defeated. However, in the elections of 1902 he acquired a seat in the Chamber of Deputies. In the last years of his life he worked towards the unification of the socialist movement, participating in the unification of the French Socialist Party and the Socialist Party of France, and towards closer relations between France and Germany (in anti-German circles he acquired the nickname "Herr Jaurès"). Moreover, he supported the formal-legal separation of church and state, including the eradication of state subsidies for church organisations (which materialised in December of 1905) as well as the inclusion of socialists into the government. He opposed, on the other hand, France's colonial policy as well as the alliance with Russia. In 1904, together with a group of socialists, he founded the paper "L'Humanité." He was murdered by a French nationalist on 31 July 1914. The literary output of Jaurès includes a considerable number of press articles as well as a few more extensive dissertations, like *The Franco-German War 1870–1871* (1908), or *The New Army* (1910).

The Marxist "orthodox" members of the Second International accused Jaurès, as well as many other socialists active in this alliance, of so-called "revisionism," which referred to not adhering to the views and postulates of Marx. V. I. Lenin in the "accusatory" document "Marxism and Revisionism," classifies him as one of the elements "least able to struggle and most vacillating and treacherous," and consequently ideologically and practically detrimental to the "great" cause, which is first of all the class struggle, and secondly the rule of the working class.[17] Jaurès gave his opinion of these allegations in a lecture delivered on the 10th of February 1900 to an academic society in Paris. The main topic of his speech was the presentation of a resounding dispute in left-wing circles of the time between Karl Kautsky and one of the most prominent "revisionists," Eduard Bernstein (the author of the formula: "the movement is everything, the final goal is nothing,"[18] which was unacceptable to the orthodox Marxists). Although he initially asserted that he "in the majority of cases supports Kautsky" ("in matters of rules and methods of socialism"),

---

[17] Cf. V.I. Lenin, "Marxism and Revisionism," in *Collected Works*, vol. 15, Moscow 1973, p. 29 ff.

[18] What he meant by it was that "[t]he socialist movement was capable of fighting successfully for many changes which would mean the realisation of more and more socialist values; if it were to live merely on the expectation of once-and-for-all cataclysm, it would not be serving the interests of the proletariat." Cf. L. Kołakowski, *Main Currents of Marxism. Its Rise Growth and Dissolution*, vol. 2, op. cit., p. 110 ff.

he added that he "partly supports Bernstein," and what is more, he believes that "the possibilities of supplementing and reviving Marxism are inherent in Marxism itself" (supported for instance by Bernstein's thesis that "each great revolution arises at the same time from slow economic evolution and from decisive intervention on the part of the oppressed class"). Generally, he said, he would "like the socialist party to be a geometric spot for all great causes, all great ideas," etc., as it is the only way to transcend "the disputes, divisions and oppositions of the contemporary schools," which may lead to the unification of the socialist movement ("so that we could delineate our socialist fraternity against the strives of the bourgeois society").[19]

The search for allies wherever possible (even at the cost of pluralistic views on social life) is characteristic for Jaurès in the whole of his activity as a politician, ideologist and an organiser of the socialist movement. In his doctoral dissertation he already attempted to bridge the realm of Luther, who was oriented towards the values of the supernatural world, and Marx, who was completely oriented towards the earthly world and negated the existence of the supernatural. After the party of anarchists appeared on the political scene and its members undertook such activities as throwing a bomb at the amphitheatre in the Palais Bourbon (August Vaillant, 9 December 1893), he attempted to enter into dialogue with the ideological leaders of the movement, M. Bakunin and P. Kropotkin. His sketch on the topic of anarchism begins with a statement which is characteristic of Jaurès: "To understand – is our primary duty," and ends with an equally symptomatic confession of faith in humanity, which "will be liberated through a threefold action: of individuals who develop their mental energy, of groups of workers who exercise free solidarity and of the proletariat organised as a class party in their rise to power."[20]

In the statement of Jaurès quoted above one could read a positive reference to liberalism. There are even more such phrases, inviting liberals to debate and co-operation with socialists, to be found in his article *Socialism and Liberty*, in a liberal magazine "Revue de Paris," published in December of 1898. He highlighted among others the fact that "too often our adversaries, who are ill-informed, confuse collective socialism, i.e., communism, with state socialism, and because it manifests itself only in acts introducing control and coercion, they think that coercion constitutes the essence of socialism. As a matter of fact, however, there is a wide gap between collectivism and state socialism."[21] In the later part he indicated further points of difference between communism

[19] Cf. J. Jaurès, "Bernstein i ewolucja metody socjalistycznej" [Bernstein and the evolution of the socialist method], in *Wybór pism* [Selected Writings], op. cit., p. 386 ff.

[20] Cf. ibidem, p. 144.

[21] Cf. ibidem, p. 326 ff.

and state socialism as well as similarities between the latter and liberalism. What is also common for both options, apart from rejecting coercion (as a method of implementation of the postulated social order), is the recognition of the right to private property ("collectivism, that is communism, by abolishing the private ownership of the means of production, creates new society..."), as well as the defence of civil liberties. He writes on the aims of the socialist struggle: "To say that political liberty and intellectual liberty will cease to exist along with the establishment of public property, is to claim that the economic dependence of the working class is the condition of freedom [...]. Never was the argument raised against the hope of improvement more ironic, never was the paradox more cruel. We share a dream that liberty and fraternal equality should enter the depth of society's everyday life, whose essence is labour. We wish no man in a factory or in the field to be another man's tool. We wish none of the working men to be the object of exploitation, nor to be excluded from the heritage of humanist patriotism, accumulated over generations. And we demand that every individual, by exercising his right to co-ownership of the means of labour, which constitute the means of support, is entitled to keep the output of his or her effort to himself or herself and to participate in the management of labour;" and hereby "grant each individual dignity," as "we liberate him or her from the economic burden," while "we grant equal rights and equal volition" and "we construct this community of thinking men on the solid and deep foundation of an economic system." This disclosure of the deepest dreams, desires and hopes of so-called state socialism comprises the essence of social rationalism for Jaurès and those socialists who did not and do not support revolution, violence and coercion by a dispersed group of fighters (who are "exalted and bitter in consequence of a defeat, hungry for revenge and terrified with the lack of contact with life"). Jaurès's view is one of "revolutionary evolution," achieved through the power of the working masses. Not by the masses, who are uneducated and driven by the thirst for revenge for the injustice and humiliation they suffered, but by the energy "inspired by the Reformation and Renaissance" and "the active will of many individuals" for change. In the cycle of articles published in the "Cahiers de la Quinzaine," which were titled *Evolutionary revolution*, he propagated not only the already mentioned "evolutionary revolution," but also appealed to readers not to obey these "exalted and bitter" fighters of the working class cause, but to follow the instructions of leaders such as Wilhelm Liebknecht, who considered the tactics of the (socialist) party to be "perforce conditional and changeable" and indicated (in the "Vorwärts" paper, the organ of the Social Democratic Party of Germany) that resorting to the argument of force (instead of the force of argument) "may become counter-revolutionary in character." Jaurès did exclude Marx from the group of the "exalted," however, at the same time he pointed out that he was wrong about more than one issue – for instance about assigning 50 years for workers to reach "political maturity to take over political power" ("the assigned time has just elapsed"), or making the victory of socialism in Western Europe dependent on the victorious wars of the progressive forces (liberal and socialist) in Eastern Europe; "It appeared to Marx that until tsarism is overthrown it is impossible to speak of revolution in Western Europe [...]. What other exterior and domestic wars did Marx think about? Presumably about the wars which were to liberate Italy and unite the German state [...]. He might also have shared the belief of Engels, who during his travels in France after the events of June 1848 wrote in his notes that socialism in France is to prevail only as a consequence of a domestic war of the workers against the peasants. Fortunately it is not and shall not be so."[22]

To an orthodox Marxists these remarks would sound like an insult (everyone may be mistaken, but Marx), and acknowledging Marx as the creator of the vision of that "magnificent revolutionary evolution" is a complete misconception – when Marx spoke of revolution (and he spoke of it many a time), it was "revolutionary revolution," that is to say such which will wipe off the surface of the earth all the exploiters, and the "revolution of all other revolutions," which will have its origin in one country and later, like a rapidly moving river, will carry all the remaining ones with it.

With these critical remarks on the prophecies of Marx, Jaurès was voicing his doubts on the rationality of the ideological thought of the founder of communism. He expressed them in a much wider range in the articles *The Question of Method* and *Proletariat and Homeland.* Although in the former he admitted that Marx contributed to "bringing the ideas of socialism and the worker's movement closer and uniting the two," at the same time he favoured the non-Marxist implementation of socialism – non-Marxist because it is not brought about through revolution, but through "the rise of the proletariat,

[22] Cf. J. Jaurès, "Ewolucja rewolucyjna" [Revolutionary evolution], in *Wybór pism* [Selected Writings], op. cit., p. 508 ff. There are many indications that Jaurès was not clear on the fact whether he was still a Marxist or not. On a number of occasions, it appeared to him that he was either close to the views of the ideological founder of socialism, or that the founder had little in common with the communism he was criticising, or that it was relatively easy to correct his mistakes in order for the "state socialist" to support them. He did attempt such minor amendments. As an example one could mention the article published in *Cahiers de la Quinzaine* (in September 1901) under the title "Socialism and life," where he claimed that "regard for life is the essence of communism," and "when the proletariat takes over the rule, when communism is introduced, the whole of human effort accumulated over the centuries, will create a favourable and serene aura, accepting all human beings since the day of their birth, granting them full development." Cf. ibidem, p. 561.

which identifies with it." It is a fundamental answer and as general as possible. When expressed in a more specific manner it amounts to definite forms: "the popular vote, trade unionism, co-operative movement, various kinds of public authorities and a democratic state." He did not wish to leave any room for doubt with regard to this method and he added "today history has eliminated the way of understanding the proletariat revolution represented by Marx, Engels and Blanqui." In *Proletariat and Homeland* he disputed the thesis that "the workers are devoid of homeland" or, synonymous to the founders of communism, that the homeland of the proletariat is the "whole world of labour" (hence the appeal, which is the final phrase of the *Manifesto of the Communist Party*: "Working men of all countries unite!"). Although Jaurès agreed with Marx that "sometimes a painful horrible cry comes from the exacerbated heart of proletarians: 'There is no homeland for us!,'" but he presented it as a voice not abolishing the idea of a homeland, but rather transforming the old ones into the new "proletarian, humane homelands," where "the exploitation of an individual by an individual as well as the exploitation of a state by a state shall be eradicated." The nations themselves – in the name of the proletariat internationalism – shall not be eradicated, nor their traditional revolutions. He noted, however, that in *the Manifesto of the Communist Party* itself, this issue is presented in a simplistic and "quite brutal" way: "Marx and Engels, despite the attempts of their dialectics and their erudition have never understood the depth of the French revolutionary tradition." This, according to him, is because it (like the revolutionary traditions in Italy, Germany, or Hungary) expresses not only the class needs but also the national needs of the oppressed and exploited classes. In the final part of this article he recalled those "heroic fighters who, besieged by the Germans in Paris of 1870, defended the integrity of the republican homeland."[23]

In the years 1905–1914, on many occasions and in various forms he stood up against the forces which strived for the armed resolution of class, national and international problems. In a lecture he was to deliver in June of 1905 to the congress of the Social Democratic Party of Germany in Berlin (from which he was incidentally banned, by order of the Chancellor of the German

[23] Cf. ibidem, p. 678 ff. This line of argumentation, which aimed to prove the thesis that the struggle of the proletariat to abolish class discrimination does not mean the struggle for abolishing national identity, was continued in the book *The New Army* (*L'Armée Nouvelle*), published in 1911. He attempted to demonstrate that the above-mentioned "new army" is supposed to be both the people's as well as national army, which means that it is to be "recruited from the citizens of all classes" and to have a control system which "corresponds to the best traditions and the most daring pursuits of the French revolutionary democracy, as well as the present requirements of national defence." Cf. ibidem, p. 782 ff.

Reich, Bülow) he summoned, in the name of socialist ideas, all the Germans and the French to resolve their internal and external problems peacefully. He wrote: "We, socialists do not fear the war. If only it breaks out we know how to face the facts, to deal with them in the best way we can, for the benefit of the independence of nations, the freedom of peoples, the liberation of the proletariat. The war evokes terror and abhorrence in us not due to some silly, nervous sentimentalism. The revolutionary accepts human suffering, it is a precondition of the great progress of mankind [...]. But now, in the present Europe, not by means of an international war will the work of freedom and justice come about, or the grievance of one nation against the other be appeased."[24] Moreover, in a dramatic appeal made several days before the outbreak of World War I – under the title *Necessary Poise* – he summoned the leaders of the European superpowers of the time to continue the politics of dialogue and to abandon power politics, and all people of good will to retain poise and clear thought: "[P]eople are in need of nerves of steel, or rather they are in need of a clear, peaceful and untroubled mind. It is necessary for us to appeal to the intellect of the nation, to its ability to think. [...] The danger is grave, but not inevitable, provided that we keep we keep a clear mind and strong will to afford simultaneously the heroism of patience and the heroism of action. A clear sense of duty will give us force to fulfil this duty."[25] The very same day this appeal was published in "Humanité," Jaurès was murdered.

Postscript

The concept of social rationality Jaurès adopted and promoted featured in many of his public speeches. It is clear in the anti-war appeal above. This might be called (after Leszek Kołakowski) *conciliarism*. I would add: a *global conciliarism*, because at its foundation lies the assumption that in order to shape rational social relations it is particularly important to find what constitutes common ground for the people of good will and clear mind, and which possibilities there are for uniting them in the development and implementation of the rules of the philosophy of dialogue over divisions. This is the only way to prevent the catastrophes of wars and social revolutions. Here the highest cause is not the well-being of one of the nations, or one of the social classes, but the well-being of all, because these conflicts do not leave any winners. On the other hand, causes which are complementary, in a more or less direct way, are the national, class and individual well-being of those who, in these wars and revolutions,

[24] Cf. ibidem, p. 796 ff.

[25] Cf. ibidem, p. 998 ff.

pay with suffering and their lives. Jaurès had no doubt that in these local and global conflicts the weakest social groups come to pay the highest price, which means that the philosophy of dialogue over divisions assumes, and, according to socialists, *must* assume a class character.

The grave implications of this fact are that, in this appeal, delivered just before the outbreak of the great world conflict, Jaurès spoke not so much of social classes, but rather of European states, and urged their governments to enter into negotiations. He assumed at the same time that there was still a chance for a peaceful resolution of existing problems, and that the ruling authorities would wish to and be able to talk peace. This assumption proved to be unfounded. However, later events revealed that the fault lied in the reasoning, not of Jaurès, but of those who supported military resolutions, and had been preparing themselves for them for a long time. They were all certain that they would emerge the victor of this confrontation. Such conviction was shared, after all, not only by the ruling authorities in the states which unleashed World War I, that is the German Reich and the countries which supported its politics of armed confrontation, but also by the majority of common Germans or Austrians.[26]

Jaurès supported the common people, including the so-called proletariat, in his conception of social rationality. He did not merely support their work, however, but also their ability to co-operate in a just cause, to develop and reach higher levels of professional dexterity, rationality, morality, patriotism, and so forth. At the same time he referred to numerous examples of their collective causative power in various fields of social life – in manufacturing material goods, unionising, exerting influence on capitalists as well as political authorities, in altering the old social structures, and even forming a new type of armed forces (People's Armies), and serving as junior commanding officers. He expressed his opinion more cautiously on the topic of appointing individual proletarians to decision-making posts in parliament, the government, the judiciary, or administrative and educational systems. Yet when it was high time to put the finishing touches on the matter, he provided rather evasive answers. In his replies to the question of who should be appointed to decision-making posts in public life he usually concluded that such an electoral system should be introduced in which the proletariat would be represented, so for instance in

[26] Characterising the situation in Germany before World War I, Jerzy Krauski writes: "It is significant that the moment the war broke out almost all Germans breathed a sigh of relief. They joined it with remarkable zest and enthusiasm. [...] They went to the front with a song on their lips, they felt good taking extreme risk just to break away from the circle of their enemies." Cf. J. Krasuski, *Historia Niemiec* [The History of Germany], Wroclaw – Warsaw – Cracow 2004, p. 312.

parliament there should be more than a few workers and also some peasants (because "there is not even one"). At the same time he highlighted the fact that representatives should not only come from the social elite, but should also be appointed from among the elite of the people. ("The elite of the people has always displayed an extra-ordinary amount of interest.")

Chapter VII

Rationality of social life according to the communists

Today, after many years of polemics between socialists and communists, it is a little easier to draw the demarcating lines between these essentially different ideologies and programmes for managing the most serious problems of social life. However, at the time of their birth in the middle of the 19th century, these troubles were shared by all, even the ideological founders of Marxism, to which a dissertation by Engels, under the title *Socialism: Utopian and Scientific*, attests.[1] In this section of the debate, however, I shall not elaborate on the concurrences and divergences of socialism and communism. I shall rather present two versions of communism and two related concepts of rationalism and the rationalisation of social life. None of them can be described (using the terminology of its creators and propagators) as "corrupted by bourgeois Utopian dreams," including the "dreams" of socialists. The first version appeared in the writings of Marx and Engels, the second in the works of Lenin.

1. Karl Marx and Friedrich Engels

Both Marx (1818–1883) and Engels (1820–1895) came from social backgrounds which they later harshly criticised and combated with great commitment. These were the circles of the middle-class, or as they themselves referred to them, the bourgeois.[2] Karl Marx's father was a lawyer and an active

---

[1] Cf. F. Engels, *Socialism: Utopian and Scientific*, Chicago 1908.

[2] It must be remembered that this expression comes from the French term *bourgeois* which meant a burgher (as well as a landlord or a landlady).

participant in the political life of the state Rhineland-Palatinate at the time. Karl was born as the eldest of ten children in Trier, and graduated from a local high school. He later undertook studies in humanities (law and philosophy) at the University of Bonn. During the Berlin period he acquainted himself with the philosophy of Hegel and for some time he was its great proponent; he even joined the association of the Young Hegelians, which brought together students who shared anticlerical and leftist views. In 1841 he defended his doctoral thesis at the University of Jena on the philosophy of Democritus and Epicurus, and in 1842 he undertook work as a journalist in a liberal newspaper called *Reinische Zeitung* which was published in Cologne, where he wrote articles on topics such as poverty and crime. In 1843 he started a family with his wife Jenny von Westphalen, who came from an aristocratic family, and a few months after his wedding he moved to Paris. He established co-operation with the French socialists and republican radicals as well as Friedrich Engels, who was also staying in Paris at the time. The latter became his closest friend and associate. In February of 1845, after intervention from the Prussian government, he was expelled from France, and he renounced his Prussian citizenship.

In the years 1845–1848 he was staying in Brussels and was actively participating in the formation of the organisational structures of the communist movement. In 1847 he joined a workers' organisation comprised mostly of German immigrants, which operated in London and was called the League of the Just. The very same year the organisation changed its name to the Communist League. In response to the needs of the League, The Communist Manifesto was written in 1848. Following the outbreak of the February Revolution of 1848 he came to Paris at the invitation of the French provisional government, and later to Rheinland where he began to work as editor of the *Neue Rheinische Zeitung*, a left-wing daily, which supported the revolutionary forces in the German states. After suppressing the workers' revolts the Prussian authorities brought Marx to trial on various chargers, one of which was tax boycotting. Although he was acquitted, the authorities declared he was a foreigner and expelled him from Prussia in May of 1849.

In the time between August of 1849 and his death he lived in London and in a financial sense he led a modest life. In the years 1850–1864 he lived with his family, including four children, in outright poverty. His main source of income was his work as correspondent for the American newspaper *The New York Tribune* as well as financial support from Engels. The financial situation of Marx and his family improved after he had become one the leaders of the International Workingmen's Association (the so-called First International) which was founded in London. In this organisation, which included English,

French and German workers, he was a member of the General Council, where he represented a socialist rather than communist position.[3] This was the assumption expressed by Mikhail Bakunin, leader of the left-wing radicals of this organisation. Marx had been engaged in fierce polemics with him and his followers until 1872, that is until the congress of the association in the Hague. Although the so-called "conciliatory faction" won, the congress proved to be the beginning of the end of the First International. On the request of Engels its headquarters was relocated from London to Philadelphia (in the United States) where it was disbanded in 1876.

At the time Marx was already well known in the workers's movement, and his three-volume work *Capital* (*Das Kapital*) had already been written and published.[4] After the dramatic events of the Paris Commune he began to distance himself once more from socialism and socialists. He expressed this among others in *Critique of the Gotha Program* (the programme of the German Social Democratic Party).[5] In the last years of his life Marx experienced two family tragedies (the death of his wife and eldest daughter) and struggled with a lung disease (which proved to be a direct cause of his death).

The collaborator closest to Marx, Friedrich Engels, came from a very wealthy middle-class family. His father was the owner of a textile factory in Barmen (in Rheinland) and co-owner of a factory in Manchester, England. After dropping out of school in Barmen a year before the final exams, his family sent him off to Bremen to work as a merchandise apprentice. He stayed there in the years 1838–1844, working in an export house and at the same time learning foreign languages (he claimed that he mastered 24 of them), and studied the literary works of the authors of the so-called "Young Germany." During this period he began his individual study of the philosophy of Hegel and acquainted himself with the views of the German anarchist Max Stirner and the Young Hegelian Bruno Bauer. In 1845 he conducted – in co-operation

[3] An argument proving this point can be found in the Inaugural Address of the International Working Men's Association, and in its General Rules. In the latter revolutionary themes recede into the background, while organisational matters, which remain close to the socialists, come to the fore. Cf. K. Marx, *Inaugural Address and Provisional Rules of the International Working Men's Association*, London 1864.

[4] In the preface to the first English edition of volume one (from the year 1867) it was presented as a work of purely scientific character. Cf. K. Marx, *Capital. A critique of political economy*, vol. 1, Moscow 1887, p. 27

[5] In the letter to W. Bracke (of 5th May 1875) he wrote that in his opinion this programme is "a thoroughly objectionable programme that demoralises the party," and "is no good, even apart from its sanctification of the Lassallean articles of faith." Cf. K. Marx, "Letter to W. Bracke," in *Marx/Engels Selected Works*, vol. 3, Moscow 1970, pp. 11–12. The above-mentioned Fredinand Lasalle was one of the leaders of the German Social Democratic Party.

with Marx – a severe critique of his beliefs.[6] He also began to write newspaper articles (under the pseudonym Friedrich Oswald). In 1841 he volunteered to join the army (for a year he served in the artillery regiment in Berlin), and in 1842 he first came across communism (as represented by M. Hess). In the years 1842–1844 he resided in Manchester, running the family textile factory and expanding his education in the field of history, even planning to write the history of England from the point of view of the emergence of the working class. At the time he met Mary Burns, an uneducated worker, with whom he remained in an informal relationship until her death in 1864. In 1844 the mentioned encounter with Marx took place, as well as the launch of a co-operation. They joined the London League of the Just together and participated in transforming it into the Communist League. After the February Revolution of 1848 was suppressed they were preparing appeals, programmes and plans of action for the workers' movement in Europe. In one of them they blamed the "German liberal bourgeois" (whom they considered to be "far more dangerous for the workers than the liberals of the past") for the defeat of the workmen's revolt, and summoned the workers to start the total revolution. ("Their battle cry must be: 'The Revolution in Permanence.'")[7]

In later life Engels divided his time between work in his family factory (which was actually quite successful as it generated sufficient income to ensure him an affluent life) and activity in the workers' movement. He wrote a number of introductions to the works of Marx which were published in various languages, and after his death he became the most eminent authority among Marxists. One of his individual accomplishments is the dissertation *Anti-Dühring* (aa critique of the German social-democrat Karl Eugen Dühring, an opponent of Marx and Marxism) and a couple of shorter studies.[8] The contents of these works as well as numerous declarations of tribute Engels paid to the accomplishments of Marx, indicate that in the process of laying the ideological and programmatic foundations of communism, his role was auxiliary (not to use the term: secondary). However, without going into details,

[6] It was included in *The Holy Family, or a Critique of Critical Criticism, Against Bruno Bauer and Company*. In characterising this work L. Kołakowski wrote: "*The Holy Family* is a radical, and one may say, ruthless challenge to Young Hegelianism. It is a virulent, sarcastic, and unscrupulous attack on Marx's former allies, especially Bruno and Edgar Bauer. The work is diffuse and full of trivial mockery, puns on his adversaries' names, etc. It sets out to display the naivety and intellectual nullity of the Hegelian 'holy family...'" Cf. L. Kołakowski, *Main Currents of Marxism. It' Rise Growth and Dissolution*, vol. I: *The Founders*, Oxford 1978, p. 147.

[7] Cf. K. Marx, F. Engels, "Address of the Central Committee to the Communist League," in F. Engels, *Revolution and Counter-revolution in Germany*, Peking 1977, p. 149 ff.

[8] Cf. e.g.. *The Origin of the Family, Private Property and the State* (1884), or *Ludwig Feuerbach and the End of Classical German Philosophy* (1888).

one could say that Marxism came into existence as the shared "offspring" of their minds and, frankly speaking, their hearts, because it consists of not only intellectual, but also emotional commitment.

The collected works of Marx and Engels comprise several dozen extensive volumes. What is surprising is not only the diversity and multifariousness of the problems they discuss (from the global to the completely incidental), but also the long list of people they want to sort out once and for all. Many names of criticised philosophers and politicians are already mentioned in the titles of dissertations; and even if not, they are invoked repeatedly throughout the work (usually in the guise of the accused). This far-reaching criticism could be partially explained by the extremely difficult situation of both the workers' movement and its ideological leaders. Only to some extent, however, since this criticism is often expressed in rather vulgar terms. For those who are not well acquainted with Marxist rhetoric and logic, it may come as a surprise that the works of Marx and Engels include so many points of critique and so little support of such fundamental matters postulated by the communist society.

This fact has also been acknowledged by some declared Marxists.[9] Generally speaking, they opposed all that led to the development of capitalism and determined its continuity, development and appropriation of subsequent areas of social life. On the other hand, it is not so obvious what they supported in their programmatic dissertations. Unless we associate this support with their theory of class struggle (till the day of the final victory of the proletariat), the theory of proletariat dictatorship (leading to the complete exclusion of class enemies from social life), or a theory of a state which is not only in control of everyone and everything but is also in possession of appropriate measures for enforcing the obedience of citizens towards authorities. Even if this is so, this only proves that Marxism – in contrast to other conceptions of social life, including socialist ones – is a theory of social confrontations of various types, and not a theory of peaceful coexistence, or dialogue across divisions. It ought to be acknowledged that while Marx and Engels did promise, after all the battles they fought and won on various fronts, the rise of a communist society, which was to constitute a "kingdom" of pure happiness, justice and welfare for all those who decide to follow their path, they were not the first to make such promises, which in time proved to be an illusion, or a non-realisable dream.

To the creators of Marxist theory and their later followers they are of course not an illusion or a non-realisable dream, but an accurate description of the actual processes of change which occur in social life and an apt prognosis

[9] Cf. e.g. S. Kozyr-Kowalski, J. Ładosz, *Dialektyka a społeczeństwo. Wstęp do materializmu historycznego* [Dialectic and society. An introduction to historical materialism], Warsaw 1972.

for the future. To their opponents they are a far-reaching simplification of these processes, and they are prophecies – prophesies which are dangerous in a social sense, as they encourage actions which are neither rational nor offer the possibility of rational outcomes. This opinion is expressed among others in *The Open Society and its Enemies* by Karl R. Popper.

According to this work, Plato was the "progenitor" of the Marxist theory of social life, including its rationality and rationalisation. Its direct precursor, that is the philosopher who had the most significant influence on the fact that it first emerged in the minds of Marx and Engels and later came into the world and began to "wander around Europe" (as a "ghost of communism") was Hegel. It was in his works that Marx and Engels were to find explanations for global and local social processes, including an indication of the driving forces which determine its dynamics, character and directions of change, and also – which has always been equally important to Marxism – justification for their general thesis that the history of the world is not the history of peace, or "theatre of happiness," but a theatre of struggle and misery of individual peoples, nations and social classes, sometimes greater, at other times lesser.[10]

According to Hegel, what underlies all of this is the almighty, all-knowing, all-understanding and self-realising *Weltgeist* ("World Spirit"), always present in what occurs in history (in the real world). It is always right, and it is the Highest Reason (in its purest form it appears as the Reason of the Universe) and always results in that which only yesterday was moderately rational to be considerably less rational today, and to be devoid of all rationality tomorrow or the day after tomorrow, or, to put it more bluntly, all that existed, exists or will exist is "by force of its destiny doomed for destruction." In order to explain this belief, which is essential to Marxist thought concerning the rationality of history, Engels wrote: "Thus the Hegelian proposition is transformed into its opposite through the Hegelian dialectic itself: All that is real in the domain of human history, becomes irrational in the course of time, is therefore already irrational by definition, is infected in advance with irrationality, and everything which is rational in the minds of men is destined to become real, however much it may contradict existing apparent reality. In accordance with all the rules of the Hegelian method of thought, the proposition about the rationality of everything real resolves itself into the other proposition: All that exists deserves to perish."[11]

---

[10] "Hegel paints a gloomy picture of what he calls 'mere customary life,' and reminds us that according to him "[t]he History of the World is no theatre of happiness. Periods of happiness are blank pages in it..." Cf. K.R. Popper, *The Open Society and its Enemies*, Princeton 1966, p. 269.

[11] Cf. F. Engels, *Ludwig Feuerbach and the End of Classical German Philosophy*, Peking 1976, p. 5.

Marx and Engels, during one of their "stopovers" on their intellectual journey to communism, parted with Hegel and the idealistic baggage of Hegelianism. Since then they followed their own path, that is of materialism, and to a Marxist Materialist everything has its beginning not in the more or less distant areas of the spirit, but in the immediate environment of the body, including its prosaic needs such as protection and defence against the unfavourable influence of the natural environment (cold, hunger, etc.). This is where it has its beginning, but of course not its end, because after these prosaic needs have been fulfilled, spiritual needs come to the fore, including the needs of human reason, such as the need to have faith in a better world, or to understand an ever-changing and in many respects imperfect world. Marx and Engels may not have devoted enough attention to the spiritual needs for those who believed in their ability to "explain everything through everything," whether it is rational or not, but they definitely put much effort into providing a general explanation of where social rationality and irrationality come from, and what is required for there to be as much of the former and as little of the latter as possible.

If we were to take their word for it, they both result from a specific logic of time. Not, as in the case of Hegel, in an "idealistic and theoretical" sense, but in a "materialistic and practical," and generally, revolutionary one, because each change for the better means revolution. In his concise exposition of these fundamental questions in the *Theses on Feuerbach*, Marx wrote that Ludwig Feuerbach, who was also a materialist, although not entirely rational in his thinking, in his *The Essence of Christianity* "regards the theoretical attitude as the only genuinely human attitude, while practice is conceived and fixed only in its dirty-judaical manifestation. Hence he does not grasp the significance of 'revolutionary,' of 'practical-critical' activity," which in consequence means that he is compelled "[t]o abstract from the historical process and to fix the religious sentiment as something by itself and to presuppose an abstract – isolated – human individual." Marxists naturally refer to the above-mentioned "historical process" and "presuppose" collectiveness (peoples, nations and social classes) – briefly speaking, they are historical materialists, or, as Karl R. Popper described them, "historicists," and more specifically "economic historicists," because in the domain of the historical means of production and distribution of material goods they search for the basic driving forces of social revolutions (economic, political, ideological, etc.).

According to the author of *The Open Society* one needs to make a clear distinction between the position of Marx himself and the position of "Vulgar Marxists." The former presented an "ingenious and highly original [...] doctrine" on the topic of "agents who are caught in the network of the social system" who behave as "mere puppets, irresistibly pulled by economic wires – by historical forces." On the other hand, "[t]he average Vulgar Marxist believes that Marxism lays bare the sinister secrets of social life by revealing the hidden motives of greed and lust for material gain which actuate the powers behind the scenes of history; powers that cunningly and consciously create war, depression, unemployment, hunger in the midst of plenty, and all other forms of social misery."[12]

In the case of the above-mentioned "Vulgar Marxist," it is not so much the issue of change that occurred in Marx's paradigm, i.e., "economic historicism," but rather a revaluation of psychological factors, such as "greed and lust for material gain," or a constant inclination towards mischievous acts. This Marxist, however, remains in the terrain of the same paradigm, from which he generates his vision of human history as a history of antagonistic and non-antagonistic socio-economic systems (in the former he includes slavery, feudalism and capitalism, and in the latter primitive community and communism), his laws of social development (the law of a gradual development of conflict between the forces of production and the relations of production and the conflict between the base and superstructure), his theory of class struggle and the revolution which accompanies it (because the forces which support the old "superstructure," i.e., the state, the law, ideologies, etc. otherwise will not give up their "class rule" without a struggle), and communism which appears in the final stage of this historical process (as its necessary and most logical culmination).

In order to explain this logic of history, which many who are not Marxists do not accept easily, Marx wrote: "The general conclusion at which I arrived and which, once reached, continued to serve as the leading thread in my studies, may be briefly summed up as follows: In the social production which men carry on they enter into definite relations of production correspond to a definite stage of development of their material powers of production. The sum total of these relations of production constitutes the economic structure of society – the real foundation, on which rise legal and political superstructures and to which correspond definite forms of social consciousness. The mode of production in material life determines the general character of the social, political, and spiritual processes of life. It is not the consciousness of men that determines their existence, but, on the contrary, their social existence determines their consciousness. At a certain stage of their development, the material forces of production in society come into conflict with the existing relations of production, or – what is but a legal expression for the same thing – with the property relations within which they had been at work before. From

[12] Cf. K. R. Popper, *The Open Society...*, op. cit., p. 293 ff.

forms of development of the forces of production these relations turn into their fetters. Then begins an epoch of social revolution. With the change of the economic foundation the entire immense superstructure is more or less rapidly transformed."[13]

This terse depiction of the Marxian theory of social life indicates such phenomena as the historical source of increasingly higher levels of rationality (at the most elementary level it comprises human labour, as the forces of production are human labour combined with the instruments of labour and workers' qualifications), the main reasons for on-going social changes (at the elementary level these are the material needs of humans), as well as regularities in on-going rationalisation (the forces of production are always the first to be subject to rationalisation, later they lead to the rationalisation of the relations of production, and subsequently they become the basis of the rationalisation of the "superstructure," including the consciousness of classes, strata and other social groups).

In his numerous works Marx described in detail the above-mentioned origins, forces and regularities. In this historical process the main part was not to be played by individuals, not even the most prominent ones, but by large groups such as classes. In the preface to *Das Kapital* he wrote that "individuals are dealt with only in so far as they are the personifications of economic categories, embodiments of particular class-relations and class-interests." It is of course the aim of communism to build a classless society, but reaching this aim requires the working class to mobilise all its capabilities, to declare absolute war with the capitalist class, to defeat them and to introduce into society, through the victorious proletariat, such forms of diktat that no social force would dare to question communism, its ideals, paradigms, authorities, rationality, laws, justice, etc.

It is not only the historical imperative of transgressing the rationality of the capitalist world that is the justification for these rather brutal measures, but also a list of injustices suffered by the proletariat of all countries in the past. In the first article of the *Communist Manifesto*, all the wrongdoers and all the wronged of former eras are enumerated ("freeman and slave, patrician and

[13] K. Marx, *A Contribution to the Critique of Political Economy. Preface*, Chicago 1904, p. 11. In the *Contribution* itself he added that a revolutionary discovery not only in the realm of economy, but in all historical sciences, was the claim that the mode of production of material life determines social, political and spiritual processes of life in general, and that such phenomena as social and state relations, or religious and legal systems, or theoretical views can only be analysed and understood through the understanding of the material conditions of every respective historical era, since it is not consciousness that determines people's existence, but it is social existence that determines consciousness.

plebeian, lord and serf, guild-master and journeyman," etc.). Subsequently the thesis is formulated that "Society as a whole is splitting up more and more into two great hostile camps, into two great classes directly facing each other: Bourgeoisie and Proletariat." And finally (literally in the final sentences of the document) he formulates the general thesis that "proletarians have nothing to lose but their chains," while "they have a world to win." It is openly declared that "their ends can be attained only by the forcible overthrow of all existing social conditions."[14]

In later years Marx and Engels put a lot of intellectual effort into cataloguing all the injustices that the working classes of all antagonistic social groups suffered, and into advocating the necessity of calling to account all those who have been responsible for injustices and made capital out of this. Marx and Engels write on the nature of the balance in feudal systems in works such as *Peasant War in Germany*, and on the capitalist system especially in Marx's *Das Kapital.*

Postscript

In "Speech at the Grave of Karl Marx," Engels calls his friend a "man of science" and considered him to be "the greatest living thinker," recalling such "epoch-making" achievements as the discovery of "the law of the development of human history," or "the special law of motion governing the present-day capitalist mode of production, and the bourgeois society that this mode of production has created."[15] Undoubtedly, it presents Marx as the greatest of the rationalists of his time. This topic is resumed by Karl R. Popper in his *The Open Society and its Enemies.* He agrees with the general thesis that Marx was a rationalist, because "[w]ith Socrates, and with Kant, he believed in human reason as the basis of the unity of mankind. But his doctrine that our opinions are determined by class interest hastened the decline of this belief."[16] In a further part of this dissertation, Popper attempts to demonstrate that the Marx's theory nevertheless "tended to undermine the rationalist belief in reason," and thsi was caused mainly by the fact that "historicist prophecy and oracular irrationalism made a frontal attack on it."

To justify this thesis he presents his interpretation of rationalism: it means to him "readiness to listen to critical arguments and to learn from experience

[14] Cf. K. Marx, F. Engels, *Manifesto of the Communist Party*, Peking 1970, p. 31 ff.

[15] Cf. F. Engels, "Speech at the Grave of Karl Marx," in F. Engels, *On Marx*, Peking 1975, p. 16 ff.

[16] Cf. K.R. Popper, *The Open Society...*, op. cit., p. 411 ff.

[...] an attitude of admitting that 'I may be wrong and you may be right, and by an effort, we may get nearer to the truth.'" He also mentions various ways of "getting nearer to the truth," such as the method of arbitration, or co-operation of parties with differing opinions (as in science, where "in the search for truth we need co-operation" and "with the help of argument, we can in time attain something like objectivity").

On the sources of weakness in the philosophical rationality of prophecies (not only in the works of Marx), Popper mentions "an irrational faith in reason," lack of criticism or the ever-present possibility of a refusal "to accept arguments" without running the risk of a logical contradiction. All this simultaneously determines the strength of irrationalism. Its social position is reinforced by the possibility of accepting all kinds of faith (in fraternity as well as hostility between people), all kinds of morality, all kinds of feelings and all kinds of passions ("according to the irrationalist, the majority of men will always have to be tackled by an appeal to their emotions and passions"). As a result, not much is required to be an irrationalist. A lot is required, on the other hand, to become and remain a rationalist, especially in the context of such a complicated matter as social life.

According to Popper, despite the acuteness of his mind and his criticism, Marx did not resist the temptation of following the direction of irrationalism. It manifests itself in the theory of social life that he adopted, by e.g. a sharp division into "class comrades" and "class enemies," and in his eventual support for solving the most eminent problems not by force of rational arguments but by force of the revolutionary proletariat. Another manifestation is the "irrational emphasis upon emotion" ("this attitude, which is at best one of resignation towards the irrational nature of human beings, at worst one of scorn for human reason, must lead to an appeal to violent and brutal force as the ultimate arbiter in any dispute").

What prompts a more profound reflection on these considerations of the rationalism and irrationalism of Marx and Marxism (as a "prophetic philosophy") is its connection to Judaism. This question arises in the context of the polemic between Popper and A. J. Toynbee. According to the latter, Marxism has its origins in the Judaic tradition (both Marx's parents were of Jewish descent), and in particular "[t]he distinctively Jewish [...] inspiration for Marxism [...] is the apocalyptic vision of a violent revolution which is inevitable because it is the decree [...] of God himself, and which is to invert the present roles of Proletariat and Dominant Minority in a reversal of roles which is to carry the Chosen People, at one bound, from the lowest to the highest place in the Kingdom of This World. Marx has taken the Goddess 'Historical Necessity' in place of Yahweh for his omnipotent deity, and the internal proletariat of the modern Western World in place of Jewry; and his Messianic Kingdom is conceived as a Dictatorship of the Proletariat."[17]

In general, Popper does not question the appropriateness of this analogy. He indicates components of the Marxist system, such as socialism, which is to constitute "the essence of the Marxian way of life." On one hand he debates the thesis that "[s]ocialism is Marx's original discovery," on the other hand he acknowledges his important achievement as his "claim to have based an old idea, socialism, upon a new, namely a rational and scientific, basis," and also that he showed ("by purely rational means") that "socialism will come and in what way it will come." In addition, he quotes Toynbee's thesis (and generally agrees with it) that "all historical thought is inevitably relative to the particular circumstances of the thinker's own time and place." It is of course fundamental to the evaluation of Marx's historical role, because it means that everything he proposed does not constitute some universal truth, but rather a historical truth, and his role in history is not timeless, but was set in a certain time and place.

What also inspires profound reflections is the Popperian evaluation of Toynbee's "historism and historical relativism." According to the author of *The Open Society*, this is an example of the paradox of the liar; "for if no genius is exempt from expressing the fashions of his social habitat then this contention itself may be merely an expression of the fashion of its author's social habitat, i.e., of the relativistic fashion of our own day." With regard to the cognitive value of Toynbee's historical analyses and theses, they ought to be considered "an apologetic anti-rationalism, born out of despair of reason, and trying to escape into both the past and prophecy of the future."[18] It is paradoxical but logical.

I do not wish to develop the topic of the complexities of the paradoxes of "historism and historical relativism." However, I would like to say a few words on the topic of what Popper called "the essence of the Marxian way of life," i.e., the relations of Marx to socialism and his contribution to socialism. Basically, if Marx was close to any of the versions of socialism of his time, it was definitely not socialism as represented by Proudhon or Jaurès, that is socialism which did not support a revolutionary, but rather an evolutionary and peaceful road to establishing social rationality and justice. It seems worth mentioning at this point that in the conclusion to his *The Poverty of Philosophy*, which was to discredit the social philosophy of Proudhon (and other "conformists" of his kind) Marx states: "It is only in an order of things in which there are no more classes and class antagonisms that *social evolutions* will cease

[17] Cf. ibidem, p. 440 ff.

[18] "This diagnosis is corroborated by many features of Toynbee's work. An example is his stress upon the superiority of other-worldliness over action which will influence the course of this world." Cf. ibidem, p. 444 ff.

to be *political revolutions*. Until then, on the eve of every general reshuffling of society, the last word of social science will always be: 'Combat or death; bloody struggle or extinction.'"[19]

Radical socialists of the time, such as Louis Blanc or Louis Auguste Blanqui, were of a similar opinion. And yet they were a minority among the socialists, and not particularly valued either by the ideological founders of communism, or by their later continuators and propagators.[20] If one was to contrast the extraordinary verbal aggression of Marx and his advanced criticism (which often evolved into hypercriticism) with the balanced judgments and postulates that Jaurès formulated, and his focus on what connects rather than divides people (including politicians), then one must reach the conclusion that these are two different worlds (of thought, emotion, desire, etc.).

2. Vladimir Ilyich Lenin

It is sometimes claimed that Marx and Engels were not the authors of communism, but Lenin (1870–1924).[21] Leszek Kołakowski, in his *Main Currents of Marxism*, views Leninism as a particular version of Marxist doctrine and tactics, and recalls the long-debated issue whether "Leninism is a 'revisionist' ideology in relation to the Marxist tradition, or a faithful application of the general principles of Marxism to a new political situation."[22] I will not even

---

[19] Cf. K. Marx, *The Poverty of Philosophy*, Peking 1978, p. 170. The emphases in this quotation come from K. Marx.

[20] W. P. Wołgin, who held a Marxist point of view in this matter, writes in his dissertation that the above-mentioned socialist radicals lack, among other things "a profound analysis of capitalism as a particular form of exploitation," and the most radical of the radicals, L. A. Blanqui, "in his understanding of the capitalist exploitation did not surpass the level of the petit bourgeois Utopians of the first half of the 19th century." Cf. W. P. Wołgin, *Poprzednicy naukowego socjalizmu* [The predecessors of scientific Socialism], Warsaw 1958, p. 320 ff.

[21] Cf. J. M. Bocheński, *Lewica, religia, sowietologia* [The political left, religion, sovietology], Warsaw 1996.

[22] Cf. L. Kołakowski, *Main Currents of Marxism. Its Rise Growth and Dissolution*, vol. II: *The Golden Age*, Oxford, p. 381 ff. Those Marxists, who, like the above-mentioned Stanisław Kozyr-Kowalski and Jarosław Ładosz, perceive Leninism as a "faithful application of general principles of Marxism to a new political situation" add that Lenin "had to undertake great scientific effort in order to free the Marxist theory of social process from deformation, simplification and certain fossilisation, which it was subjected to in the works of the leading theoreticians of the Second International." In contrast to those who "knew the works of Marx and Engels practically by heart," but to a certain extent misconstrued it, "he grasped it outstandingly, which means that he was able to adopt the Marxian style of thinking fully, to elicit with great insight the theoretical premises and consequences included in the analyses of specific empirical problems, that were carried out by the authors of historical materialism, to unveil complex theoretical structures

attempt to resolve the matter at this point. It is sure, however, that his concept of social life is not identical to that in the works of Marx and Engels.

For Marxists, the question of Leninist orthodoxy towards Marx and Engels is of course fundamental. However, for the present reconstruction of the Leninist concept of rationalism and rationalisation of social life, it is of secondary importance. What is worth considering is Lenin's biography. As in the case of many other ideologists and political activists, it offers a number of significant circumstances in which he formulated his views, judgements, oppositions and propositions. He was born in Simbirsk as one of five children of Ilya and Maria Ulyanov. His father was initially a teacher in a secondary school and later an inspector and a headmaster of public schools in the Simbirsk Governorate (in acknowledgement of his services he was awarded with hereditary nobility). His older brother, Alexander, was an activist in the so-called Narodniks movement. He certainly exerted some influence on the future leader of the revolution in Russia in terms of his choice of the career. After graduating in 1887 from a gymnasium in his home town he continued his education at the Faculty of Law in Kazan. After several months he was expelled from the university for participating in an illegal student movement. He later applied to be readmitted at the university, but in view of the lack of assent of the authorities he was forced to prepare for the exams independently (he passed them externally in 1891 at the Faculty of Law of the University of Saint Petersburg). After receiving a diploma he took up practice in a notarial office in Samara. At the same time he learned more about the views of the social Narodniks (including N. Chernyshevsky and P. Tkachev) and about Marxism (mainly as represented by G. Plekhanov). In 1889 he joined the Marxist circle operating in Kazan, and in 1893 he moved to Petersburg and got involved with the proponents of Marxism active at the local university. At the time he proved himself to be a declared opponent of Narodnism (he presented a critique of it in a pamphlet called "What 'the Friends of the People' are and How they fight the Social-Democrats") and a supporter of radical socialists (summoning the proletariat to carry out a revolution). In 1895, supported ideologically among others by G. Plekhanov, who was staying abroad, he led the unification of Marxist circles in Saint Petersburg and became involved in agitation work among the local workers. On December 1895 he was arrested for this

that were to be found in the brief, aphoristic statements of Marx." Cf. S. Kozyr-Kowalski, J. Ładosz, *Dialektyka a społeczeństwo...* [Dialectic and Society...], op. cit., p. 28 ff. Remarks of this sort constitute an interesting contribution not only to the Popperian thesis that the Marxist "prophetic philosophy," stemming from "hard-core" rationalism, pretty swiftly turned into "revolt against reason" (and lapsed into a phase of irrationalism), but also the thesis that it began to assume the form of a new religion, with its "Apostles," martyrs, fanatics, etc.

activity, put on trial and sentenced to three-year exile to Siberia (he served the sentence in the Shushenskoye village located in the Yeniseysk Governorate). He made the acquaintance of Nadezhda Krupskaya, who also was there in exile, ond married her in 1898. During his sentence he wrote, among others, a dissertation titled *The Development of Capitalism in Russia*, where he made an attempt to demonstrate that Russia, despite its economic backwardness, is heading towards capitalism.

After serving his sentence he left for Germany in June of 1900 and joined the Russian socialists operating in exile (Plekhanov, Zasulich, Martov and others). He participated in the establishment of the newspaper *Iskra* [Spark] and began to sign his articles published there with the name 'Lenin.' He propagated among others the need for organising "the revolutionary proletariat party," which would conduct an armed revolution. In a pamphlet titled "What Is To Be Done?" (an extended version of the article "Where to Begin," published in May 1901 in *Iskra*) he argued against the social-democrats who caused the democratic party to be transformed into a democratic party of reform (the "Revisionists"). In order to defend the "orthodox" heritage of Marx and Engels he demanded "battle with socialist opportunism" and a return to the "revolutionary trend," which meant in practice a suspension of the right to criticise within the socialist movement ("'[f]reedom of criticism' is undoubtedly the most fashionable slogan at the present time, and the one most frequently employed in the controversies between the Socialists and democrats"), re-establishment of the "revolutionary theory" of Marx and Engels ("Without a revolutionary theory there can be no revolutionary movement"), making workers aware of their class position and indicating the way out of this difficult situation.

In this pamphlet, Lenin did not negate the need for "the economic struggle of the workers against the employers and the government," but he considered it, just like political struggle, or "training in revolutionary activity," as a necessary stage, only preparatory to the confrontation which would determine the future of the proletariat, which was "the nation-wide armed insurrection." In the final fragments of this pamphlet he wrote: "Everyone will probably now agree that we must think of this and prepare for it" – prepare by doing such work which "would guarantee the highest probability of success in the event of an uprising. Such work would strengthen our contacts with the broadest strata of the masses of the workers and with all those strata who are discontented with the autocracy, which is of such importance for an uprising. Precisely such activity would cultivate the ability to estimate the general political situation properly and consequently, the ability to select the proper moment for an uprising."[23]

---

[23] Cf. V.I. Lenin, *What Is To Be Done?*, Peking 1973, p. 9 ff.

In the same pamphlet he postulated the establishment of an organisation which would manage the preparations for this uprising. In 1903 the editors of *Iskra* inspired the formation of such an organisation, which was called the Russian Social Democratic Labour Party. At its Second Congress two factions emerged: the majority (the Bolsheviks) headed by Lenin and the minority (the Mensheviks), in which the leading role was played by Martov from *Iskra* newspaper and people associated with the magazines *Bund* and *Raboczyje Dieło*. In the pamphlet "One Step Forward, Two Steps Back," Lenin presented both the circumstances of this split and the Bolshevik assessment of the standpoint and views of his opponents. He accused them among others of "inconsistency of principle," "oversimplification and caricature," "opportunism in matters of organisation," and several other "sins" ("empty phrases," "domestic unpleasantness," "utter contradictoriness and inconsistency").[24]

The Second Congress of the Russian Social Democratic Labour Party ended with the adoption of a resolution which brought about the victory of the Mensheviks (proving that the Bolsheviks were in fact a minority faction). They were concerned with the character of the party: Lenin asserted it ought to be professional and consist of "professional revolutionaries," Martov believed that it ought to include everyone who "accepts its programme and who supports the Party both financially and by personal participation in one of the Party organisations." This did not bring an end to the dispute between the Bolsheviks and the Mensheviks. Lenin even made an attempt to transform his "majority" faction into an independent party (in 1912 he called the Conference of the Bolshevik faction in Prague with this end in view), but the outbreak of WWI hindered the realisation of this plan.

At the time he was living in exile in Cracow, Poland at the time. After the outbreak of this conflict Austrian authories arrested him on suspicion of espionage for Russia. Due to the efforts of the Austrian social-democrats he was released from prison and allowed to depart to Switzerland (at first he lived in Bern and later in Zurich). At that time he argued that the war in Europe should be ended quickly and all the proletariat forces united in the struggle against capitalism. In an article published in the magazine *Sotsial-Demokrat* he wrote that "the victory of socialism is possible first in several or even in one capitalist country alone. After expropriating the capitalists and organising their own socialist production, the victorious proletariat of that country will arise against the rest of the world – attracting to its cause the oppressed classes of other countries, stirring uprisings in those countries against the capitalists, and

---

[24] Cf. V. I. Lenin, "One Step Forward, Two Steps Back," in *Collected Works*, vol. 7, Moscow 1965, p. 201 ff.

in case of need using even armed force against the exploiting classes and their states."[25] These views were not met with considerable support in the Second International; Lenin presented them during this association's 1915 conference in Zimmerwald and in 1916 in Kiental. His reaction was an accusatory dissertation called *Opportunism, and the Collapse of the Second International*, where he talks about "social-chauvinism" (which "is a consummated opportunism") and about "counter-revolutionaries" such as Georgi Pekhanov ("a typical representative of the social-chauvinists of the Quadruple Entente"), or Karl Kautsky (who "advanced his theory of 'ultra-imperialism'"). Lenin turned away from these ideologists and directly to the workers, formulating radical postulates and assessments, like "We've had enough of empty talk, and of prostituted 'Marxism' *à la* Kautsky [...] Opportunism is rotten-ripe; it has been transformed into social-chauvinism and has definitely deserted to the bourgeois camp."[26]

He continued this attack against "social-chauvinists" in the pamphlet "Imperialism as the Highest Stage of Capitalism," written in 1916. In its preface (written in 1917) he says they openly and "shamelessly [...] screen the annexation of their capitalists." In the preface to the French and German edition (written in 1920) he accuses the activists of the Second International of being "the principal social (not military) prop of the bourgeoisie. For they are the real agents of the bourgeoisie in the working-class movement, the labour lieutenants of the capitalist class, real vehicles of reformism and chauvinism." These words, that were intended to be fatal to the "social-chauvinists" were expressed after the events which caused first the overthrow of tsarism in Russia (in February 1917) and later the defeat of the Provisional Government in the power struggle, along with the Mensheviks and the Esers (members of the Socialist Revolutionary Party) who supported it. Lenin wrote about Kerensky, its leader, that he was never a socialist, but a Trudovik. In October 1917 Lenin and the Bolsheviks seized power in this vast country.

The pace at which these events took place as well as the scale of the changes which occurred in such a short period of time may amaze even the most experienced historians. At the time of the outbreak of the February Revolution in 1917, caused by the defeats on the front and famine in the country (the motto of the demonstrations was: "bread and peace"), Lenin was living in Switzerland. He learned about the events which took place in Russia mainly from newspapers. He made an effort to return to the country, but the states of the Entente did not allow emigrants to cross their territories.

25 V. I. Lenin, "On the Slogan for a United States of Europe," in *Collected Works*, vol. 21, Moscow 1974, p. 342 ff.

26 V. I. Lenin, "Opportunism, and the Collapse of the Second International," in *Collected Works*, vol. 21, Moscow 1974, p. 438 ff.

He came to an understanding with the Germans through the Swiss socialist F. Platten, which allowed him first to reach Sweden and then travelled in an extraterritorial carriage (protected from interference) to Russia. In April 1917 he made his appearance in Petrograd (formerly known as Saint Petersburg) and presented, first at the meeting of the Bolsheviks, and later at the meeting of the Bolsheviks and the Mensheviks, his famous work "The April Theses." His postulates included: "(a) that the power pass to the proletariat and the poorest sections of the peasants aligned with the proletariat; (b) that all annexations be renounced in deed and not in word; (c) that a complete break be effected in actual fact with all capitalist interests." A few days later he published its extended and more moderate (language-wise) version in the newspaper *Pravda*.[27] Both the first and second version caused many readers to be confused and perplexed. Plekhanov was under the impression that these theses were delirious, and in terms of their content they "were both a concrete programme and a utopian one;";"concrete demands were an end to the imperialist war, fraternization with the enemy, and confiscation of large landholdings and nationalisation of all lands, which were then to come under the control of the local soviets. All these demands were directed toward the Provisional Government [...]. The utopian parts of the program – the abolition of the police, the army, and civil service; the election of officials subject to recall at any time, with salaries not to exceed those of an average worker's – were the promises of a future government."[28]

The "Theses," in spite of their conciseness, represent an eminent chapter in the history of communism, and include the formation of its concept of rationality of social life, dealing with at least three priority issues. The first and the most important for Leninist communism is the question of power and social rule. Although only general remarks are made in the vein of power "in the hands of the proletariat and the poorest sections of the peasants," it became apparent over the course of time that this was basically all about power for the revolutionary leaders of communism, or, as they were later called, "the avant-garde of the proletariat." In theory it referred to the most class-conscious and militant part of the proletariat. In practice, power was shared by only a few of the most trusted communists, who were focused around the "Great Leader of the Great Revolution."

This trend in thinking about power and the way it is exercised by communists began to mark itself more and more clearly as the decisive clash with

[27] Cf. V.I. Lenin, "The Tasks of the Proletariat in the Present Revolution," in *Collected Works*, vol. 24, Moscow 1964, p. 21 ff.

[28] Cf. M. Heller, A. Nekrich, *Utopia in Power: the History of The Soviet Union from 1917 to the Present*, New York 1988, p. 30 ff.

the powers in the way of taking control over society was approaching. In "On Slogans" written in June 1917, Lenin distinguishes revolutionary Soviets from those "organs collaborating with the bourgeoisie" who never shared this revolutionary zeal, or lost it ("these Soviets are like sheep brought to the slaughterhouse and bleating pitifully under the knife").[29] Later, in the turbulent days of the October Revolution, when the fate of the upheaval brought about by the communists was still uncertain and their opponents could start to gain victory at any time, he once more began to speak of handing over the power to "the Soviets of Workers,' Soldiers' and Peasants' Deputies" who were to secure a true revolutionary order, and even stated (in "The Decree on Land") that "[t] he landed estates, as also all crown, monastery, and church lands [...] shall be placed at the disposal of the volost land committees and the uyezd Soviets of Peasants' Deputies pending the convocation of the Constituent Assembly." However, when the greatest threat to the communists' power came to an end, instead of referring to proletariat rule he began to speak of proletariat work, competition etc. If he ever mentioned ruling in writing or in his speeches, then (as in the "Declaration of Rights of the Working and Exploited People") it was about measures taken by the "Soviet Government" such as the abolishment of bourgeois anachronisms like private banks, or private property. The Soviets are mentioned in this document, but in a professional character as "the Council of Peoples Commissars."

The second important question raised in the "April Theses" is the "absence of violence," which meant espousing peace and implementing the principles of peaceful existence and coexistence. Lenin explained this in detail in his article "The Tasks of the Proletariat in our Revolution" which was published on April 10th, 1917 in *Pravda.* He condemns the Provisional Government as "a government for the continuation of the imperialist war, a war that is being waged in alliance with the imperialist powers – Britain, France, and others, for division of the capitalist spoils and for subjugating small and weak nations," and proposes (on behalf of "the Soviets of Workers' and Soldiers' Deputies") "an immediate armistice to all the belligerent nations."[30] He spoke in a similar vein in a speech delivered on June 4th, 1917 at the First All-Russia Congress of Soviets of Workers' and Soldiers' Deputies. He urged the assembled delegates: "The first step we should take ["we," i.e., communists – Z. D.] if we had power would be to arrest the biggest capitalists and cut all the threads of their intrigues. Without this, all talk about peace without annexations and

[29] Cf. V. I. Lenin, "On Slogans," in *Collected Works*, vol. 25, Moscow 1977, p. 185 ff.

[30] Cf. V. I. Lenin, "The Tasks of the Proletariat in Our Revolution," in *Collected Works,* vol. 24, op. cit., p. 58.

indemnities is utterly meaningless."[31] In the mentioned article "On Slogans" he added: "'All Power Must Be Transferred to the Soviets' was a slogan [...] on that peaceful path of development." He also mentioned the "peaceful development of the revolution" in the "Letter to the Central Committee" of 13–14 September 1917, and in "The Tasks of the Revolution" (a paper from 8 October) he argued that "The Soviet Government must *straight away* offer to *all* the belligerent peoples to conclude an immediate general peace on democratic terms..." (i.e. simultaneously both to their governments and to the worker and peasant masses). However, a resolution which was written by him and adopted by the Central Committee of the Russian Social Democratic Labour Party two days later states that "an armed uprising is inevitable," and in the "Letter to Bolshevik Party Members" (of 18 October), Lenin mentions that "the Party has been discussing the question of an insurrection since September," and argues that previously "it was only a question of elections, whereas now it is a question of an insurrection for the conquest of power." Four days later in the "Letter to Central Committee Members" he states that "everything now hangs by a thread," and declares that "the seizure of power is the business of the uprising; its political purpose will become clear after the seizure. [...] the people have the right and are in duty bound to decide such questions not by a vote, but by force [...]. The government *is tottering. It must be given the death blow at all costs.*" His later speeches frequently included remarks on peace, but as the communist power grew stronger, the actual (as opposed to the declarative) peace seemed increasingly distant, becoming at the climax of communist rule something like a "flickering light" at the end of a long and dark tunnel.

The third important question raised in the "April Theses" concerns "a complete break [...] in actual fact with all capitalist interests." Read alongside other pronouncements of Lenin this meant depriving bourgeoisie and landowners of their property and handing it over – not to the workers, but to the state. In "The Tasks of the Proletariat" he writes that "The proletarian party strives to create as large a state as possible, for this is to the advantage of the working people" and indicates solutions to this problem such as "the nationalisation of the land, of all the banks and capitalist syndicates, or, at least, the *immediate* establishment of the *control* of the Soviets of Workers' Deputies." "The Tasks of the Revolution," written a few days before the communists took power, contains slogans such as "land for the working people," and the text itself declares that the Soviet government will take measures "which do not deprive either the middle peasants, the Cossacks or the small handicraftsmen

[31] Cf. V. I. Lenin, "First All-Russia Congress of Soviets of Workers' and Soldiers' Deputies," in *Collected Works*, vol. 25, Moscow 1977, p. 15 ff.

of a single kopek." During the time when the fate of this government hung by the proverbial thread he claimed (in "The Decree on Land") that "[a]ll land [...] shall [...] become the property of the whole people, and pass into the use of all those who cultivate it." After the rise of communist power, it became apparent that the land did indeed become their "property," just as the factories and plants became the "property" of the workers, but only in the sense that they could work there and be productive for the sake of the communist state. Decisions concerning the course of this work, the production and distribution of the goods, however, generally remained in the hands of the "all-knowing" and almighty Soviet government.

The civil war in Soviet Russia in the years 1918–1921 and the political and economic mistakes made by this government lead to widespread famine. Initially the communists tried to resolve their problems by means of terror. The All-Russian Extraordinary Commission for Combating Counter-Revolution, Profiteering and Corruption (often shortened to Cheka) was appointed. An example of such an attempt to improve the political and economic situation is the organisation of "party weeks" by the communist government in order to review (from the point of view of ideology) the personnel of the communist party and accept only the most ideologically sophisticated workers and peasants, as well as the introduction of the so-called "communist subbotniks," which referred to mobilising all those who are able to work (not only on Saturdays, but also after hours). About the last of the so-called "Great Initiatives" Lenin wrote in December 1919 that it "is the beginning of a revolution that is more difficult, more tangible, more radical and more decisive than the overthrow of the bourgeoisie."

When it transpired that all this was not sufficient to improve the drastic political and economic situation of the country, the authorities decided on the so-called "New Economic Policy" (NEP). This was implemented in the years 1922–1927 and meant an effective and not only declarative empowerment of the part of society referred to as small-scale manufacturers.[32] This

[32] In the resolutions of the CC, RCP (B), that is the Russian Communist Party (the Bolsheviks), which came into existence after the purge at the RSDLP (B), which announced this policy, it is stated that "the New Economic Policy introduces a number of changes in the position of the proletariat [...]. The great bulk of the means of production in industry and the transport system remains in the hands of the proletarian state. [...] the Communist Party and the Soviet government are now adopting special methods to implement the general policy of transition [to communism – Z. D.] [...]. In particular, a free market and capitalism, both subject to state control, are now being permitted and are developing; on the other hand, the socialised state enterprises are being put on what is called a profit basis..." Cf. V. I. Lenin. "Role and Functions of the Trade Unions. Under the New Economic Policy," in *Collected Works*, vol. 33, Moscow 1965, p. 188 ff.

policy produced certain effects (it improved the situation of the food market as early as 1923). However, the battle fought at the highest level of communist power between the so-called "Trotskyists" (including, apart from Trotsky, Krupskaya, Kamenev, Piatakov, Radek, Rakovsky and Zinoviev), and the so-called "Stalinists," caused this programme to be abandoned, and its authors, coordinators and executors on the levels of individual establishments met with severe repressions.[33]

Lenin was already dead at this time (he died on 21 January 1924 from a stroke), and it is difficult to say how he would have reacted to the reversal from politics of authentic dialogue with society towards politics of "monologue," based on the assumption that the executive committee of the communist party imposes on society what they should think, feel, do, etc. Much has been written on the reaction of society to both these styles of politics. The authors of the *Utopia in Power* claim that the October Revolution was not so much of Lenin and the Bolsheviks' making, but rather a result of World War I and the social problems that Russia experienced at the beginning of the 20th century – turbulent economic development of which changes in power structures could not keep abreast. ("The governmental system evolved at a much slower pace than the economic, social, and cultural structure.") Social dissatisfaction had been deepened further by the defeat in the war with Japan, as well as the aroused but unsatisfied aspirations of individual social groups like the large peasantry, which admittedly received (in 1906) an enfranchisement decree, but this was being implemented inefficiently. As a result, society generally greeted the outbreak of the war with satisfaction, in some circles even with enthusiasm. The defeats suffered on the fronts (caused, among others, by insufficient numbers of officers and poor army supply lines), as well as a deep crisis of power (beginning at the highest level, that is Tsar Nicholas II) quickly stifled this zeal and the public mood changed from pro-government to decidedly anti-government. The authors of *Utopia in Power* state that the country was in "an uproar because it was sick of the war. All segments of the population were beginning to see the source of their misfortunes in the tsar, the tsarina, and Rasputin" ("the illiterate Siberian muzhik reputed to have cast a spell over the imperial family and to be shamelessly officiating in Petrograd").

Despite this deep social discontent, during the early years of the war the revolutionary agitation was not particularly supported by the nation, and the positions of the revolutionary parties were weakened by infiltration and vari-

[33] Cf. S. Courtois, N. Werth, J.-L. Panné, A. Paczkowski, K. Bartosek, J.-L. Margolin, *The Black Book of Communism*, Cambridge – London 1999, p. 145 ff.

ous provocations by the police.[34] The crisis of social trust towards the tsarist government deepened when, in the spring of 1917, the people started to suffer notably from the increase in food prices and problems with supplies. This was particularly felt in the big cities, such as Petrograd and Moscow. Here could also be found the main audience of the power struggle – initially between the liberal-democratic powers and the monarchists, and later between the socialists (the Esers and the Mensheviks) and the communists. During this brief and turbulent period, much changed in Russia, but two of the basic social expectations – that is "Bread and Peace" – remained unchanged. Lenin was very well aware of this and tried to make use of these sentiments as long as possible, reaching for power only when "the streets were literally paved with it."[35]

It soon transpired that, even though it was not difficult to acquire power, it was very difficult to meet the expectations of Russian society, especially to provide it with "bread and peace." When it became clear that the communists were not willing or not able to satisfy these expectations, first local, and later mass revolts were triggered. In response, the communist government declared an actual war against the dissatisfied part of the society. This lasted until 1921 and went down in history as the "civil war," or, as the authors of *The Black Book of Communism* describe it, the "dirty war." The so-called "social masses" participated in it on both sides. In the camp of the forces defending the October achievements (the so-called "Reds") the leading role was played by the Bolsheviks and common workers, while the the counter-revolution (the so-called "Whites") was led by the members of various parties abolished by the Bolsheviks (from monarchists to anarchists), officers of the tsarist army and common peasants.

This confrontation ended in the defeat of the "Whites," and the price for this victory, as the authors of *Utopia in Power* assert (citing official data of the Soviet Central Statistical Office), was ca. 10 180 000 killed, great destruction of the country, and the emergence of famine on a mass scale. According to these authors, it resulted in the death of 5 053 000 people in 1921–1922. To this account ought to be added over 5 million victims of famine and a vast number of victims of communist terror, which lasted for the entire period of this war and continued (with varying intensity) in later years.[36]

---

[34] Cf. M. Heller, A. Nekrich, *Utopia in Power...*, op. cit., p. 20 ff.

[35] According to the authors of *The Black Book of Communism*, "the number of direct participants in the Great Socialist October Revolution was very limited – a few thousand soldiers, sailors from Kronstadt, Red Guards who had rallied to the cause of the PRMC, and a few hundred militant Bolsheviks from factory committees." Cf. *The Black Book of Communism*, op. cit., p. 51 ff.

[36] The authors of *The Black Book of Communism* provide a "global accounting of the crimes" committed by the Soviet communists between the years 1918–1945. The victims

It could be said that, at least during the first years of communist rule, the societies of Russia and a few other Soviet Republics behaved in the way that the majority of societies would behave, namely that those who had benefited from the introduced changes, or at least were hoping for an improvement of their situation, supported the government, while those who were disadvantaged or felt deceived by the communists either went against it, or emigrated abroad (it is estimated that by 1922 ca. 1 million people had left Russia). During the period of the NEP (New Economic Policy), many groups demonstrated that if the authorities do not hinder their normal life and social functioning, they can cope quite well without them. The only problem was that this called into question the grand slogans of communism related to class struggle and rule, the alliance of the working masses of town and country, and the leading role of the party and its leaders. This was bound to come to a bad end for all those who believed they could do without communism and communist government.

The wave of repression affected this society considerably, not only altering its ways of thinking, but also what seem to be natural human instincts, that is the instinct to rebel, or to sympathise with those who are treated in an inhuman way by the authorities. As early as the beginning of the 1930s the participation of ordinary citizens in mass demonstrations in support of the communist government was mainly driven by fear of repression or the human need for peace and quiet. However, a few years later, many began to consider it their duty and a spiritual need. The authors of *Utopia in Power* note in the chapter titled "Socialism Achieved and Won (1935–1938)" that "[d]uring the May Day parade in 1935 [...] the demonstrators carried thousands of portraits of him [Stalin]. There were also carvings and statues of the leader, and his name, repeated a million times that morning, was cast in metal, embroidered on transparent gauze, and spelled out in chrysanthemums, roses and asters. [...] Especially popular (the poster circulated in the millions) was a photograph of Stalin with a dark-eyed, high-cheekboned little girl named Gelya Markizova [...], even though Gelya's father was shot as an 'enemy of the people' and her mother was arrested and later committed suicide."[37]

include: "The execution of tens of thousands of hostages and prisoners without trial, and the murder of hundreds of thousands of rebellious workers and peasants from 1918 to 1922; The liquidation of almost 690,000 people in the Great Purge of 1937–38; The deportation of 2 million kulaks (and so-called kulaks) in 1930–1932; The destruction of 4 million Ukrainians and 2 million others by means of an artificial and systematically perpetuated famine in 1932–1933; The deportation of hundreds thousands of Poles, Ukrainians, Balts, Moldovans, and Bessarabians from 1939 to 1941, and again in 1944–45." Cf. ibidem, p. 9 ff.

[37] Cf. M. Heller, A. Nekrich, *Utopia in Power...*, op. cit., p. 281 ff.

Postscript

Many works have been written on the circumstances of the birth, development and functioning of communism in Russia. Yet it is still difficult, using rational categories, to account for the great success of this handful of men who, at the beginning of their road to power, were only a faction of the Second International, which was relatively unknown in Russia, and after only some years became the greatest political power in a country so vast and culturally varied. They took control of the power and exercised it in such a way that it was initially impossible to criticise it in public, and later even in one's thoughts. Those who dared to do so were subject to the most severe repressions. This means that communism passed the stage of prophecy and rebellion against reason and entered the stage of creating and implementing a new type of rationality, or, as a matter of fact, two essentially different and complementary rationalities: the rationality of communist power, and the rationality of an ordinary citizen. In the case of the former the most important cause and principal "guideline" of the tasks undertaken became communist rule and the spreading it as widely as possible. The price that had to be paid for this was basically of secondary importance. In the case of the latter, on the other hand, the cause and guideline became survival – initially as social groups (of former landowners, capitalists, craftsmen, intelligentsia etc.), later as ordinary citizens, and finally, at the climax of communist terror, biological survival of individual people.

The role that Lenin played in creating this specific communist rationality was, if not decisive, then at least highly significant. Undoubtedly Stalin (born Iosif Vissarionovich Dzhugashvili, 1878–1953) contributed to some extent. He was capable, above all, of skillful "exploitation" of those of its layers of which his Master and Teacher might have not even have been aware.

This rationality is not completely original. It shares elements with for instance Plato's *Republic*. K. R. Popper pointed this out in his *Open Society and Its Enemies*. I would like to mention that in light of this work these "enemies" are thinkers such as Plato, Hegel and Marx. There is little to suggest that the works of Plato were Lenin's favourite reading, or that their social message had a significant influence on him. Yet some of the message did reach him – partly through Hegel, but above all through Marx and Engels, whose views he generally shared. He interpreted them in such a way that they would suit both the specific social situation in Russia as well as his own ambition, and the ambition of the comrades of his party who supported him. The final outcome does not resemble Plato's "Kingdom of Philosphers" (which is overintellectualised as far as the requirements and abilities of the Bolsheviks go), and also differs essentially (particularly in its practical application) from the "kingdom of communist happiness" about which many Utopians later spoke and wrote.

That is to say, Leninist communism is not an utopia in the sense intended by Thomas Moore, and later supported by a large group of Utopians of different provenance (from the deeply religious to the non-religious). It is not, and it cannot be, because none of them perceive it coming to power and exercised by the use of force as principal means. It can be understood as an eulogy for "social engineering" and "the Great Engineer" – under the condition that such "engineering" and such an "Engineer" possess inherent force, an ordinary and often brutal physical force that was capable of breaking and forcing to submission the toughest characters. This "engineering" and "Engineer" are not completely devoid of morality. However, communist morality does not have much in common with either Platonic virtues or with the morality of the average citizen of the Western civilised world, who appeals to values such as human rights, and who at least makes an effort to apply these principles to his or her everyday life.

Chapter VIII

Rationality of social life according to the contemporary liberals

It appears impossible to give a crisp and unequivocal depiction of the rationalisation of social life as it has been postulated and implemented by liberals. This is because it is so frequently amended and changed to fit the concrete realities of social life. One could nonetheless point to a few elements which seem indispensable to a liberal doctrine. Following John Gray, these would have to include: 1. individualism ("it asserts the moral primacy of the person against the claims of any social collectivity"); 2. egalitarianism (liberalism "confers on all men the same moral status"); 3. universalism (liberalism "affirms the moral unity of the human species"); 4. ameliorism (liberals proclaim "its affirmation of the corrigibility and improvability of all social institutions and political arrangements").[1] To this list I would add: 5. the respect of liberals for the sanctity of private property, 6. the limits liberals impose on the role of the state in social life, as well as 7. the demand for public and civic powers to be divided, so that society has the ability to control the ways in which public authorities operate, and remove them from power when they do not fulfil their functions properly. These different elements of the liberal doctrine have been presented, justified and implemented in various ways, both in theory and practice. In this respect, I share the general thesis of John Gray that in European culture liberal thought not only had multiple different meanings, but also "it has been given concrete historical embodiment in diverse ways."

On the other hand, I would not be eager to subscribe to Gray's presentation of liberalism, which makes it seem as if all the best ideas liberalism had to offer

---

[1] Cf. J. Gray, *Liberalism*, Minneapolis 1995, p. xi.

originated and developed on the British Isles, and developments brought about by other nations were only of secondary importance. This view permeates his *Liberalism*, starting from an in-depth analysis of the position of Thomas Hobbes (who, according to him, "gives voice to an intransigent individualism"), then providing a rather superficial treatment of Benedict Spinoza ("Spinoza shared many of Hobbes's assumptions about man and society"). He mentions John Locke frequently ("Locke's thought harbours a number of themes which confer a distinctive complexion on English liberalism"), but mentions liberals and liberalism in France and other Catholic countries such as Italy and Spain only in passing. He arrives at the liberal era, dominated by either English thinkers (for example J. S. Mill or H. Spencer) or authors who wrote in English. He discusses an abundant selection of American liberals, including those temporarily residing in the British Isles or the United States,[2] and also two liberals who will be discussed at length in the present context, namely, F. A von Hayek and J. Rawls.

1. Friedrich August von Hayek

In Gray's *Liberalism*, von Hayek (1889–1992) is presented as the one scholar and political philosopher who "more than any single figure is responsible for the revival of classical liberalism in the post-war period." Gray considers his *The Constitution of Liberty*[3] (1959) a masterpiece. The other notable work by Hayek is obviously the *The Road to Serfdom* (1944), but a complete list of Hayek's important influences on contemporary liberalism would be much longer. His works include various elements which broaden and deepen our views on social rationality and the rationalisation of social life.[4] Let us begin, however, with some general information concerning the author.

Hayek was born in Vienna and studied law at the University of Vienna, obtaining two doctorates: one in law (1921) and another in psychology (1923). Economics turned out to be his main area of interest, but at the time there was

[2] This "anglophile" skew is surprising as John Gray refers to *The History of European Liberalism* by Guido de Ruggiero, which shows the great variety of European liberalisms. Cf. G. de Ruggiero, *The History of European Liberalism*, Boston 1959.

[3] "Hayek's work is significant in containing the most sophisticated reconstruction of the central ideas of the Austrian School of Economics which had dominated intellectual life at the London School of Economics in the 1930s when it was led by Hayek and Lionel Robbins." Cf. H. Gray, *Liberalism*, op. cit., p. 38.

[4] Apart from these works, F. A. von Hayek is also the author of *Geldtheorie und Konjukturtheorie* (1929); *The Pure Theory of Capital* (1941); *Individualism and Economic Order* (1948); *The Counter-Revolution on Science. Studies on the Abuse of Reason* (1952); *Law, Legislation and Liberty. A New Statement of the Liberal Principles of Justice and Political Economy* (vol. 1–3, 1973–1979).

no chair of economics at the University of Vienna. A crucial influence on his development came in his participation in a private seminar organised by Ludwig von Mises (1881–1973), the author of works such as *Die Wirtschaftsrechnung im sozialistischen Gemeinwesen* (1920), as well as *Socialism. An Economic and Sociological Analysis* (1922).[5] In 1927, L. von Mises founded the Austrian Institute for Business Cycle Research, and it was Hayek who was entrusted with managerial duties, which he assumed until his move to London, where he was invited to give a series of lectures on the business cycle at the London School of Economics.

London was an important centre of economic thought at the time, and one of the principal English economists was John Maynard Keynes (1883–1946), a proponent of state intervention in situations where economic crises occur.[6] Hayek would argue against Keynes and in defence of the self-regulating power of the free market (one forum for this debate was facilitated by *The Economic Journal*). The on-going economic crisis of the early 1930s, as well as the events of the Second World War and the overall dire economic situation many states were facing seemed to favour Keynes and his adherents.[7]

The Road to Serfdom comes from this period of debate with Keynes, and this "political book" – as Hayek himself would call it in the introduction – is dedicated to the "socialists of all parties," and constitutes a liberal polemic against the ideologies and social programmes of these parties. It generated much interest in the United States,[8] and helped Hayek to be named professor

[5] Both books constitute a criticism of the socialist way of management. According to Miłowit Kuniński, "Hayek abandoned any socialist sympathies under the influence of Mises." Cf. M. Kuniński, *Wiedza, etyka i polityka w myśli F.A. von Hayeka* [Knowledge, ethics, and politics in the thought of F. A. Hayek], Cracow 1999, p. 16 ff.

[6] Keynes' theory proposed among other things 1. progressive taxation with respect to the wealthy; 2. reduction of taxes on investments; 3. utilisation of public funds for investments and the organisation of public works. In general his point was that there should be an active state policy in the fiscal, monetary and social spheres. Cf. J. M. Keynes, *The General Theory of Employment, Interest and Money,* New York 1936.

[7] This is admitted by Gray, who nevertheless criticises the school from a liberal standpoint.. "Macroeconomic theory – as found in Hayek's contemporary J. M. Keynes – leads easily to the mistake of conferring on statistical fictions and aggregative judgements a causal role which they cannot possess in the real world. Hayek's microeconomic perspective, and the individualist and subjectivist methodology which supported it, went out of favour in the Second War and the long period of postwar expansion in which Keynes's ideas appeared to be vindicated." Cf. J. Gray, *Liberalism*, op. cit., p. 38

[8] According to M. Kuniński it gathered wide response not only among those professionally concerned with the problems of politics, but also among the general public: "Hayek's criticism of collectivism – or to put it in modern terms, of totalitarianism [...] and the rejection of state intervention considered to be an early form of totalitarianism, were something truly astonishing in the days of increasing popularity of statist ideas..." Cf. M. Kuniński, *Wiedza, etyka i polityka...*, [Knowledge, ethics, and politics...], op. cit., p. 18.

of social and moral sciences at the University of Chicago, where he worked until 1962. In this "American" period of his life and work, he wrote his *magnum opus*, *The Constitution of Liberty*. After returning to Europe, he initially became a professor of economic policy at the University of Freiburg, and later (in 1968) at the University of Salzburg. In 1974, he received the Nobel Prize in Economics together with Gunner Myrdal for "for their pioneering work in the theory of money and economic fluctuations and for their penetrating analysis of the interdependence of economic, social and institutional phenomena."

An in-depth analysis of the works from different periods of Hayek's life indicate not only to the evolution of his thinking, but also a general change in the nature of his interests.[9] To simplify the task of reconstructing his standards of rationality of social life, I shall stick mainly to his *Constitution of Liberty*, which in itself is a book spanning an impressive array and diversity of themes. It does have one main protagonist, that is, freedom. However, it faces so many different challenges in so many different situations that one gets the impression that no aspect of social life remains indifferent to Hayek in pursuing his agenda. Rationally conceived and enjoyed freedom remains a key element of this agenda.

What is challenging in this context is that freedom has been conceived of and used in so many different ways that "[i]n the struggle for the moral support of the people of the world, the lack of firm beliefs puts the West at a great disadvantage."[10] It is also problematic that "those men from the less advanced nations who became purveyors of ideas to their own people learned, during their Western training, not how the West had built up its civilisation, but mostly those dreams of alternatives which its very success had engendered." Yet another problem stems from the fact that no single nation of the Western world is the sole creator and depositary of the freedom which underlies the greatness of the Western culture. Even these difficulties, indicated in the introduction to *The Constitution of Liberty*, seem to constitute a good enough justification for commencing the exposition of liberal ideals from the most basic, elementary principles. This is the task that the first part of the book, "The Value of Freedom," has been devoted to, and one should perhaps add to this that it is the value of freedom as much as the value of reason which is under consideration, as from the course of the argument it becomes clear that true freedom and true reason are mutually necessary phenomena.

---

[9] When it comes to the evolution of his ideas, cf. A. Gamble, *Hayek: The Iron Cage of Liberty*, Cambridge 1966.

[10] "This was a time when the intellectuals of the West had to a great extent abandoned the very belief in freedom which, by enabling the West to make full use of those forces that are responsible for the growth of all civilisation, had made its unprecedented quick growth possible." Cf. F. A. von Hayek, *The Constitution of Liberty*, Chicago 2011, p. 48.

In Chapter I Hayek presents different ways of understanding freedom, starting from the most basic conception of a "condition of men in which coercion of some by others is reduced as much as is possible in society," through more complex and socially nuanced conceptions, ending with the consideration of such situations where freedom and coercion are not juxtaposed, but actually complement each other mutually, in a rational way. Just coercion, which is "[c]oercion according to known rules, which is generally the result of circumstances in which the person to be coerced has placed himself, then becomes an instrument assisting the individuals in the pursuit of their own ends and not a means to be used for the ends of others."

In Chapter II, Hayek explores the "creative powers of a free civilisation." In the opening stages of these considerations his main focus is already on such human reason that is capable of co-operating and co-existing with nature, and a human reasonableness that is capable of utilising the civilizational advances of previous generations. ("The growth of knowledge and the growth of civilisation are the same only if we interpret knowledge to include all the human adaptations to environment in which past experience has been incorporated.") These considerations on true human reasonableness lead to the same aim as those of the previous chapter, i.e., depicting the kind of freedom in which the man of the West should participate.

The general thesis of these considerations amounts to the statement that true reasonableness depends on "the recognition of the inevitable ignorance of all of us concerning a great many of the factors on which the achievement of our ends and welfare depends." For most people this means that "Our necessary ignorance of so much means that we have to deal largely with probabilities and chances." For the liberals, however, it means that they have to accept both the fact of their own ignorance as well as of the ignorance of even the wisest, and that "all institutions of freedom are adaptations to this fundamental fact of ignorance, adapted to deal with chances and probabilities, not certainty."

Towards the end of this chapter the attention shifts from rationality and rationalism to the rationalist himself, who in his desire to subject everything to human reason, faces a real dilemma: "The use of reason aims at control and predictability. But the process of the advance of reason rests on freedom and the unpredictability of human action," or to put it in other words, he faces the problem of spontaneity.[11] In a sense, this constitutes a *votum separatum* with respect to rationalism and rationality, which stems from the desire for rational cognition, control and prediction of all that appears in social life, accompanied

[11] According to Norman Barry, this idea of the spontaneity of human action and its effects (such as social institutions) constitutes a foundational idea for the edifice of Hayek's theory. Cf. N. Barry, *Hayek's Social and Economic Philosophy*, London 1979, p. 9 ff.

by the instinct to supress all the elemental forces that stand in the way of realising this desire. In Hayek's view, this would be deeply irrational, as it would entail opposition to the forces which make progress possible.

The demonstration of the irrationality of this desire is presented in Chapter III of this part of *The Constitution of Liberty*. That is why so much of the discussion focuses on the negative (opposition to the belief in boundless progress, opposition to intellectuals who doubt the existence of progress), while relatively little emphasis is put on positive arguments (support for such conceptions of progress, which uncover the errors of reason, support for the conception of progress that does not equate it merely with technical progress and the wealth of the West, but also includes the capacity to reduce inequality and the eradication of poverty through redistribution.

Chapter IV, in broad terms, states that there can be no reason if it does not involve learning from the mistakes of the past. In this respect crucial inputs have been given by the English and the French: "Though these two groups are now commonly lumped together as the ancestors of modern liberalism, there is hardly a greater contrast imaginable than that between their respective conceptions of the evolution and functioning of a social order and the role played in it by liberty. The difference is directly traceable to the predominance of an essentially empiricist view of the world in England and a rationalist approach in France. The main contrast in the practical conclusions to which these approaches led has recently been well put, as follows: 'One finds the essence of freedom in spontaneity and the absence of coercion, the other believes it to be realised only in the pursuit and attainment of an absolute collective purpose.'"[12]

Hayek seems closer to the English (or perhaps more correctly the British) tradition, with key representatives such as David Hume, Adam Smith and Adam Ferguson. ("Those British philosophers have given us an interpretation of the growth of civilisation that is still the indispensable foundation of the argument for liberty.") This is not referred to as the rationalist tradition, as rationalism is understood in this chapter in the sense defined by Groethuysen: as a tendency "to regulate individual and social life in accordance with principles of reason and to eliminate as far as possible or to relegate to the background everything irrational."

In the light of the standards of rationality assumed by these British philosophers and Hayek, the tendency or desire to regulate is essentially irrational.

---

[12] "[...] one stands for organic, slow, half-conscious growth, the other for doctrinaire deliberateness; one for trial-and-error procedure, the other for an enforced solely valid pattern." It is the second view, as J. L. Talmon has shown in the book from which this description is taken, that has become the origin of totalitarian democracy." Ibidem, p. 111; cf. J. L. Talmon, *The Origins of Totalitarian Democracy*, London 1952.

The reasons for this view were explained in preceding chapters. In this chapter, Hayek provides further arguments pointing to this irrational character. Some of these may seem surprising to those whose understanding of rationalism follows the French tradition, and to some extent even to those sticking to the British tradition. For the former, it would not be astonishing to learn that "[t]he anti-rationalist tradition is here closer to the Christian tradition of the fallibility and sinfulness of man," which has been widely accepted ever since the publication of Max Weber's studies on the ascetic varieties of Protestantism. Yet it certainly would be surprising to read that, in the view of the British philosophers "man was by nature lazy and indolent, improvident and wasteful, and that it was only by the force of circumstances that he could be made to behave economically or would learn carefully to adjust his means to his ends." The claim that the notion of *homo oeconomicus* "was explicitly introduced, with much else that belongs to the rationalist rather than to the evolutionary tradition, only by the younger Mill" could also be read with some incredulity, as of all people John Stuart Mill has always been associated with the British rather than the Continental liberal tradition. In short, it seems that Hayek articulates his standards of rationality not only in opposition to the French tradition, but also in many aspects to the British tradition, or at least to what is commonly associated with it.

In such a cursory examination of the standards of rationality assumed by Hayek, there seems to be no space for an in-depth analysis of the way he distances himself from both liberal traditions, or to be more precise, from the visions of these traditions disseminated by historians. For the sake of signalling the direction in which this discussion of the nature of reason seems to be heading, I would just like to point out that what is taken to be meant by rationality for Hayek has its origins in Cartesian thought. What might perhaps arouse more suspicion is the fact that he identified to Sparta as the model for this kind of rationality in the social dimension. It seems important then to remind ourselves that Descartes actually assumed a disparaging attitude towards traditions as well as those who base their thinking on them.[13]

What remains vital to this reflection on rationality are not these details, which interest mostly historians of philosophy, but something more general in the form of the standards of true rationality. From this point of view it is crucial that they are not assumed to pre-exist – as in the Cartesian pre-existing human reason which devises various social institutions – nor is any kind of social contract legitimising these institutions, or some law-giver endowed with wisdom that knows everything best and proposes the most advantageous solu-

[13] According to Descartes such references can only play a moralising role, and any kind of knowledge based on them can only have the charm of a fairy-tale. Cf. R. Descartes, "Discourse on the Method," in *The Philosophical Writings of Descartes*, vol. I, Cambridge 1985.

tions to social problems, envisaged. What is assumed is merely the existence of freedom, spontaneity, and reasonability which might not be perfected but is in fact being perfected with time, and, even more importantly, being spread to larger groups of people.

In the considerations concluding this chapter of *The Constitution of Liberty*, Hayek advances a number of generalisations important to his standards of rationality. The first relates to Reason itself: "Reason undoubtedly is man's most precious possession. Our argument is intended to show merely that it is not all-powerful and that the belief that it can become its own master and control its own development may yet destroy it." The second concerns true reasonableness, or what Hayek refers to as "intelligent use of reason." It has to find its expression not only in thinking but also, and perhaps primarily, in social action founded upon "co-operation of many separate minds." Thirdly, it is noted with respect to changing the world that "In all our endeavour at improvement we must always work inside this given whole, aim at piecemeal, rather than total, construction, and use at each stage the historical material at hand and improve details step by step rather than attempt to redesign the whole." Finally, the concluding remark is made that "None of these conclusions are arguments against the use of reason, but only arguments against such uses as require any exclusive and coercive powers of government."[14]

These comments close this rather general part of Hayek's reflection on the standards of rationality, and in the subsequent parts we find mostly concretisations or applications of these conclusions to specific problems of social life. The list of such problems is obviously long. When it comes to the most important ones, Hayek mentions questions of responsibility, equality, merits, the rule of the majority as well as the wage and independent labour. These are considered in the remaining chapters of the first part of *The Constitution of Liberty*. Predictably, in all these specific cases it turns out that there can be no virtues or social values without true freedom accompanied by true rationality. These are neither easy to achieve, nor to maintain, let alone enlarge. It is, however, all to easy to confuse them with their phantoms.

One such issue where it seems all too easy to confuse true social rationality with its phantom reflection is the question of democracy. This confusion arises whenever the rule of majority is treated not as a means to an end but as the end itself. According to Hayek, this kind of approach is founded on the groundless assumption that higher wisdom springs not from the decisions of the most intelligent and best prepared minority but from the decisions of the majority of individuals forming a society. The author of *The Constitution of Liberty* does indeed admit that democracy is a means of defending free-

[14] Cf. ibidem, p. 79 ff.

dom and even that "Though democracy is probably the best form of limited government, it becomes an absurdity if it turns into unlimited government. Those who profess that democracy is all-competent and support all that the majority wants at any given moment are working for its fall."[15]

In Part II of the book, Hayek points to the rule of law which has facilitated the necessary limitations on the functioning of democracy in the West. These are closely connected with the system of freedom, including the operation of the free market. Such an economy is based on free competition between the producers of various commodities and the providers of services. However, "all these activities of government are part of its effort to provide a favourable framework for individual decisions; they supply means which individuals can use for their own purposes." There also exist areas of social life where this activity should go further. "To this latter group belong all those services which are clearly desirable, but which will not be provided by competitive enterprise because it would be either impossible or difficult to charge the individual beneficiary for them. Such are most sanitary and health services, often the construction and maintenance of roads, and many of the amenities provided by municipalities for the inhabitants of cities." However, even in these domains, "In most instances [...] it is by no means necessary that government engage in the actual management of such activities."[16]

In the remarks closing this chapter, Hayek states that "within the limits set by the rule of law, a great deal can be done to make the market work more effectively and smoothly; but, within these limits, what people now regard as distributive justice can never be achieved." What follows is that "distributive justice requires an allocation of all resources by a central authority; it requires that people be told what to do and what ends to serve. Where distributive justice is the goal, the decisions as to what the different individuals must be made to do cannot be derived from general rules but must be made in the light of the particular aims and knowledge of the planning authority."[17] Justice so conceived stands in conflict with both the liberal ideals of freedom and the rule of law. The remaining parts of *The Constitution of Liberty* are to a large extent a polemic against those who have been actively advocating the practical introduction of such an ideal of justice into social life.[18]

---

[15] Ibidem, p. 183.

[16] "The services in question can generally be provided, and more effectively, by the government's assuming some or all of the financial responsibility but leaving the conduct of the affairs to independent and in some measure competitive agencies." Ibidem, p. 333.

[17] Cf. ibidem, p. 232.

[18] According to Hayek, this question arose in the days of the French revolution and would frequently be revived with the different waves of social change: "The four chief movements

Postscript

Hayek himself wrote something of a post scriptum to *The Constitution of Liberty* when he answered the question "Why am I not a conservative?" It is worth taking a closer look at this response, as it contains an attempt to make key liberal ideas more specific by juxtaposing them to those of its most formidable opponent until the dawn of socialism, but also an effort to eliminate certain crucial conceptual misunderstandings concerning liberalism, conservatism and socialism. This confusion over terms has to a large extent arisen from the fact that many American radicals and socialists "began calling themselves 'liberals.'" As a result, the term 'liberal' in the United States is the cause of constant misunderstandings today. In Europe, on the other hand, conceptual misunderstandings "would arise because the predominant type of rationalistic liberalism has long been one of the pacemakers of socialism." Thus we must address the question why a liberal is not a socialist. In Hayek's view, the conceptual framework is a tripartite one, where the position on the right wing is occupied by conservatism, and on the left by socialism – with liberalism positioning itself somewhere in the centre.

Starting with the adherents of conservatism, Hayek states that it is impossible for him or any other liberal – given his understanding of liberalism – to accept the attitude and convictions of a conservative, as these amount to an attitude principally opposed to radical change, while "Liberalism is not averse to evolution and change; and where spontaneous change has been smothered by government control, it wants a great deal of change of policy." This is only the beginning of a longer list of various differences between the conservative and liberal doctrines. These include 1. "one of the fundamental traits of the conservative attitude is a fear of change, a timid distrust of the new as such, while the liberal position is based on courage and confidence, on a preparedness to let change run its course even if we cannot predict where it will lead;" 2. the lack of faith in "the spontaneous forces of adjustment which makes the liberal accept changes without apprehension, even though he does not know how the necessary adaptations will be brought about;" 3. "The conservative feels safe and content only if he is assured that some higher wisdom watches and supervises change, only if he knows that some authority is charged with keeping the change 'orderly'" (it goes without saying that a liberal does not require such assurances). According to Hayek, "the most objectionable feature

which operated in this direction were, in descending order of importance, legal positivism, historicism, the "free law" school, and the school of 'jurisprudence of interest.'" Ibidem, p. 344.

of the conservative attitude is its propensity to reject well-substantiated new knowledge because it dislikes some of the consequences which seem to follow from it – or, to put it bluntly, its obscurantism [...]. By refusing to face the facts, the conservative only weakens his own position. Frequently the conclusions which rationalist presumption draws from new scientific insights do not at all follow from them. But only by actively taking part in the elaboration of the consequences of new discoveries do we learn whether or not they fit into our world picture and, if so, how." This method of undermining the stock of social knowledge obviously does not have a rational justification, nor is it likely to bring about new scientific discoveries.

Hayek's observations concerning socialism appear both in fragments where he points to the differences between liberalism and conservatism (such as the inclinations to economic protectionism or the lack of respect for free enterprise) and in those passages where he discusses the conceptual frames and social practices specific to socialism ("the crude rationalism of the socialist, who wants to reconstruct all social institutions according to a pattern prescribed by his individual reason"). On the whole, however, the remarks on socialism have a distinctly fragmentary nature within this passage.

A much more expansive analysis of socialism is included in *The Constitution of Liberty*, and especially in the 17th chapter of Part III ("Freedom in the Welfare State"). Hayek states, for instance, that "The common aim of all socialist movements was the nationalisation of the "means of production, distribution, and exchange," so that all economic activity might be directed according to a comprehensive plan toward some ideal of social justice."[19] This type of collectivisation under the slogans of social justice ended in great disenchantment and the fall of socialism, yet it was not so long ago that "doctrinaire socialism appeared as the main danger to liberty."

His other treatise mentioned above, *The Road to Serfdom*, also stems from the period when socialism presented a viable threat to freedom. In this book many different types of liberalism were treated the same, and various distinctions between the different kinds of socialism were ignored. This simplification seemed justified by the consciously employed device of bipolar juxtaposition of friends and foes, which remains typical of political publications. The list of the enemies of freedom is headed up by the French utopian socialist from the early decades of the 19th century, and concluded by the Soviet communists of the first half of the 20th century. What unites them is the slogan of emancipation from the tyranny of political power, the tyranny of material needs

[19] "Socialism meant the common ownership of the means of production and their 'employment for use, not for profit.'" Ibidem, p. 368.

as well as many other kinds of tyranny. Those who place their trust in such slogans, and followed the paths they described, did not find the promised land of freedom, but one of serfdom – the unfreedom of the socialist organisation of life, the oppression of more complete centralisation of the economy, and thus oppression by the central planners and their belief in the possession of superior knowledge concerning the actual needs and duties within society. All this in fact boils down to submission to various forms of totalitarianism – starting with the totalitarianism of the power which holds all the decision-making capacities, and ending with the totalitarianism of propaganda, which proves "destructive of all morals because they undermine one of the foundations of all morals, the sense of and the respect for truth."[20]

A supplement to this criticism of socialism is *The Fatal Conceit*, a book Hayek published in 1988. Its central thesis is directly connected to issues of rationality and irrationality, especially in relation to social planning and implementation in social life. This thesis implies that those who, like socialists, "demand a deliberate arrangement of human interaction by central authority based on collective command over available resources," are in fact falsely assuming that "since people had been able to generate some system of rules coordinating their efforts, they must also be able to design an even better and more gratifying system." This task of planning and implementing a perfect systemic solution is supposed to be undertaken by the Reason which socialists ascribe to central authorities.[21] The problem with this belief is not only that the trust in the existence of such a superior Reason is groundless, but also that it can easily "destroy much of present humankind and impoverish much of the rest."

It is in this text that Hayek indicates the wrong assumptions and beliefs underpinning socialism, and juxtaposes them to the assumptions and beliefs shared by liberals, which can in turn demonstrate their rationality in approaching social life. Most of these have already been mentioned, including: 1. the notion of "an extended order that runs counter to some of their strongest instincts;" 2. the notion of a human mind that "is not a guide but a product of cultural evolution, and is based more on imitation than on insight or reason;" as well as 3. a social rationality that does not and indeed cannot have fully

[20] Cf. F. A. von Hayek, *The Road to Serfdom*, London 2001, p. 159.

[21] "This book, like some of my earlier studies, is directed against the traditional norms of reason that guide socialism: norms that I believe embody a naive and uncritical theory of rationality, an obsolete and unscientific methodology that I have elsewhere called 'constructivist rationalism.'" Cf. F. A. von Hayek, *The Fatal Conceit. The Errors of Socialism*, Chicago 1988, p. 8. This is Hayek's reference to his *Law, Legislation and Liberty* (London 1973). According to M. Kuniński, "Hayek is opposed to any conceptions which include the element of axiological creationism, whatever their concrete nature – be it rationalism or voluntarism." Cf. M. Kuniński, *Wiedza, etyka i polityka...* [Knowledge, ethics, and politics...], op. cit., p. 216.

specified aims, because in the extended order most objectives are assumed unconsciously and without reflection, but a social rationality that remains a form of rationality as long as it does not fall into the fatal conceit of reason. A detailed analysis of these elements would surely bring vital extensions to the treatment of Hayek's conception of rationality.

2. John Rawls

Rawls (1921–2002) studied philosophy at Princeton, and later at Cornell University as well as Oxford University (Christ Church). He spent the academic year of 1952/53 at Oxford as a Fulbright Scholar, which allowed him to take part in seminars led by Isaiah Berlin and Stuart Hampshire. After his return to the United States, he became an assistant professor at Cornell University. In the years 1960–1962 he was a professor at MIT, and later on at Harvard University until his retirement in 1991. He received most acclaim for two works: *Theory of Justice* (1971) and *Political Liberalism* (1992). It was here that he presented the creed of political liberalism, but also his doctrine of social rationality.

His key "intuitive ideas" were already outlined in the first four paragraphs of the first chapter. At the outset of these considerations he assumes "the first virtue of social institutions," which is that "the rights secured by justice are not subject to political bargaining or to the calculus of social interests."[22] These two fundamental assumptions are complemented by the further stipulations that 1. "a society is a more or less self-sufficient association of persons who in their relations to one another recognise certain rules of conduct as binding and who for the most part act in accordance with them;" and 2. "these rules specify a system of co-operation designed to advance the good of those taking part in it." However, he also writes that "a society is well-ordered when it is not only designed to advance the good of its members but when it is also effectively regulated by a public conception of justice. That is, it is a society in which 1. everyone accepts and knows that the others accept the same principles of justice, and 2. the basic social institutions generally satisfy and are generally known to satisfy these principles." From this, it follows that "[o]ne may think of a public conception of justice as constituting the fundamental charter of a well-ordered human association." It seems clear, therefore, that badly ordered human associations do not have an overreaching and commonly shared concept of justice.[23] However, even in well-ordered associations a cer-

[22] Cf. J. Rawls, *Theory of Justice*, Cambridge, Mass. 1999, p. 5 ff.

[23] This is what happens whenever "[d]istrust and resentment corrode the ties of civility, and suspicion and hostility tempt men to act in ways they would otherwise avoid." Ibidem, p. 6.

tain divergence of opinion may persist as to the question of what is actually just or not. The crux of the matter is that it is not necessary for all members to assume one understanding of rationality, but rather to accept some general principles of justice.

According to Rawls, one should seek these rules in "the way in which the major social institutions distribute fundamental rights and duties and determine the division of advantages from social co-operation." This he calls the "basic structure of society," capable of generating such norms as "the legal protection of freedom of thought and liberty of conscience, competitive markets, private property in the means of production, and the monogamous family." It goes without saying that individuals in society occupy different starting positions (for instance, due to birth) as well as different life-chances (determined by political as well as economic circumstances), and social institutions tend to favour some over others. While these inequalities might be inevitable within the basic structure of any society, "they cannot possibly be justified by an appeal to the notions of merit or desert." It is nevertheless possible, and advisable, to treat individuals according to such rules that allow for an equal distribution of life chances, which in Rawls' view constitutes one key procedural rule of fairness.

In the third paragraph of this chapter, fairness is presented as the main idea behind the theory of justice. Rawls describes the principles that "free and rational persons concerned to further their own interests would accept in an initial position of equality as defining the fundamental terms of their association." To this he adds that "[j]ustice as fairness begins, as I have said, with one of the most general of all choices which persons might make together, namely, with the choice of the first principles of a conception of justice which is to regulate all subsequent criticism and reform of institutions. Then, having chosen a conception of justice, we can suppose that they are to choose a constitution and a legislature to enact laws, and so on, all in accordance with the principles of justice initially agreed upon." Later on he also mentions social systems where individuals endowed with both rationality and an understanding of justice apply reasonable restrictions upon themselves."

In the fourth paragraph of this chapter we find some further specifications of the "original situation", including remarks expanding on the understanding of the notion of rationality. This notion is not only conceived of as a cognitive quality of the individual, but also implies modes of action, which imply the selection of actions which are characterised by superior rationality, from the social point of view. ("This connects the theory of justice with the theory of rational choice.") Choices can be considered rational whenever they have some justification not only in the knowledge of the choosing agents, but can also be justified from the point of view of the "original situation," and in relation to the social consequences of those choices. "The aim is to rule out those principles that it would be rational to propose for acceptance, however little the chance of success, only if one knew certain things that are irrelevant from the standpoint of justice."[24]

What comes next is the reference to the concept of 1. *understanding* ("each man is presumed to have the requisite ability to understand and to act upon whatever principles are adopted"); 2. *veil of ignorance* (accompanying both the choices of the principles of action and their implementation). These mean that "One excludes the knowledge of those contingencies, which sets men at odds and allows them to be guided by their prejudices." Thus, such principles are implied which are able to guide us, when needed, by reference to our strongest convictions.

After providing this justification for the initial situation, Rawls presents a short description of the mode of operation which allows for reaching the strongest possible convictions: "We begin by describing it so that it represents generally shared and preferably weak conditions. We then see if these conditions are strong enough to yield a significant set of principles. If not, we look for further premises equally reasonable. But if so, and these principles match our considered convictions of justice, then so far well and good. But presumably there will be discrepancies. In this case we have a choice. We can either modify the account of the initial situation or we can revise our existing judgments, for even the judgments we take provisionally as fixed points are liable to revision. By going back and forth, sometimes altering the conditions of the contractual circumstances, at others withdrawing our judgments and conforming them to principle, I assume that eventually we shall find a description of the initial situation that both expresses reasonable conditions and yields principles which match our considered judgments duly pruned and adjusted. This state of affairs I refer to as reflective equilibrium."[25] However, this remains a relative and transient equilibrium as it does not rest upon self-evident truths ("A conception of justice cannot be deduced from self-evident premises or conditions on principles"), but rather on consideration whose value remains purely hypothetical, and one has to take into account that the consideration of specific cases might lead to the corroboration or falsification of particular hypotheses. This opens the forum for discussing the criteria of choosing the hypotheses.

[24] "[...] if a man knew that he was wealthy, he might find it rational to advance the principle that various taxes for welfare measures be counted unjust." Ibidem, p. 16.

[25] "This state of affairs I refer to as reflective equilibrium. It is an equilibrium because at last our principles and judgments coincide; and it is reflective since we know to what principles our judgments conform and the premises of their derivation." Ibidem, p. 18.

In the foreword to the *Theory of Justice*, Rawls states that the utilitarians (such as Hume, Smith, Bentham and Mill) "were social theorists and economists of the first rank; and the moral doctrine they worked out was framed to meet the needs of their wider interests and to fit into a comprehensive scheme." In the opening paragraphs of the first chapter, he provides further justification for holding the utilitarians in such high esteem, and also outlines the foundations of their ideas. These foundations comprise such a conception of man, whereby "each man in realising his own interests is certainly free to balance his own losses against his own gains." Given that he seems to be good at what he is doing, "why should not a society act on precisely the same principle applied to the group and therefore regard that which is rational for one man as right for an association of men?" Subsequently, Rawls enumerates all the reasons for the rationality and attractiveness of the utilitarian approach, including the combination of individual utility with that of a group, or combining the understanding of social rationality with the principle of "rational prudence applied to an aggregative conception of the welfare of the group."

In a subsequent paragraph, Rawls indicates mismatches between the idea of justice as fairness and the idea of justice as utility. In the former, the basic freedoms are treated as self-evident and hence the laws based on justice cannot be subject to political haggling or the calculus of social utility, while in the latter view they can. "A second contrast is that whereas the utilitarian extends to society the principle of choice for one man, justice as fairness, [...] assumes that the principles of social choice [...] are themselves the object of an original agreement. [...] The last contrast that I shall mention now is that utilitarianism is a teleological theory whereas justice as fairness is not. By definition, then, the latter is a deontological theory, one that either does not specify the good independently from the right, or does not interpret the right as maximising the good..."[26]

These and other differences between these two conceptions are supposed to lead to the conclusion that utilitarianism might be a rational approach, although its rationality remains weaker than that of Rawls's conception. In justification of this view, Rawls suggests a discussion of intuitionism (also referred to as "pluralism"), as a perspective enriching his own views, yet, just as utilitarianism, requiring substantial improvements.[27] These improvements concern both the principles of justice and the procedures of their selection.

[26] "The question of attaining the greatest net balance of satisfaction never arises in justice as fairness; this maximum principle is not used at all." Ibidem, p. 27.

[27] "Now there is nothing intrinsically irrational about this intuitionist doctrine. Indeed, it may be true. We cannot take for granted that there must be a complete derivation of our judgments of social justice from recognisably ethical principles. The intuitionist believes to the

In the second chapter of *Theory of Justice*, Rawls lists the two principles of justice, which are situated at the level of the "initial situation." The first states that "each person is to have an equal right to the most extensive scheme of equal basic liberties compatible with a similar scheme of liberties for others." The second stipulates that "social and economic inequalities are to be arranged so that they are both (a) reasonably expected to be to everyone's advantage, and (b) attached to positions and offices open to all."[28] In the rest of the chapter, Rawls attempts to demonstrate that the choice of these two principles is not only in itself the most rational one, but also that it brings about social outcomes which prove rational, such as rational expectations, rational priorities or rational planning.

In the third chapter, he comes back to the analysis of the initial situation, with special attention devoted to examining the rationality of attitudes and ways of thinking and acting of the particular social agents. He states that "I have assumed throughout that the persons in the original position are rational," which means that they try to pursue their interests to the best of their ability. Without the capacity to "know his conception of the good, the particulars of his rational plan of life, or even the special features of his psychology such as his aversion to risk or liability to optimism or pessimism." Rawls's way out of this situation is the assumption of such an understanding of rationality in the light of which "a rational person is thought to have a coherent set of preferences between the options open to him. He ranks these options according to how well they further his purposes; he follows the plan which will satisfy more of his desires rather than less, and which has the greater chance of being successfully executed."

Such an understanding of rationality has the qualities of an ideal type, with the complementary assumption that "a rational individual does not suffer from envy."[29] In practice, people have preferences that vary when it comes to the degree of their coherence, and are sometimes free from and on other

contrary that the complexity of the moral facts defies our efforts to give a full account of our judgments and necessitates a plurality of competing principles." Ibidem, p. 35.

[28] "These principles primarily apply [...] to the basic structure of society and govern the assignment of rights and duties and regulate the distribution of social and economic advantages." Ibidem, p. 53.

[29] "He is not downcast by the knowledge or perception that others have a larger index of primary social goods. Or at least this is true as long as the differences between himself and others do not exceed certain limits, and he does not believe that the existing inequalities are founded on injustice or are the result of letting chance work itself out for no compensating social purpose" (ibidem, s. 199). A broader discussion of the idealisations present in the thought of J. Rawls and the political philosophy of liberalism is contained in P. Przybysz, "O ideale liberalnym. Uwagi o zastosowaniu idealizacji w filozofii politycznej liberalizmu" [On the Liberal

occasions enslaved by envy. What Rawls is concerned with are not so much the particulars of human action, but a general pattern we should be able to refer to while discussing justice and the kind of social rationality that it implies.

The treatise *Political Liberalism* contains important expansions of Rawls' idea of rationality, but also certain modifications of his theory of justice as fairness. Too some extent it can be seen as a polemic in response to the communitarian criticisms of his theory. He readily admits to lacking some crucial elements in his theory, including "1. the idea of justice as fairness as a freestanding view and that of an overlapping consensus as belonging to its account of stability; 2. the distinction between simple pluralism and reasonable pluralism, together with the idea of a reasonable comprehensive doctrine; and 3. a fuller account of the reasonable and the rational worked into the conception of political (as opposed to moral) constructivism, so as to bring out the bases of the principles of right and justice in practical reason."[30] In general, Rawls is convinced that his explanations would lead to a better understanding of political liberalism, as well as improved comprehension of its underlying concepts of reasonableness and rationality.

The content of the book is based on academic lectures, the first three chapters on lectures delivered at Columbia University in 1980. He attempts to sketch a general philosophical background of political liberalism, embedding it in the notion of practical reason. This general background includes 1. a democratic society which enables "social co-operation between citizens characterised as free and equal," as well as a political culture "marked by a diversity of opposing and irreconcilable religious, philosophical, and moral doctrines. Some of these are perfectly reasonable, and this diversity among reasonable doctrines political liberalism sees as the inevitable long-run result of the powers of human reason at work within the background of enduring free institutions." Inquiry into the first of these tenets leads to the question: "What is the most appropriate conception of justice for specifying the fair terms of social co-operation between citizens regarded as free and equal, and as fully co-operating members of society over a complete life, from one generation to the next?" With respect to the second tenet the following question arises: "What are the grounds of toleration so understood, given the fact of reasonable pluralism as the inevitable outcome of free institutions?"

The problem of reasonableness and rationality is involved in the attempt to answer both of these questions. In the first case, it comes into play in the following way: "The problem of political liberalism is to work out a concep-

Ideal. Remarks on the Uses of Idealisation in the Political Philosophy of Liberalism], *Principia*, XV, 1996, pp. 107–122.

[30] Cf. J. Rawls, *Political Liberalism*, Expanded Edition, New York 2005, p. 30.

tion of political justice for a constitutional democratic regime that the plurality of reasonable doctrines – always a feature of the culture of a free democratic regime – might endorse."[31] The solution is sought, and in Rawls' view actually found in the principle of justice as fairness "that fits into and can be supported by various reasonable comprehensive doctrines that endure in the society regulated by it." The analysis of this match between justice and reasonable doctrines leads to the idea of a "well-ordered society," i.e., one that satisfies the following conditions: 1. "a society effectively regulated by a public political conception of justice; 2. "its basic structure – that is, its main political and social institutions and how they fit together as one system of co-operation – is publicly known, or with good reason believed, to satisfy these principles;" 3. "its citizens have a normally effective sense of justice and so they generally comply with society's basic institutions, which they regard as just."[32] Towards the end of this analysis, Rawls returns to the idea of reasonable pluralism, that is one that, unlike simple pluralism, is more than the inevitable result of the operation of human free will, but actually leads to the superior organisation of society, including the legalisation and strengthening of "an enduring and secure democratic regime, one not divided into contending doctrinal confessions and hostile social classes," which must be "willingly and freely supported by at least a substantial majority of its politically active citizens."

Before further analysis of this pluralism and the attempt to answer the second of the two key questions stated in *Political Liberalism*, Rawls considers the question: "What is it that distinguishes the reasonable from the rational?" To formulate an answer he claims that "persons are reasonable in one basic aspect when, among equals say, they are ready to propose principles and standards as fair terms of co-operation and to abide by them willingly, given the assurance that others will likewise do so." On the other hand, the reasonable is connected to the rational, but also distinct, and it "applies to a single, unified agent (either an individual or corporate person) with the powers of judgment and deliberation in seeking ends and interests peculiarly its own. The rational applies to how these ends and interests are adopted and affirmed, as well as to how they are given priority. It also applies to the choice of means, in which case it is guided by such familiar principles as: to adopt the most effective means to ends, or to select the more probable alternative, other things equal."[33]

Further on he notes that "rational agents are not limited to means-ends reasoning, as they may balance final ends by their significance for their plan of

[31] "Gaining this support of reasonable doctrines lays the basis for answering our second fundamental question..." Ibidem, p. 10.

[32] "In such a society the publicly recognised conception of justice establishes a shared point of view from which citizens' claims on society can be adjudicated." Ibidem, p. 35.

[33] Ibidem, p. 50.

life as a whole, and by how well these ends cohere with and complement one another. Nor are rational agents as such solely self-interested." He states that "rational agents may have all kinds of affections for persons and attachments to communities and places, including love of country and of nature; and they may select and order their ends in various ways." In short, such a picture of rationality has many different facets and is intertwined with many different spheres of social life and human co-operation. A similar observation holds true of reasonableness – although it is a complementary idea to rationality and both of them need each other, neither can be seen as determined by the other, because the former contains "the particular form of moral sensibility that underlies the desire to engage in fair co-operation as such, and to do so on terms that others as equals might reasonably be expected to endorse." This and other differences between the rational and the reasonable discussed in *Political Liberalism* underlie, in Rawls's view, the misunderstanding of this part of the *Theory of Justice*, where it is stated with regard to the original situation that it "connects the theory of justice with the theory of rational choice."[34]

In the second lecture published in *Political Liberalism* – "Powers of Citizens and Their Representation" – the analysis of the reasonable and the rational is two-pronged, in that it oscillates between answering the first and the second question. For instance, in the second section of this lecture, Rawls starts with the statement that "the first basic aspect of the reasonable, then, is the willingness to propose fair terms of co-operation and to abide by them provided others do. The second basic aspect [...] is the willingness to recognise the burdens of judgment and to accept their consequences for the use of public reason in directing the legitimate exercise of political power in a constitutional regime." In places he connects both of these aspects to the reasonable, for instance in the case of "reasonable disagreement." Soon enough, however, he moves to the discussion of the rational: "As reasonable and rational we have to make different kinds of judgments. As rational we have to balance our various ends and estimate their appropriate place in our way of life; and doing this confronts us with grave difficulties in making correct judgments of rationality." Among other things he connects this to the problem of reasonableness, because "as reasonable we must assess the strength of peoples' claims."[35] In the final passages of this lecture we encounter a reference to the multi-faceted "reasonable moral psychology," with some of its many aspects, such as the

[34] "What should have been said is that the account of the parties, and of their reasoning, uses the theory of rational decision, though only in an intuitive way." Ibidem, p. 53, footnote 7.

[35] "In addition, there is the reasonable as it applies to our beliefs and schemes of thought, or the reasonable as appraising our use of our theoretical (and not our moral and practical) powers." Ibidem, p. 56.

capacity to retain a conception of good, or judgements concerning justice. In spite of moments in other lectures where he attempts to discern the exact moment when we should stop referring to the reasonable and start speaking of the rational, in the end we can justify the opinion that we must be resigned to rather intuitive understandings.

Rawls investigated the nature of such intuitive understanding in the third lecture, devoted to the tenets of "political constructivism," which he distinguishes from Kantian moral constructivism and from "rational intuitionism as a form of moral realism." In Rawls's view the idea of political constructivism boils down to the belief "that the principles of political justice (content) may be represented as the outcome of a procedure of construction (structure)."[36] In constructivism of this kind "the procedure of construction is based essentially on practical reason and not on theoretical reason." The remaining lectures allow for at least a partial elucidation of the meaning of this assertion.

Before concluding this exposition of Rawls's views, I would just like to mention briefly the content of the remaining lectures. In lecture five he analyses the problem of the "priority of right" ("it has a central role in justice as fairness"), as well as uses of the notion of the good where "accepting the political conception does not presuppose accepting any particular comprehensive religious, philosophical, or moral doctrine." In the conclusion of these analyses he states that in such cases it also proves crucial to relate to the distinction between the reasonable and the rational made in political liberalism. In lecture six, he focuses on "the idea of public reason," not only to distinguish between "nonpublic reasons of churches and universities and of many other associations in civil society," but also to be able to prove that it is characteristic of a democratic society. Lecture seven discuses "the basic structure as subject" to demonstrate what this structure is and how it is supposed to influence individuals. Lecture eight discusses "basic liberties," not only listing them, but also presenting the reasons underlying their special status, inherent to assuming their primacy in the original situation.

Postscript

Political Liberalism contains a polemic against challenges to the theory of justice as fairness, as formulated by the communitarians. Their general allegation amounts to the contention that the liberal individualism assumed by this theory generates a series of negative consequences for public life and social bonds.

---

[36] "In this procedure rational agents, as representatives of citizens and subject to reasonable conditions, select the principles to regulate the basic structure of society." Ibidem, p. 93.

One of these communitarians was Alasdair MacIntyre, the author of *After Virtue*.[37] In his view, Rawls and the other defenders of liberal individualism do not recognise that allowing for a high degree of moral pluralism when it comes to diversity of human convictions makes public discourse on moral questions degenerate into endless squabbling, without the possibility of objective superiority of some moral standards over others. In short, pluralism in the domain of morality is supposed to lead towards arbitrariness and instrumentalism, with the impossibility of distinguishing instrumental from non-instrumental social relations. At the same time, with regard to consciousness it is supposed to lead to the defence of the modern ego, conceived as a set of open possibilities without any necessity. In the sphere of norms and judgements it is seen to lead to de-standardisation, which means modern man lacks a proper anchor in the social structure, and is resigned to a hopeless drifting without direction or destination.[38]

Theory of Justice has also been criticised from the communitarian standpoint by Michael Sandel. He claimed, for instance in *Liberalism and the Limits of Justice*, that due to the assumption that a human being is an agent choosing aims rather than receiving them, this theory leads or at least may lead to deep social disintegration and to the breaking of social bonds which determine both the social identity and the common interests of the participants in social life. In his view, this could be countered by taking pro-active stances in defence of the social majority, for example one should allow for a city to ban pornography "on the grounds that pornography offends its way of life."[39]

The solutions based on the theory of justice as fairness were also criticised by Michael Walzer. In the treatise *Philosophy and Democracy* he countered the liberals in offering a defence of the non-philosophical majority from the philosophical minority. In his view, "Democracy has no claims in the philosophical realm, and philosophers have no special rights in the political community."[40] As to the question of what stands behind the authority of the law, the thinks that it is not the reason of philosophers, but rather the social will, and therefore people are likely to accept not what is rational but whatever they find agreeable. From Walzer's point of view, and that of other communitarians (such as John Hart Ely, the author of *Democracy and Distrust*), democracy cannot entirely dispense with philosophers, as they have an important role to play when it

---

[37] Cf. A. MacIntyre, *After Virtue*, Notre Dame 1981. A polemic against the assumptions made in the *Theory of Justice* can also be found in his PhD thesis entitled *Whose Justice? Which Rationality?*, Notre Dame 1988.

[38] Cf. A. MacIntyre, *After Virtue*, op. cit., p. 30.

[39] Cf. ibidem, p. 6.

[40] Cf. M. Walzer, "Philosophy and Democracy," *Political Theory*, 1981, no. 9, p. 388.

comes to the rational criticism of irrational prohibitions and demands. Setting the standards of such a critique, Walzer writes that it should be an immanent critique, looking not so much for the ideal city, but for an ideal dwelling for a small community.

In response to these and other criticisms of the theory of justice as fairness, Rawls recapitulates what is meant by "first subject of justice," i.e., the basic structure, and why he declares its primacy. ("We must begin somewhere, and this starting point may turn out to be justified by how well the theory that results hangs together.") He also explains the status of the rules established at this point Their status is conventional, i.e., they are a sort of social contract created by free, equal and moral individuals capable of rational thought and conduct. He subsequently addresses the question of how theoretical unity can be reached within such contracts, by claiming that the parties should move forward in a way which respects that "the principles of each later agreement are to be subordinate to those of all earlier agreements, or else adjusted to them by certain priority rules. The underlying unity is provided by the idea that free and equal moral persons are to construct reasonable and helpful guidelines for moral reflection in view of their need for such organising principles and the role in social life that these principles and their corresponding subjects are presumed to have."[41]

After answering these questions Rawls moves on to challenges posed from the libertarian perspective, and his stance can be reduced to the statement that "libertarianism has no special role for the basic structure," while he argues that "a minimal state limited to the narrow functions of protection against force, theft, fraud, enforcement of contracts, and so on, is justified; and that any state with more comprehensive powers violates the rights of individuals." Rawls admits that his presentation of the libertarian stance is based on Robert Nozick's *Anarchy, State and Utopia*.[42] In the Seventh Lecture of *Political Liberalism*, Rawls is chiefly concerned with the argument against the idea of a minimal state – a state that he sees as derived from the state of nature, and striving to retain as much as possible from that state. Libertarians seem to defend the idea of such a state, within which there are no entitlements or principles, and "there are no powers or rights lawfully exercised by associations, including the state, that are not rights already possessed by each individual acting alone in the initial just state of nature."

---

[41] Cf. J. Rawls, *Political Liberalism...*, op. cit., p. 262.

[42] In this book R. Nozick not only presents the idea a minimal state but also declares in the introduction that no larger form of statehood can be justified. Cf. R. Nozick, *Anarchy, State, Utopia*, New York 1974, p. 8 ff.

In the Eighth Lecture, Rawls takes on the criticism of Herbert Hart, that the theory of justice has two major gaps, because "the grounds upon which the parties in the original position adopt the basic liberties and agree to their priority are not sufficiently explained," and furthermore, "when the principles of justice are applied at the constitutional, legislative, and judicial stages, no satisfactory criterion is given for how the basic liberties are to be further specified and adjusted to one another as social circumstances are made known." To a certain extent, Rawls accepts the merits of these challenges, although he claims that the deficiencies were clarified in his "Dewey Lectures" and also indicates 1. "the special status of basic liberties" ("They have an absolute weight with respect to reasons of public good and of perfectionist values"); 2. the concept of a human person assumed on the basis of his theories (a person that can be understood in relation to such concepts as *homo politicus, homo economicus* as well as *homo faber*); 3. the assumed concept of the good and definition of the "primary goods."

In summarising these extensions, Rawls claims that "Hart is correct in saying that the priority of liberty cannot be argued for by imputing this ideal of the person to the parties in the original position; and he is right also in supposing that a conception of the person in some sense liberal underlies the argument for the priority of liberty. But this conception is the altogether different conception of citizens as free and equal persons; and it does not enter justice as fairness by imputation to the parties. Rather, it enters through the constraints of the reasonable imposed on the parties in the original position as well as in the revised account of primary goods." In this way, Rawls confirms that an indispensable role is played in his theory by freedom and equality, as well as the reasonable and the rational. It appears indisputable that his description and explanation of the "basic structure" cannot do without them. What remains disputable, however, is the decision as to which of these should be primary from the point of view of contemporary Western societies, while Rawls's opinion is firm, that primacy should be assigned to the reasons for maintaining basic liberties.

Bibliography

Aristotle, *Nicomachean Ethics*, Cambridge University Press, Cambridge 2000.
Aristotle, *Politics*, trans. B. Jowett, Oxford University Press, Oxford 1908.
Alberti L. B., *The Family in Renaissance Florence*, University of South Carolina Press, South Carolina 1969.
Barry N., *Hayek's Social and Economic Philosophy*, Macmillan, London 1979.
Baszkiewicz J., *Historia Francji* [The History of France], Zakład Narodowy im. Ossolińskich, Wroclaw 1974.
Beccaria C., *An Essay on Crimes and Punishments*, International Pocket Library, London 1983.
Bocheński J. M., Lewica, religia, sowietologia [The political left, religion, sovietology], Morex, Warsaw 1996.
Courtois S., Werth N., Panné J.-L., Paczkowski A., Bartosek K., Margolin J.-L., *The Black Book of Communism*, Cambridge, Harvard University Press, Cambridge – London 1999.
Descartes R., *Discourse on the Method*, in *The Philosophical Writings of Descartes*, vol. I, Cambridge University Press, Cambridge 1985.
Diogenes Laertius, *The Lives and Opinions of Eminent Philosophers*, George Bell and Sons, London 1853.
Drozdowicz Z., *Liberalizm europejski* [European Liberalism], Wydawnictwo Forum Naukowe, Poznan 2005.
Duroselle J. B., *Les débuts de catholicisme sociale en France (1822–1870)*, Presses universitaires de France, Paris 1951.
Engels F., *Ludwig Feuerbach and the End of Classical German Philosophy*, Foreign Languages Press, Peking 1976.
Engels F., "Speech at the Grave of Karl Marx," in F. Engels, *On Marx*, Foreign Languages Press, Peking 1975.
Engels F., *Socialism: Utopian and Scientific*, Charles H. Kerr and Company, Chicago 1908.
Fauget É., *Liberalizm* [Liberalism], Lwów (n d.).
Fauré Ch. (ed.), *Les déclarations des droits de l'homme de 1789*, Paris 1988.
Filozofia niemieckiego Oświecenia. Wybrane teksty z historii filozofii [Philosophy of German Enlightenment. History of Philosophy: Selected Sources], PWN, Warsaw 1973.
Friederick II, *Die Politischen Testamenten*, Verlag Heinz Treu, München 1941.
Gamble A., *Hayek: The Iron Cage of Liberty*, Polity Press, Cambridge 1966.
Gray A., *Liberalism*, University of Minnesota Press, Minneapolis 1995.

Hayek F. A. von, *Law, Legislation and Liberty*, Routledge, London 1973.

Hayek F. A. von, *The Constitution of Liberty: The Definitive Edition (The Collected Works of F.A. Hayek)*, R. Hamowy (ed.), vol. 17, University of Chicago Press, Chicago 2011.

Hayek F. A. von, *The Fatal Conceit. The Errors of Socialism*, University of Chicago Press, Chicago 1988.

Hayek F. A. von, *The Road to Serfdom*, Routledge, London 2001.

Heller M., Nekrich A., *Utopia in Power: The History of the Soviet Union from 1917 to the Present*, Summit Books, New York 1988.

Himmelfarb G., *The Roads to Modernity. The British, French, and American Englightenments*, Knopf, New York 2004.

Hobbes T., *Leviathan; Or, The Matter, Form, and Power of a Commonwealth Ecclesiastical and Civil*, George Routledge and Sons, London 1886.

Jaurès, J., "Bernstein i ewolucja metody socjalistycznej" [Bernstein and the evolution of the socialist method], in *Wybór pism* [Selected Writings], Książka i Wiedza, Warsaw 1970.

Jaurès J., "Ewolucja rewolucyjna" [Revolutionary evolution], in *Wybór pism* [Selected Writings], Książka i Wiedza, Warsaw 1970.

Jaurès J., "U źródeł socjalizmu niemieckiego" [The origins of German socialism], in *Wybór pism* [Selected Writings], Książka i Wiedza, Warsaw 1970.

Johansson U., *Transformation of Gendered Work: Dualistic Stereotypes and Paradoxical Reality*, Lund University, Lund 1997.

Keynes J. M., *The General Theory of Employment, Interest and Money*, Harcourt, New York 1936.

Klapisch-Zuber Ch., "Women and the family," in J. Le Goff (ed.), *Medieval Callings*, University of Chicago Press, Chicago 1990.

Kołakowski L., *Main Currents of Marxism. Its Rise Growth and Dissolution*, vol. I: *The Founders*, Oxford University Press, Oxford 1978.

Kołakowski L., *Main Currents of Marxism. Its Rise Growth and Dissolution*, vol. II: *The Golden Age*, Oxford University Press, Oxford 1978.

Kozyr-Kowalski S., Ładosz J., *Dialektyka a społeczeństwo. Wstęp do materializmu historycznego* [Dialectic and society. An introduction to historical materialism], PWN, Warsaw 1972.

Krasuski J., *Historia Niemiec* [The History of Germany], Zakład Narodowy im. Ossolińskich, Wroclaw – Warsaw – Cracow 2004.

Kuniński M., *Wiedza, etyka i polityka w myśli F.A. von Hayeka* [Knowledge, ethics, and politics in the thought of F. A. von Hayek], Księgarnia Akademicka, Cracow 1999.

Le Goff J., *Medieval Callings*, University of Chicago Press, Chicago 1990.

Lenin V. I., "First All-Russia Congress of Soviets of Workers' and Soldiers' Deputies," in *Collected Works*, vol. 25, Progress Publishers, Moscow 1977.

Lenin V. I., "Marxism and Revisionism," in *Collected Works*, vol. 15, Progress Publishers, Moscow 1973.

Lenin V. I., "On Slogans," in *Collected Works*, vol. 25, Progress Publishers, Moscow 1977.

Lenin V. I., "One Step Forward, Two Steps Back," in *Collected Works*, vol. 7, Progress Publishers, Moscow 1965.

Lenin V. I., "On the Slogan for a United States of Europe," in *Collected Works*, vol. 21, Progress Publishers, Moscow 1974.

Lenin V. I., "Opportunism, and the Collapse of the Second International," in *Collected Works*, vol. 21, Progress Publishers, Moscow 1974.

Lenin V. I., "Role and Functions of the Trade Unions. Under the New Economic Policy," in *Collected Works*, vol. 33, Progress Publishers, Moscow 1965.

Lenin V. I., "The Tasks of the Proletariat in Our Revolution," in *Collected Works*, vol. 24. Progress Publishers, Moscow 1964.

Lenin V. I., *What Is To Be Done?*, Foreign Language Press, Peking 1973.

Locke J., *Four Letters on Toleration*, Alexander Murray, London 1870.

Locke J., *Two Treatises on Government*, T. Tegg, London 1823.

MacIntyre A., *After Virtue*, University of Notre Dame Press, Notre Dame 1981.

MacIntyre A., *Whose Justice? Which Rationality?*, University of Notre Dame Press, Notre Dame 1988.

Machiavelli N., *Discourses on Livy*, University of Chicago Press, Chicago 1996.

Machiavelli N., *The Prince*, Oxford University Press, Oxford 2008.

Manent P., *An Intellectual History of Liberalism*, trans. R. Balinski, Princeton University Press, Princeton 1995.

Mannheihm K., *Ideology and Utopia. An Introduction to the Sociology of Knowledge*, Routledge & Kegan Paul, London 1954.

Marx K., *A Contribution to the Critique of Political Economy. Preface*, Charles H. Kerr & Company, Chicago 1904.

Marx K., *Capital. A critique of political economy*, vol. 1, Progress Publishing, Moscow 1887.

Marx K., *Inaugural Address and Provisional Rules of the International Working Men's Association*, Cautley Newby, London 1864.

Marx K., "Letter to W. Bracke," in *Marx/Engels Selected Works*, vol. 3, Progress Publishing, Moscow 1970.

Marx K., Engels F., "Address of the Central Committee to the Communist League," in F. Engels, *Revolution and Counter-revolution in Germany*, Foreign Languages Press, Peking 1977.

Marx K., Engels F., *Manifesto of the Communist Party*, Foreign Languages Press, Peking 1970.

Marx K., *The Poverty of Philosophy*, Foreign Languages Press, Peking 1978.

Montesquieu, *Persian Letters*, trans. J. Davidson, Routledge and Sons, London 1891.

Montesquieu, *The Spirit of Laws*, trans. M. Richter, Hackett Publishing Company, Indianapolis 1900.

Nozick R., *Anarchy, State, Utopia*, Basic Books, New York 1974.

Plato, *Państwo* [Republic], Antyk, Kęty 2006.

Plato, *The Laws of Plato*, The University of Chicago Press, Chicago – London 1988.

Plato, *The Republic*, Basic Books, New York 1991.

Plato, *The Republic; Statesman*, Walter Dunne Publisher, New York 1901.

Popper K. R., "Przedmowa do czytelnika polskiego" [A foreword to the Polish reader], in *Społeczeństwo otwarte i jego wrogowie* [The Open Society and its Enemies], vol. 1, PWN, Warsaw 1993.

Popper K. R. *The Open Society and its Enemies*, 5th edition revised, Princeton University Press, Princeton 1966.

Popper K. R., *The Poverty of Historicism*, Routledge, London 2002.

Proudhon P.-J., "O sprawiedliwości w rewolucji i w Kościele" [Of Justice in the Revolution and the Church], *Wybór pism* [Selected Writings], vol. 1 and 2, Książka i Wiedza, Warsaw 1974.

Proudhon P. J., *The Evolution of Capitalism. A System of Economical Contradictions, or The Philosophy of Misery*, Kessinger Publishing, Champaign 2004.

Proudhon P. J., *What is Property?*, B. R. Tucker, Princeton 1876.

Przybysz P., "O ideale liberalnym. Uwagi o zastosowaniu idealizacji w filozofii politycznej liberalizmu," [On the Liberal Ideal. Remarks on the Uses of Idealisation in the Political Philosophy of Liberalism], *Principia*, XV, 1996.

Quesnay F., "Farmers [abridged]," *The Encyclopedia of Diderot & d'Alembert Collaborative Translation Project*, trans. N. S. Hoyt and T. Cassirer, MPublishing, Ann Arbor 2005.

Quesnay F., "General Maxims of the Economical Government of in an Agricultural Kingdom," in O. J. Thatcher (ed.), *The Library of Original Sources*, vol. VI: *Advance in Knowledge 1650–1800*, University Press of the Pacific, reprinted from the 1901 edition, 2004.

Quesnay F., "Grains [abridged]," *The Encyclopedia of Diderot & d'Alembert Collaborative Translation Project*, trans. N. S. Hoyt and T. Cassirer, MPublishing, Ann Arbor 2005.

Quesnay F., *Pisma wybrane* [Selected Writings], Cracow 1928.

Ranke L. von, *The History of the Popes: Their Church and State*, Henry G. Bohn, London 1851.

Rawls J., *Political Liberalism*, Expanded Edition, Columbia University Press, New York 2005.

Rawls J., *Theory of Justice*, Belknap Press of Harvard University Press, Cambridge, Mass. 1999.

Reale G., *A History of Ancient Philosophy. II: Plato and Aristotle*, State University of New York, Alabany 1990.

Romano R., *Między dwoma kryzysami. Włochy Renesansu* [Between Two Crises. Italy in the Renaissance], PIW, Warsaw 1978.

Rossi P., *Filozofowie i maszyny* [Men and Maschines], PWN, Warsaw 1978.

Rossi P., *Philosophy, Technology and the Arts in the Early Modern Era*, Harper and Row, New York 1970.

Ruggiero G. de, *The History of European Liberalism*, Beacon Press, Boston 1959.

Shaftesbury A. A. C., *Life, Unpublished Letters, and Philosophical Regimen*, Swan Sonneschein & Co., New York 1900.

Smith A., *An Inquiry into the Nature and Causes of the Wealth of Nations*, P. F. Collier & Son Company, New York 1909.

Talmon J. L., *The Origins of Totalitarian Democracy*, Mercury Books, London 1952.

"The Communist Manifesto," in K. Marx, F. Engels, *Manifesto of the Communist Party*, Peking 1970.

Titone V., *La storiografia dell'illuminismo in Italia*, Mursia, Milano 1969.

Trevelyan G. M., *English Social History: From Chaucer to Victoria*, Longmans, Green & Co., London 1942.

Turgot A. R. J., "Discours sur l'histoire universelle," in *Oeuvres*, vol. II, Paris 1844.

Turgot A. R. J., *Reflections on the Formation and Distribution of Riches*, Macmillan Guillaumin, London 1911.

Walzer M., *On Toleration*, Yale University Press, Yale 1997.

Walzer M., "Philosophy and Democracy," *Political Theory*, 1981, no. 9.

Weber M., *Economy and Society: an Outline of Interpretative Sociology*, University of California Press, Berkeley 1978.

Weber M., *The Protestant Ethics and the Spirit of Capitalism*, Scribner, New York 1930.

Witwicki W., "Wstęp od tłumacza" [Translator's foreword], in *Państwo* [Republic], Antyk, Kęty 2006.

Wołgin W. P., *Poprzednicy naukowego socjalizmu* [The predecessors of scientific Socialism], PWN, Warsaw 1958.

Wollstonecraft M., *A Vindication of the Rights of Woman*, Walter Scott, London 1891.

Zins H., *Historia Anglii* [The History of England], Zakład Narodowy im. Ossolińskich, Wroclaw – Warsaw – Cracow 2001.

Index of persons

* References to footnotes are in italics.

Development in Humanities

edited by Zbigniew Drozdowicz (General Editor) and Sławomir Sztajer (Adam Mickiewicz University, Poznán/Poland)

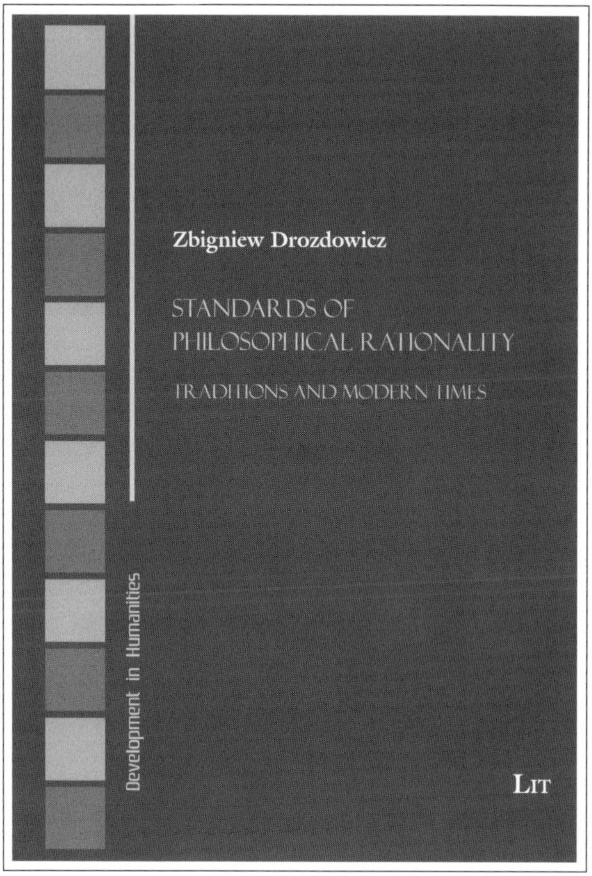

Zbigniew Drozdowicz
Standards of Philosophical Rationality
Traditions and Modern Times
An attempt at pointing out the standards of philosophical rationality corresponds to a philosophy that aspires to be more than wisdom stemming from and addressing everyday human needs. Such extraordinary philosophy searches for those standards that would, as it were, show the way to philosophical wisdom to anyone who is willing and able to assess and appreciate it. One of the problems here is that people have had a different understanding of the basic concept of rationality, which is the rationale.
Zbigniew Drozdowicz is a full professor at Adam Mickiewicz University in Poznan, and the head of the Chair of Religious Studies and Comparative Research
vol. 1, 2013, ca. 160 pp., ca. 29,90 €, br., ISBN-CH 978-3-643-90388-4

LIT Verlag Berlin – Münster – Wien – Zürich – London
Auslieferung Deutschland / Österreich / Schweiz: siehe Impressumsseite

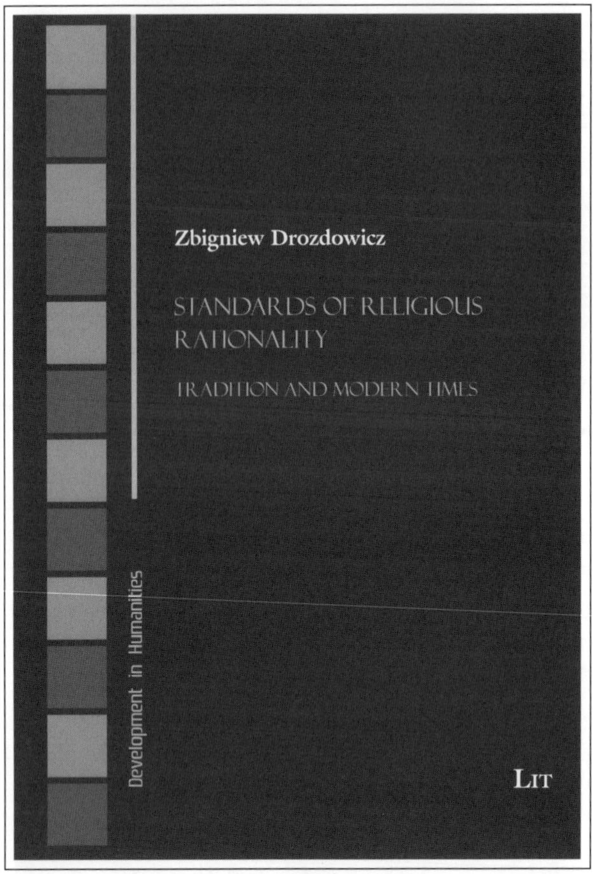

Zbigniew Drozdowicz
Standards of Religious Rationality
Tradition and Modern Times
The leading motive of the book deals with the past and present standards of rationality of religion, which functioned as significant regulators of thoughts and practical actions of various social groups. Determining these standards of rationality requires several general assumptions. One is, for example, that religion is of this world and serves the needs of this world. Another assumption is represented in Leibniz's principle *nothing is without reason* (*nihil esse sine ratione*).
Zbigniew Drozdowicz is a full professor at Adam Mickiewicz University in Poznan, and the head of the Chair of Religious Studies and Comparative Research.
vol. 2, 2013, ca. 160 pp., ca. 29,90 €, br., ISBN-CH 978-3-643-90389-1

LIT Verlag Berlin – Münster – Wien – Zürich – London
Auslieferung Deutschland / Österreich / Schweiz: siehe Impressumsseite

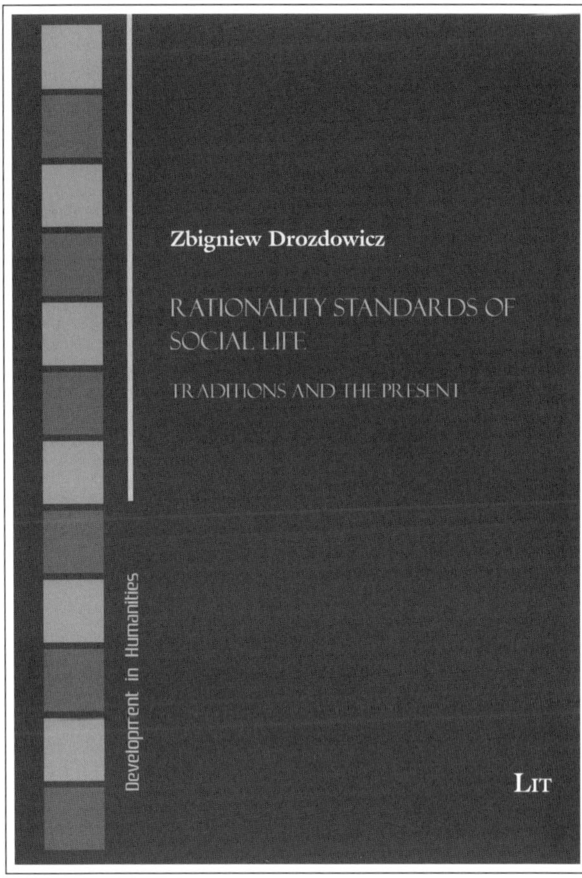

Zbigniew Drozdowicz
Rationality Standards of Social Life
Traditions and the Present

The standards of rationality are treated in the book as certain regulators of social life. They are compared to the rudders of the great vessels constituted by social communities. The diversity exhibited by those standards do not only result from the differences of time and space of their implementation, but also from the differences in the sets of ideas put forward by the leading social thinkers accompanied by the different characteristic of their designated audiences.

Zbigniew Drozdowicz is a full professor at Adam Mickiewicz University in Poznan, and the head of the Chair of Religious Studies and Comparative Research.

vol. 7, 2013, ca. 160 pp., ca. 29,90 €, br., ISBN-CH 978-3-643 90376-1

LIT Verlag Berlin – Münster – Wien – Zürich – London
Auslieferung Deutschland / Österreich / Schweiz: siehe Impressumsseite

Marian Golka
The Sociology of the Artist in the Postmodern Era
Pride and Uncertainty
The artistic profession is not easy to characterize. Various fields of artistic work are coupled with a range of different artistic attitudes, and these, in turn, with a variety of social positions assumed by artists, various historical conditions in which the profession functions as well as the diverse courses of artistic careers. There are those who say that this profession is not an occupation, but a vocation of an almost mystical nature. Yet it is tempting to examine the phenomenon of the artist, at least to the extent that it is possible in view of the scarcity of historical data.
Marian Golka is a sociologist of culture and cultural anthropologist and professor in the Institute of Sociology at Adam Mickiewicz University in Poznan.
vol. 8, 2013, ca. 160 pp., ca. 29,90 €, br., ISBN-CH 978-3-643-90377-8

LIT Verlag Berlin – Münster – Wien – Zürich – London
Auslieferung Deutschland / Österreich / Schweiz: siehe Impressumsseite

Józef Baniak
THE IMAGE OF THE PRIEST IN THE AWARENESS OF POLISH YOUTH
A SOCIOLOGICAL STUDY
Development in Humanities
LIT